REPORTI

Praise for *Reporting Disasters*

'*Reporting Disasters* makes a powerful case for a better understanding of the causes of hunger. Franks shows how the way starving people in Ethiopia were portrayed on TV during the famous "Biblical famine" of 1984 distorted the world's response, inspiring aid deliveries that may have done more harm than good. This is the best kind of history — one that challenges stereotypes and asks uncomfortable questions.' — David Loyn, BBC International Development Correspondent

'The cause and effect relationship between media and policy-making in crises continues to be dominated by ill-informed assumptions more than examination of hard facts from all angles. Suzanne Franks' interviews and access to historical records reveal compelling evidence that often challenges the orthodox view that images and powerful TV reporting in particular drive the most appropriate, pro-active policy response. Her important analysis has applications far beyond humanitarian disasters.' — Nik Gowing, international broadcaster and journalist

'The compelling story of a groundbreaking news event. Famine footage from Ethiopia allied to the pop star glamour of Live Aid confirmed the predominance of television news and changed the aid business forever. Thirty years on, with fresh revelations from inside Government and the BBC, Suzanne Franks' study takes on contemporary significance.' — Peter Gill, journalist and author of *Famine and Foreigners: Ethiopia Since Live Aid*

'This fascinating book is a must-read for anyone with an interest in the enduring effects on the aid industry of the nexus of global politics, celebrity and the media of the mid-1980s. Franks' sweeping narrative offers an unprecedented insight into events which were to define a generation's view of Africa.' — Leigh Daynes, Executive Director of Médecins du Monde in the UK

'A comprehensive and detailed analysis of the profound impact of an iconic 1984 BBC film, exploring the relationship between the media and humanitarian organisations — their overlapping and sometimes conflicting interests and the ways in which they are reconciled. Impressive.' — John Borton, Overseas Development Institute

'A fascinating, thoroughly researched and eminently readable book which makes a major contribution to our understanding of television's impact on politics, policy-makers and audiences. Highly recommended for anyone interested in the relationship between media and politics.' — Steven Barnett, Professor of Communications, University of Westminster

SUZANNE FRANKS

To Julia

Reporting Disasters

Famine, Aid, Politics and the Media

Best wishes

[signature]

HURST & COMPANY, LONDON

First published in the United Kingdom in 2013 by
C. Hurst & Co. (Publishers) Ltd.,
41 Great Russell Street, London, WC1B 3PL
© Suzanne Franks, 2013
All rights reserved.
Printed in India

Distributed in the United States, Canada and Latin America by
Oxford University Press, 198 Madison Avenue, New York, NY 10016,
United States of America.

The right of Suzanne Franks to be identified as the author of
this publication is asserted by her in accordance with the
Copyright, Designs and Patents Act, 1988.

A Cataloguing-in-Publication data record for this book
is available from the British Library.

ISBN: 9781849042888

www.hurstpublishers.com

This book is printed on paper from registered sustainable
and managed sources.

CONTENTS

LIST OF ILLUSTRATIONS

PREFACE AND ACKNOWLEDGEMENTS

The BBC coverage of the Ethiopian Famine in 1984–85 was an iconic news event. It is widely believed to have had an unprecedented impact, challenging perceptions of Africa and mobilizing public opinion and philanthropic action in a dramatic new way. It offers a remarkable case study of how the media can affect public opinion and the policy making process. This research, using for the first time privileged access to BBC and government archives, examines and reveals the internal factors which drove the BBC news. It constructs the process which accounts for the immensity of the news event, as well as following the response to public opinion pressure into the heart of government. And it shows that, whilst the reporting and the altruistic festival that it produced were to trigger remarkable and identifiable changes, the ongoing impact was not what the conventional account claimed it to have been.

The configuration of aid, media pressure, NGOs and government policy today is still directly affected, and in some ways distorted, by what was—as this narrative reveals—also an inaccurate and misleading story. In popular memory the reporting of Ethiopia and the humanitarian intervention were a triumph of journalism and altruism. Yet alternative interpretations give a radically different picture: that the reporting was misleading and the resulting aid effort did more harm than good. This book explains the event within the wider context of international news broadcasting, especially by the BBC, and looks at the way it has influenced the reporting of humanitarian disasters in subsequent years.

The research which was the catalyst for this project began with a seminar at London's Frontline Club. I would like to thank the original semi-

PREFACE AND ACKNOWLEDGEMENTS

nar participants and, following on from that, the many interviewees who gave so generously of their time: in particular the late Alasdair Milne, Michael Buerk, the late Sir Timothy Raison, Sir Malcolm Rifkind, Sir Mark Tully, Nik Gowing, Paddy Coulter, Tim Allen, Mike Appleton, Sir Brian Barder, Cathy Corcoran, Chris Cramer, Professor Nicholas Deakin, Peter Gill, Libby Grimshaw, Myles Wickstead, the late Brian Hanrahan, Roger Laughton, David Loyn, Graham Mytton, Ron Neil, Charles Stewart, John Seaman, Tony Vaux and Michael Wooldridge. Through Freedom of Information applications I was able to access files at the Department of International Development and I would like to thank the officials there for their help. The other key part of the research was access to the BBC files in Caversham. Under the auspices of the BBC Official History project I was allowed access to material that had not been made available for public inspection. I would like to acknowledge help from the BBC History unit, Robert Seatter, and the BBC Written Archive Centre at Caversham and to thank in particular Anthony McNicholas who knows his way around there better than most. Steve Barnett, Colin Seymour-Ure, Beate Planskoy made helpful comments on the manuscript, and many thanks to the very helpful team at Hurst, Michael Dwyer, Rob Pinney and Georgie Williams. Above all I would like to express my gratitude to Jean Seaton, official historian of the BBC, adviser and friend, whose patience and help were, as ever, tireless. And finally a tribute goes to my irrepressible and adored family—John, Emma, Hannah and Ben—who have been supportive and uplifting in so many ways.

INTRODUCTION

ARGUING ABOUT FAMINE

'We used to think, those of us who were writers, that novels would change the world. No, it's television that changes the world.'

Norman Mailer, 2007[1]

On 23 and 24 October 1984, BBC Television news broadcast a series of reports about a famine in Ethiopia. The story led both the lunchtime and the early evening 6pm bulletins on BBC1 and ran on each occasion at six minutes or longer—which was remarkable for a foreign news story set in a developing country and without any British angle. The footage was re-cut and featured later that evening on the BBC1 *Nine O'Clock News*, viewed by an audience of 7.4 million.[2] Over the following days the news images from Ethiopia, shot by a Kenyan based Visnews cameraman, Mohamed Amin, and presented by the BBC South Africa correspondent Michael Buerk, were seen by almost a third of the adult population of the UK.[3] At the same time it was re-broadcast by many hundreds of TV stations across the world, including the American network NBC, where it featured prominently on Tom Brokaw's evening news show. The footage contained harrowing images of starving people of all ages who were arriving in their thousands at feeding stations in northern Ethiopia.

The first report, transmitted in the bulletins on 23 October, opened with a wide panning shot across a group of desperate famine victims,

1

who had congregated on the outskirts of a town in Tigray. The commentary began:

Dawn, and as the sun breaks through the piercing chill of night on the plain outside Korem, it lights up a biblical famine, now, in the 20th century. This place, say workers here, is the closest thing to hell on earth. Thousands of wasted people are coming here for help. Many find only death. They flood in every day from villages hundreds of miles away, felled by hunger, driven beyond the point of desperation. Death is all around. A child or an adult dies every 20 minutes. Korem, an insignificant town, has become a place of grief.[4]

Michael Buerk's reports from the Ethiopian highlands, broadcast on BBC TV news in October 1984, were to become landmark news items. John Simpson, the BBC's World Affairs editor, considers that 'The famine in Ethiopia was probably the biggest news story BBC Television News broadcast in the 1980s, until the fall of the Berlin Wall.'[5] It acted as an international siren telling the world about the plight of the famine victims in Ethiopia, and eventually spurred on the biggest humanitarian relief effort the world had ever seen and a spectacular new strand of raising funds and awareness.[6]

Yet the question remains, why did this particular coverage become so significant, and what were its wider implications both for institutions and attitudes towards giving, as well as the dilemmas of humanitarian intervention? The coverage of the Ethiopian famine, because it had such profound effects, is significant both in itself and as a historical case study that illuminates much wider problems. It was an example of a huge and worldwide news event, but one which ultimately involved major misunderstandings and misconceptions. Despite the multiple myths and assumptions that have since arisen, there is substantial evidence to indicate that the media perception of the famine in Ethiopia was far from accurate. But this was not the only famine that was misunderstood. In preceding and succeeding years there have been other occasions in the reporting of the developing world (and in particular Africa) where in hindsight the media also got things badly wrong. So the media coverage of the Ethiopian famine needs to be seen in a wider context, because it played a pivotal role in how Western countries have understood and reported Africa in the latter part of the twentieth century. It also had an unexpected and transforming effect upon private charitable institutions in the West. And largely as a result of the extraordinary response to the media coverage, foreign relief NGOs grew at an unprecedented rate and their relationship with the media was radically and permanently altered. In fact, the response to the Ethiopian famine was a key driver in the sudden growth and significance of non-governmental aid agencies and helped to precipitate what have become the 'decades of the NGOs'. This presented a distinct set of challenges for broadcasters, in particular the BBC, who were involved in the sharp rise in fundraising that in turn brought the various agencies to such prominence. Indeed, the famine also marked a significant stage in the developing relationship between media and aid agencies. And furthermore it is now perceived as a turning point in the development of humanitarian intervention and the doctrine of 'neutral humanitarianism'.

* * *

Our awareness of nearly all humanitarian disasters is defined by the media. There is a fundamental sense in which the 'media may not be successful in telling people what to think, but it is stunningly successful in telling its readers what to think about.'[7] Although this observation might apply in a general way, it is particularly important in our awareness of distant places, because there are rarely alternative sources of information. The media are the only way of finding out about such faraway events. In more recent years this has also included social media and citizen journalism which have become an additional source of knowledge about remote places and especially faraway humanitarian crises.[8] Yet even then the mainstream media have played a pivotal role of validating and providing a coherent, reliable gatekeeper to the information about such crises.

Aid workers know well that 'Most of the world's horrors never get any air time at all.'[9] It is this that has precipitated many aid agencies in recent years to establish their own sophisticated reporting operations, as a means of trying to convey a message about distant suffering—and stimulate a response. Yet even in an age of social media this only works for them when they can then use their pictures and reports to attract the interest of mainstream media. Despite social media, it remains the case that even in a period of global communication, many thousands could be dying, yet a catastrophe in a far off place may remain completely unknown about in other parts of the world. In the era which preceded widespread social media this was even more apparent. Two of the greatest catastrophes of the late twentieth century, the Chinese famine of

1959–61[10] and the war in the Congo in the late 1990s, in which many millions died, were almost 'invisible' to the rest of the world. Indeed, 'it can be said that disasters do not exist—except for their unfortunate victims and those who suffer in their aftermath—unless publicised by the media … the media actually construct disasters.'[11] This makes their role in reporting a foreign, faraway disaster a vital one. And the reporting of the Ethiopian famine in 1984 is particularly important in that context because it is an unusual incident of overwhelming and mainstream media attention focused upon a crisis in a distant and generally unreported part of the world.

Yet even if the media are covering the story, the question still arises, to what extent does the reporting have any influence? Can media reporting really affect the foreign policy decisions of governments? The term 'CNN effect' was first formally used during the first Gulf War in 1991 to describe the way that real time news coverage of foreign news stories appeared to affect the decision-making of political elites, either directly or through the influence it had upon domestic audiences.[12] The phrase eventually became used retrospectively in analyzing the effects of media coverage of previous foreign crises which occurred long before CNN or any 24 hour TV news channels. It was even linked to events as far back as the Vietnam war, where media reporting was considered by some to have influenced policy decisions.

In the period since 1991, as the concept of the CNN effect developed, there have been further arguments about cases, including Ethiopia, where, retrospectively, media coverage appeared to have an effect upon foreign policy or at least prompted action in relation to foreign events. The former Conservative foreign secretary, Douglas Hurd, felt strongly about the inappropriate pressure of media coverage as an influence in policy making, in particular during the Balkan crises of the 1990s. He gave a speech in 1993 entitled 'The Power of Comment' which *The Times* reported as 'Foreign Secretary warns of media role'[13] and the *Daily Telegraph* as 'Hurd hits out again at media'.[14] Later that month the journalist George Kennan made similar disapproving observations about US policy and intervention in Somalia. Writing in the *New York Times* he argued that the media were effectively dictating foreign policy making and had triggered the ill-thought-out US intervention.[15] Two years later in 1995, the former secretary of the United Nations, Boutros Boutros Ghali, argued that CNN operated like the sixteenth member of the Security Council:

INTRODUCTION: ARGUING ABOUT FAMINE

We have 16 members in the Security Council: the 15 country members plus CNN. Long-term work doesn't interest you because the span of attention of the public is limited. Out of 20 peacekeeping operations you are interested in one or two ... And because of the limelight on one or two, I am not able to obtain the soldiers or the money or the attention for the other 17 operations.[16]

In 1999 Tony Blair, the British prime minister, made a similar observation in his Chicago speech on foreign policy when he remarked that politicians were 'still fending off the danger of letting wherever CNN roves be the cattle prod to take a global conflict seriously.'[17] And in subsequent years there have been arguments about whether liberal interventionism was sometimes a knee jerk reaction to unpleasant media images.

Philip Seib argues that Blair and other politicians are protesting too much. He quotes the legendary US TV correspondent Peter Jennings (once depicted in the Hollywood film *Live from Baghdad*): 'Political leadership trumps good television every time. As influential as television can be it is most influential in the absence of decisive political leadership.'[18] So the CNN effect will only take place in a policy vacuum. Seib concludes unambiguously that the argument that 'televised images, especially heart-wrenching pictures of suffering civilians, will so stir public opinion that government officials will be forced to adjust policy to conform to that opinion' may sound appealing, but although 'There is a certain logic to the theory and it cheers [some] journalists who like to think that they are powerful ... there is a fundamental problem: it just ain't so, at least not as a straightforward cause and effect process.'[19] The analysis offered here of the Ethiopian famine supports this view. It might have appeared that powerful media coverage had an effect upon policy—but the reality gleaned from internal documents tells a different story. The government of Mrs Thatcher was generally one of strong policy positions and this was no exception.

It is self-evident that the notion of a CNN effect is only really meaningful within a democratic framework and where there is a free press. It was Amartya Sen, the distinguished Indian economist, who focused on the effects of media coverage upon decision making within a democracy. He outlined the relationship between famine and entitlement, demonstrating that famine was not necessarily due to a decline in the availability of food but was crucially linked to the lack of entitlements amongst certain vulnerable parts of the population.[20] Sen went on to investigate the role of public action in the prevention of famine,[21] concluding that famine was unlikely to occur in a country with a robust plural polity and a free press, because the press would have a vital role in alerting wider public opinion and those holding power, as a crisis loomed. This would in due course lead to popular pressure upon government to provide sufficient entitlements to the groups facing starvation so that the crisis would be averted.

Although there are criticisms of this interpretation from economists and development theorists who see it as over-simplified,[22] it does provide a very useful framework to assess media reporting of famine. Sen highlights the crucial role that domestic reporting of a famine will have to ameliorate a situation and argues that freedom of expression leads, in effect, to food entitlements. However, there is also a more dilute effect that media coverage may have within a wider global setting and in relation to international media coverage. When there is a famine in a highly authoritarian country such as Ethiopia was in 1984, the media coverage at an international level can have an influential role, at least in the provision of aid. It may provoke international institutions, other governments and even concerned individuals to action, and thereby encourage the provision of humanitarian relief. It can also, in an indirect way, influence domestic governments, who are shamed and embarrassed by international opinion of the famine. This demonstrates the potential interaction between Sen's framework and the operation of the CNN effect. However, there may be subsequent concern beyond the provision of relief, because the authoritarian government may not always choose to use the aid to relieve the starving victims: indeed, in Ethiopia it was positively used for other purposes, and according to some interpretations caused more harm than good.

Sen is also questioning the meaning of so-called 'natural' disasters, because of the way he characterized famine as a social, rather than natural, phenomenon. This is an important distinction which has been successively refined over the years by a range of work. Onora O'Neill has written from a philosophical point of view how famine is neither a natural disaster nor something that just 'breaks out' every so often,[23] which is the way it appears in much media reporting. As a result of this work and others the neat historic division between natural and man made disasters has subsequently been superseded by a much more nuanced interpretation which recognizes the 'man made' element in almost all disasters. In many cases the media reporting fails to capture the social, political and military dimensions that are so crucial in the understanding of famine as opposed to general chronic malnutrition. In the case of Ethiopia, as in subsequent crises, the repeated depiction of famine as a 'sudden' disaster was clearly inadequate. However, if the media are not telling an accurate story—if, for example, they portray famine as a natural disaster caused by drought—there are few alternative sources for correcting this. One of the rare sources available is the interpretation of aid agencies, but on occasion they may well reinforce these misperceptions—either unintentionally or for a range of institutional reasons.

Historically, the role of emergency relief was conceived as a matter of providing help to victims suffering as a result of a disaster. This was the model of the Red Cross, which from the nineteenth century sought to provide help regardless of political affiliation. However, in the wake of the Biafra crisis in the 1960s, the Cambodian crisis in the 1970s and, much more so, the Ethiopian famine in the 1980s, and in subsequent complex emergencies there was a growing realization that it may not be straightforward to find a 'neutral space' and that relief itself is unavoidably a highly political act because it is being delivered into a complicated scenario. A crucial part of this was the acceptance that famine was not a natural disaster but a social and political crisis. It therefore followed that providing aid in such circumstances had a vital political dimension. There was no longer any guarantee that aid itself would 'do no harm' and could simply help the victims, without any other consequences.[24]

The emergence of humanitarianism over this period and the way that aid operates is now part of wider arguments about emergency assistance, development, and the way a large industry functions in complicated circumstances.[25] In retrospect it appears that the reaction of aid agencies to the provision of relief in Ethiopia in 1984/85 was a key moment in the understanding of the wider implications of aid, and it was partly the sheer scale of the operation that made it so significant. Beyond that, the nature of the fundraising—especially the Band Aid and Live Aid message—depicted the crisis as simply a matter of sending money to feed the innocent starving victims which would solve the problem for good. And crucially there was the question of the way that the famine was perceived and the issue of the underlying political causes, which most of the aid operation did not engage with. There was the additional dilemma of dealing with a highly authoritarian and repressive regime that was engaged in a huge, but secret, counterinsurgency war and diverting aid towards its own military operations. In the midst of this the French NGO Médecins Sans Frontières (MSF) took an outspoken stand, criticizing the regime, resulting in its expulsion from Ethiopia. Meanwhile other agencies became concerned that the Ethiopian government was preventing the vast majority of victims, who were in the rebel areas, from being reached. Some of the smaller agencies engaged in a controversial operation to distribute aid across the border from Sudan directly into the rebel areas in direct contravention of the UN, with its belief in the paramount significance of sovereign states—although it has since become apparent from dissident voices that the recipients of that aid were not entirely transparent in their dealings.[26] In engaging with these problems some agencies, but certainly not all, were becoming aware of the highly political nature of the relief operation. This was further compounded by the widespread misuse of aid in the Ethiopian government's drive to 'resettle' the famine victims, sometimes with the use of extreme force and by manipulating the aid programmes.

These dilemmas for the aid effort produced a variety of responses in Ethiopia, ranging from NGOs that took a high profile position of opposition, such as MSF, to the other extreme of those agencies which believed it was best to co-operate with the regime and even assist in the controversial resettlement programme. Similar themes, such as the search for a neutral space, and the dilemmas of 'complex emergencies', were to recur several times in the decades that followed. The Ethiopian famine was a crucible for many of these issues, 'a milestone in the recent history of the humanitarian movement'[27] with aid agencies attempting to work out—often in retrospect—how they should position themselves. It was becoming apparent that 'the humanitarian boom was amplified and accelerated by the existence of television.'[28] The famine and its aftermath highlighted other problems, which have surfaced many times in the intervening years, notably the tensions between fundraising and development goals within charities, the complicated relations between different NGOs, and the pressures that aid agencies experience to tell a partial or at least simplified story about a crisis, in order to maximize donations.

This famine occurred in Africa. Hence the reporting of it does not belong to any abstract 'famine reporting' but needs to be considered within the wider context of how 'Africa' was reported. There is ongoing evidence[29] about the limited and largely inadequate way that the developing world continues to be reported in the Western press and in news and current affairs programmes on television. Although there were some differences in the configuration of programming and news reporting in the 1980s, many of the wider conclusions of the various studies which discuss the reporting of Africa can be applied in the same way to this earlier decade. These relate to issues such as the superficiality of reporting, the lack of context or background, the reliance upon stereotypes when compared with conventions used in reporting of the developed world.

There were also, in fact, some earlier analyses which echoed many of those same conclusions, such as the *Images of Africa Report* co-ordinated in 1987 by Oxfam and other aid agencies[30] in the wake of the Ethiopian coverage and the examination of these problems by UNESCO.[31] Much of the work which was done to press for a New World Information and Communication Order, under the auspices of UNESCO, voiced some of these same arguments, criticizing the inadequate way that developing countries were explained and described.[32] And the same themes still recur—the limited way that Africa continues to be covered and also the consequences of this inadequate reporting and understanding.[33]

The opening chapter provides a narrative of how the famine story was reported. It is also an exploration of why this became such a prominent news story. The subsequent two chapters examine the wider effects which were a direct consequence of that high profile coverage, first (with the use of official documents) the impact it had, largely through the mobilization of public opinion, on the policy process and then on the world of charitable fundraising, where the famine coverage produced substantial long-term changes. The next two chapters (four and five) analyze the way the story of the famine was interpreted and explained. They demonstrate how this reporting was actually misconceived, both at the time and in historical memory, first by the media and then by the humanitarian agencies. The analysis also attempts to explain why, despite the enormous impact of the reporting, this misunderstanding took place, and to set that within a wider framework of reporting disasters and the development of broadcast appeals. Chapter six offers an overview of the longer-term changes that the coverage of the famine brought about within the aid agencies as institutions and in particular their developing relationships with the media. And underlying that analysis is the continuing question of how news from Africa is reported in the international media, which is the subject of chapter seven. In conclusion the final chapter assesses the overall impact of the famine reporting and examines what longer-term lessons and observations might be drawn.

1

HOW FAMINE CAPTURED THE HEADLINES

'You can't remain untouched when there are people dying as far as the eye can see.'

Mohamed Amin, cameraman.

'Is waiting for the media inevitable? ... It is the media and not the monitoring that brings awareness.'

Tony Vaux, Oxfam Report 1985

'This was the TV camera being used as a window on the world. It was a relationship between the camera lens and human beings ... one of those very rare occasions when we were turning the incredibly significant into the interesting—we cover many stories that are incredibly significant but they are dull—this was realising something was incredibly significant and making it interesting at the same time.

'Sadly for decades we can look at people dying and think nothing of it and just go off to the supermarket. This was connecting the dots for the audience in a way that we rarely do—all the way from the conception of the story to the execution and the post-production. All of those things were perfect and that is unusual—mostly you just throw it on the air and move on.'

Interview with Chris Cramer, BBC TV Foreign News editor, 1984

Early warnings

It is an uncomfortable fact that news from poor and remote parts of the developing world only rarely makes a major impact in the Western media. Many studies have highlighted the uneven way in which foreign news is covered and the resistance of mainstream television commissioning editors and news editors to the coverage of serious stories in faraway places.[1] By October 1984, plenty of people, including government officials, aid workers and journalists, had already been trying to draw attention to a developing food crisis in the Horn of Africa, but without much success.[2] So the 'story' of a famine in Ethiopia was known well before Michael Buerk's report, but it had failed to capture much attention. Yet famine in Ethiopia was already a familiar theme in Western news rooms. The broadcaster Jonathan Dimbleby had made an important film for ITV about the 1973/74 famine in Ethiopia, which occurred under the regime of Emperor Haile Selassie.[3]

Less than a decade after Dimbleby's film, towards the end of 1982, there had once again been several famine warnings both by the Ethiopian government's Relief and Rehabilitation Commission (R&RC) based in Addis Ababa and by a number of the overseas aid agencies operating in the field. Journalists had been taken on press tours of some of the affected areas, but there had been little reaction to the growing food crisis. In response to the warnings and local appeals a few brief articles had appeared in the UK press, but there was no wider media interest.[4] Save the Children Fund had reported to its headquarters concerns about declining food supplies, and possible imminent starvation. As a result the broadcasters had agreed to mount an appeal for donations. Esther Rantzen, the well known presenter of *That's Life*, made the appeal on BBC TV, which was broadcast on 31 March 1983. Her script referred to thousands of homeless, starving people descending on the little town of Korem and warned that up to two million were at risk of famine as a result of months of drought. She mentioned the 200,000 who had died in the famine ten years previously and urged viewers to donate so that the same tragedy would not happen again.[5] ITV broadcast a similar appeal, using Jonathan Dimbleby, who had made the original film about the 1973 Ethiopian famine.[6]

Despite these appeals the early media coverage of the developing story did not stir much public attention. In the early 1980s Mike Wooldridge was the BBC's East Africa correspondent, based in Nairobi, and he had been trying to cover the famine story since the start of 1983. Wooldridge had joined BBC News in 1970 after a stint with the Voluntary Service Overseas (VSO) in Uganda and had been based in Nairobi as East Africa correspondent since 1982. He demonstrated a tireless interest in Africa and in 2002 was awarded an OBE for services to broadcasting in developing countries. Wooldridge was first alerted to the growing food crisis in Ethiopia in March 1983. He was aware that Shimelis Adugna, head of the Ethiopian government's Relief and Rehabilitation Commission, had been speaking both at the United Nations and in London about the growing food crisis, indicating that Ethiopia in 1983 would need substantially more food aid than it had required in the previous years because of the failure of successive harvests:

Save the Children suggested to me in Nairobi, and also to ITN in London, that we should go and have a look at this on the ground. We were given authorisation by the relief commissioner, Shimelis Adugna, a personal decision of his to authorise the trip at a time when the Ethiopian government was not at all keen. They were keen to have food aid but not keen that this should be reported as a potential growing famine.[7]

After receiving the vital authorization Wooldridge set off on the filming trip. Accompanying him, to visit what were then the most threatened areas, was the Kenyan cameraman Mohamed Amin, well known in African news reporting as an energetic operator. They travelled with the regional representative of Save the Children, Mark Bowden. And as they went round Ethiopia in one direction over a period of five or six days, David Smith of ITN was being accompanied the opposite way around the country.

Now what we saw on the ground then was quite obviously a crisis with very great potential, we indeed saw people apparently dying of hunger already. When we went to Korem in particular we saw funerals of people who we were told had died essentially of hunger; it was already an iconic image of the famine that came out of that particular trip when we filmed in a church just on the edge of Korem a priest giving out just the very little grain he had to give and all the people holding out their upturned hands to receive it, that became one of the strong moving and still images of the famine that was to come.

Wooldridge's material from that trip received a certain amount of attention; some of it appeared on BBC national bulletins. David Smith's material went out on ITN and there was some coverage on radio in the form of radio packages.[8]

Wooldridge returned the following year in March 1984, sponsored by the Office of the United Nations High Commissioner for Refugees to report on the repatriation of refugees who had become stranded over the years on either side of the borders between Somalia, Ethiopia and Djibouti. In retrospect, he says:

13

That was again quite an eye-opening trip. We got to places where famine was now biting more deeply, as there had been the failure of more harvests and, indeed, we did more reports out of that trip, though they were then hugely overshadowed by what was to happen in October 84. It got some attention at the time and not just what I was doing for radio.[9]

Wooldridge was travelling again with Mo Amin, who wrote a story in the *Daily Nation* Newspaper in Nairobi saying that millions of Ethiopians faced starvation, based on what he had seen on the ground and what they had been told by Ethiopian officials at that time.[10] Yet despite this limited coverage and the evidence now apparent on the ground, there was no wider or sustained editorial involvement in the story. Throughout this period aid officials were concerned that it was proving hard to interest governments, journalists or the public in the emerging crisis.

In May 1984 Libby Grimshaw was a Save the Children Fund fieldworker working in Tigray. She recalls her severe disappointment at failing to get much attention from journalists to the worsening situation.[11] In common with other aid officials, she felt some frustration that television in particular was good at portraying extremes, in particular the starving child, but it was not so good at telling the complicated story of the build-up to famine which the agencies were trying to alert them to.[12] Médecins Sans Frontières had tried to persuade French TV to make a film about the Ethiopian famine in the spring of 1984, but it had been turned down. Similarly, CBS in the US had rejected a proposal on the same subject on the grounds that it was 'not strong enough'.[13]

In March 1984 the Ethiopian Relief and Rehabilitation Commission made an appeal for 450,000 tonnes of grain (which was itself only half of the total which it really thought was required) but even this reduced assessment was not taken seriously. Five months later only 87,000 tonnes had been pledged and little of that had actually materialized.[14] Although there were some official contributions to food aid in Ethiopia, this was on a small and limited scale. There were several reasons for this reluctance to help; partly it was due to the unpopular international image of the Ethiopian government. Western governments, in particular in the US and Britain, were reluctant to assist a client of the Soviet Union.[15] There is plenty of evidence to indicate that the UK government was well aware throughout this period of the scale of the food shortages, but there appears to have been little will to do much about it. A telegram from Michael Smith, a member of the British Embassy staff in

Addis Ababa, sent already in December 1982, discussing the Ethiopian Food Security Reserve, refers to 'continuing problems both of drought and excessive rain (the latter of which I can personally corroborate!) which will result in at least 4 million people needing help this year.'[16] Similarly, a telegram in March 1983 from Brian Barder, the British ambassador, describes a 'serious situation now worsening ... estimated 27,000 refugees in Korem (normal pop 8,000) living in shelters ... estimates of total numbers at risk 2–3 million'.[17]

The following year, in a lengthy report in early October 1984, Brian Barder discusses the question of increased aid and mentions the close links which Ethiopia had with the Soviet Union, arguing that there was no point in doing things to improve relations with such an 'obnoxious, repressive and anti-western regime'.[18] He recommends that the British line should, rather, be to 'undermine the Soviet influence in Ethiopia'. However, at the same time he observed the growing humanitarian crisis: 'the UK has played our part fully in contributing to the international famine relief effort, although the situation has deteriorated so dramatically in recent months that enormously more is going to be needed if a massive human disaster is to be averted or controlled.'

This was a reflection of the continuing tension in the question of helping Ethiopia—there was a recognition of the suffering of the population but a reluctance to assist a regime which was a Soviet client. Ultimately, it appears that the Cold War strategic imperative trumped all other considerations.

The ongoing British hostility to Soviet presence in this area is supported by evidence from the Foreign Office. In one key paper on the subject under the heading of 'Current Policy Objectives in Policy on Ethiopia', the first item states that 'Our long term aim is to supplant Soviet with Western influence in the Horn, especially Ethiopia.'[19] However, it is clear that individual members of the government were starting to feel that in spite of the distasteful regime more ought to be done to help the unfortunate people concerned. Malcolm Rifkind, as a junior minister in the Foreign Office, made this point quite forcibly in a memo to the foreign secretary, Sir Geoffrey Howe, in early October 1984:

I am very concerned about the extent of Britain's response to the famine in Ethiopia. Reports from embassy ... and several voluntary agencies and press reports that the famine is serious and widespread ... While the present level of our aid is not insignificant it hardly matches the scale of the problem ... Save the Children Fund has estimated that 60,000 tonnes are needed by Ethiopia each month until end of 1985. That figure puts the 3,000 tons which we announced last week into perspective. Our response appears still less adequate in the context of a record European grain harvest.[20]

Yet despite this awareness there was no change in government policy regarding food aid for Ethiopia, until the issue surfaced on television at the end of October 1984.[21]

It is also apparent that the attitude of the Ethiopian government itself did not encourage outsiders (at least from Western countries) to help. Despite the R&RC appeals there was great ambivalence about formally admitting that there was a food problem, as Mike Wooldridge confirms. Indeed, the relief and rehabilitation commissioner, Shimelis Adugna, was subsequently sacked from his position for authorizing the first press trip which Wooldridge made in 1983 to cover the food shortages.[22] The continuing paradox at this point was that the Ethiopian government, or at least parts of it, wanted to receive international food aid, but they were reluctant to accept the idea of international (or indeed domestic) publicity about the famine. Indeed they only ever referred to the subject as one of drought, never famine.

Adugna's replacement at the R&RC was Dawit Wolde Giorgis. A short time later, at the end of 1985, he defected to the West and subsequently wrote *Red Tears*,[23] which was an account of the famine from inside Ethiopia. It provides a fascinating counterpoint to all the contemporary misinformation and speculation. According to Giorgis the crisis was already clear to the Ethiopian government by early 1983. He made several tours in the northern provinces during 1983 and observed growing problems of food shortages, anticipating that potentially five million people faced the prospect of famine. According to Giorgis' own figures, in March 1984 16,000 people a week were already dying from starvation, which is little different from the scale of death that the journalists found when they eventually came in October. On a visit in April 1984 to Korem he reported the terrible sight of a quarter of a million people converging on a town which normally housed only a few thousand. 'Korem had become the death bed of thousands ... the talk of saving these people was truly monumental ... meanwhile Marx and Lenin posters and flags decorated the roads for the forthcoming celebrations'.[24]

Giorgis had held a donor conference in Addis in November 1983, and in subsequent months he toured European capitals asking for aid, but there was little response from the international community. Meanwhile Giorgis not only had difficulties in convincing foreign donors, but faced a similar struggle internally with his own government. In March 1984 there was a meeting of the Politburo to determine the next ten-year plan, but Giorgis called it fantasy budgeting. Over three days' discussion there was no mention of famine, civil war or the defence budget, which, he estimated, was running at two thirds of national expenditure. When he tried to speak out about the famine, the head of Ethiopia's government, Colonel Mengistu Haile Mariam,[25] replied that the ten-year plan was a long-term document and the food shortage was just a passing, temporary setback.[26] According to other former officials, the cover-up was even more draconian. Anyone who tried to discuss the true magnitude of the crisis was accused of 'working for imperialism' or even worse, being an agent of the CIA.[27]

The Ethiopian government was extremely secretive, especially in view of the fierce fighting against the rebel movements in the north, which was closely linked to the issue of food shortages and potential famine.[28] There was also international scepticism about the amounts of grain requested and, whatever was in fact needed, whether there was an adequate transport system and infrastructure to distribute the grain if it arrived.[29] Moreover, the World Food Programme (WFP) in May 1984 had made its own assessment of the grain requirement which was far short of that of the Relief and Rehabilitation Commission's, and indicated no great urgency in the situation. In the months that followed there was great criticism of the UN agencies and their inadequate assessment on Ethiopia. They had confused project aid with emergency aid, and mistaken pledges as actual deliveries of aid, so that the overall conclusions grossly misunderstood and underestimated the gravity of the situation.[30]

As a consequence of the WFP conclusions about Ethiopia's apparent needs, the UN agencies had not at this stage galvanized any support for an aid effort. Yet equally significant was the absence of any media presentation of a serious problem, despite considerable evidence of the growing crisis. The agency Earthscan observed grimly at the time that 'the public's impression of disasters is formed not by relief agencies, but by journalists.'[31] This raises again the question of to what extent disasters 'exist' without the media. Clearly, as far as those who witnessed what was happening in Ethiopia were concerned, the crisis was very real, and yet there was a frustrating disjunction when they tried to communicate the problem to the rest of the world. Howard Wolpe, a US Democratic Congressman from Michigan, was one of those who went on a fact-finding mission to Ethiopia in 1983 and tried, without much success, to raise awareness of the impending famine back in Washington. He later wrote in the *Washington Post* on 21 November 1984, after the story broke, 'The facts were there for anyone who wanted to see them two years ago. To say that we were taken by surprise is only to say that we didn't want to see before.'[32]

In support of Wolpe's assertion, the American authorities, like the UK government as the documents make clear, were well aware of the food crisis in Ethiopia months before the issue became a media event. An urgent cable was sent from the US Embassy in Addis to the State Department on 4 April 1984 about the prevailing food situation. It stated that 'a very serious situation could develop in Ethiopia this year and we will be remiss if we are not adequately informed and prepared.'[33] The facts on the ground were well known. Yet for months, if not years, the international media were not interested in reporting the story and Western governments were not inclined to pay much attention.

Emergency appeal

During this period, in the spring of 1984, the ITV company Central TV had been in Ethiopia filming a documentary on soil erosion and drought, partly funded by the Television Trust for the Environment. The film director was Charles Stewart, a distinguished documentary maker with a wide experience in the developing world. He had intended the filming in Ethiopia to form part of a longer series on the environment, provisionally entitled 'Seeds of Hope'; but when Stewart and his crew started to film in Ethiopia and discovered the scale of the starvation—which some of the agencies had been trying to communicate but the media had largely ignored—he found himself making a rather different kind of film and the title was changed to 'Seeds of Despair'.[34] In view of the grave food problems a decision was made to bring forward transmission of the documentary to July 1984 and ITV scheduled a slot on 17 July 1984. The Independent Broadcasting Authority (IBA) anticipated that the revelations in the film about food shortages would provoke spontaneous offers of assistance by viewers and requested that the Disasters Emergency Committee (DEC)[35] should handle these. Meanwhile a request had also been made by the Catholic Agency for Overseas Development (CAFOD) through the DEC that an emergency TV appeal should be linked to the transmission of the documentary in order to raise funds for famine relief in Ethiopia.[36]

When BBC News heard about the request for a DEC emergency appeal in July 1984, just days before Charles Stewart's film was due to be screened on ITV, they contacted the resident BBC correspondent in South Africa, Michael Buerk. The news desk had heard about the Central TV documentary which contained shocking images of imminent starvation, so they requested Buerk to find a story on famine somewhere in Africa and obtain some footage to use in the appeal, as well as conveniently scooping ITV's famine story by filming a news item on the subject. Michael Buerk clearly remembers the competitive pressures he was under:

Charles Stewart had made a very well crafted and brilliant film, and the BBC, I think, felt wrong footed about this. I wouldn't like to say that their competitive instincts were totally vainglorious but they were challenged by this idea. So in a matter of about seven days before this appeal was about to go out I got a rather alarmed phone call from the foreign desk instructing me to find some starving Africans in order to actually film something to use in the appeal, but also to run in parallel a piece on the BBC News … It would be wrong to characterise it as a spoiler, as the tabloids call it, to spike ITV's guns, because this was a brilliant documentary and all I was doing was a cheap and cheerful news piece, actually a cheap and cheerless news piece on this particular occasion.[37]

The trouble was that Buerk was now faced with finding a famine story in double quick time.

The problem of reporting in Africa, particularly if you are reporting for television where you can't kind of sidle in and make a few notes and sidle out again, … is getting permission from authoritarian regimes to actually get to areas where this was happening. My instincts were to go to Mozambique, where an awful lot of people were suffering and it was closer to Johannesburg and I knew it, but I also knew that the previous time I had been there it had taken fifteen days to get permission to get out of the capital and I didn't have that time.[38]

Instead Buerk contacted the Oxfam press office with a telex that was to become legendary. It remained pinned up in the Oxfam offices for many years. 'Help. Have had request from BBC in London relating to an appeal to be televised next Thursday entitled 'Famine in Africa' …

need urgent advice on where I can leap in and out quickly with pictures of harrowing drought victims etc to be edited and satellited ... money no object, nor distance, only time'[39] Paddy Coulter, the head of communications at Oxfam, suggested he should film in Ethiopia and Buerk was eventually granted permission to film in Wolayita, where Oxfam had a small operation, about a day's drive south of Addis Ababa. This was far from the worst of the famine areas in the north but even here there were already sufficient signs of malnutrition and problems with food shortages. Buerk spent a few hours there and flew out to Nairobi where he edited the material and sent it back to London via satellite.[40] His news story scooped the ITV documentary by a few hours and his footage was subsequently used by the Disasters Emergency Committee famine appeal on 19 July, which was fronted on BBC TV by the former sports presenter Frank Bough (and on ITV by the actress Joanna Lumley).[41]

No news ...

By all previous standards the DEC broadcast appeal was a remarkable success, raising initially over the summer of 1984 a total of nearly £2 million,[42] and that was where the media coverage of the famine almost ended. Interestingly, it was probably the news coverage rather than the documentary that encouraged public attention and led to such a high level of donations. Robert Lamb, the producer of 'Seeds of Despair', commented that 'sometimes five minutes on the news is worth 45 minutes of a documentary.'[43] The film, even though it was a significant and important programme, received the smallest viewing figures of any documentary shown that year on Central TV. However, because the documentary itself encouraged news coverage, albeit a short and superficial item, there was sufficient attention to make the appeal so successful. BBC News wanted to follow up the item and report on the way the donations were being used. Instead, the coverage from Ethiopia stopped altogether for a few months.

During the months of August and September 1984 foreign journalists were forbidden from travelling outside Addis Ababa to the affected areas, because the Derg, the Marxist-Leninist 'committee' which ruled Ethiopia, was celebrating ten years in power after the overthrow of Emperor Haile Selassie and wanted no awkward distractions. All possible resources were diverted towards the festivities, which were orchestrated by the North Koreans—with their unparalleled expertise in co-ordinating mass audience events. Even the 450 staff of the Relief and Rehabilitation Commission, whose job was to collect data on famine and to make requests for assistance, were diverted for weeks into banner waving practice.[44] In a report of a donor meeting in Addis Ababa in 1983 the British embassy noted that it had discovered that the port of Assab (which was the crucial entry point for aid) had been commandeered for several months to deal solely with the enormous volume of cement imports required for the building projects concerned with the anniversary festivities. It also emerged later that the special taxes raised to finance the celebrations were in part responsible for the extent of the famine in the southern region of Wolayita (where Michael Buerk had filmed in July).[45]

There were strange echoes of the media coverage of the 1973/4 Ethiopian famine. On that occasion, whilst the countryside had starved, Emperor Haile Selassie had been preoccupied with the lavish tenth anniversary celebrations of the Organization of African Unity, closely followed by the wedding of his daughter. Destitute peasants flocked to the city in search of food. They were beaten and turned back because their presence on the streets would have been a diversion from the aesthetic display of the festivities. The TV journalist Jonathan Dimbleby quite by chance—through an old Sri Lankan college acquaintance—learned of the famine in the highlands and managed through a series of connections to get permission to film there. He went on to make 'The Unknown Famine', which was broadcast by Thames Television on ITV and contained graphic footage of appalling starvation. Dimbleby would later describe the filming as 'the worst ten days of my life'.[46] The programme also presented a devastating view of the imperial regime by contrasting the starvation in the northern highlands with the opulence of the royal celebrations. Sections of it were eventually transmitted in Ethiopia, and they caused such revulsion that this was credited with helping to overthrow Haile Selassie in 1974 and bring into power a new regime that soon turned into the communist government of Colonel Mengistu Haile Mariam. For some years Dimbleby was hailed as 'a hero of the revolution' by the new Ethiopian government, although his continuing tendency to probe and criticize eventually aroused their displeasure.[47]

In August and September 1984 the Marxist-Leninist regime spent an estimated small fortune on celebrating its tenth anniversary in power.[48]

It used the occasion to declare the establishment of a new Marxist Workers' Party of Ethiopia and welcomed guests and observers from around the world to enjoy the festivities. The East German leader Erich Honecker was the guest of honour. However, the Ethiopian authorities were careful to make sure that on this occasion, unlike ten years previously, foreign observers were not distracted by bad news up north. Mike Wooldridge was one of the journalists reporting from Addis Ababa at that time and remembers vividly the grand military parades and the clampdown on freedom of movement. He tried to get out of the capital to visit Korem and Mekele but was flatly refused permission. Travelling clandestinely was not possible either, as all foreigners were closely watched by the secret police.[49]

Meanwhile in Britain, the public had by the start of October donated £9.5m to the DEC 'Famine in Africa' appeal, and it was scheduled to finish on 19 October. At that point it was reported as 'a record total in the 20 year history of the DEC'.[50] Yet agencies like Oxfam now warned that the situation in the north of Ethiopia was catastrophic. Oxfam had taken its time becoming aware of the seriousness of the food shortages. In the internal confidential retrospective assessments of the crisis produced by Tony Vaux and then by Robert Dodd, there was criticism of Oxfam's procedures and monitoring on the ground. The reports highlighted the continuing tensions within aid agencies (and in Oxfam in particular during this period) between focusing on long-term development, which was the ostensible work of the Oxfam operation in Ethiopia, and the immediate pressures of being diverted by short-term emergency relief.[51] There was, in particular, criticism of the local field director who was absent during the critical summer months in 1984. Tony Vaux, an experienced Oxfam employee, observed that there should have been adequate cover arrangements and he also points to the pivotal role of the media as a catalyst for action. He refers to the rain failures in 1982 which had already led to TV film of famine and prompted the DEC appeal on 31 March 1983. Vaux questions why this early indication of a crisis had not been properly followed up, either by the agency or the media.

Vaux points out that in March 1983 Save the Children had convened a meeting of the DEC and reported on evidence of growing food insecurity. Malnutrition had already been observed in the Wollo area of northern Ethiopia in September 1982 and populations were on the move to towns such as Korem; 'this appeared to mean that either there was a severe famine in the local area or else this was a sign of a famine on a much larger scale.' The DEC raised £1.9 million on this occasion (when Esther Rantzen and Jonathan Dimbleby presented the broadcasts) and kept the appeal open until the end of September 1983. Lord Hunt, the chairman of the DEC, sent a letter to the *Radio Times* thanking all those who had donated and expressing satisfaction with the outcome of the appeal.[52] As a result of this original appeal Oxfam sent a team from its Oxford headquarters to monitor the situation in Ethiopia, but crucially there was almost no reporting of the problem once the appeal was over. In his subsequent report, Tony Vaux points to a critical 'gap in publicity' over this period until a news bulletin announced the *Seeds of Despair* programme in July 1984, when 'Once again it was the media, not the monitoring, that brought awareness'.[53]

Robert Dodd, another Oxfam official, took up this theme in an especially detailed and trenchant assessment of the way Oxfam responded to the crisis.[54] His confidential report was written in 1986 after extensive interviews with all those involved. Dodd is critical of the field director's failure to venture into the northern areas to make his own assessment until he went to accompany a Thames Television *TV Eye* crew in October 1984, observing that it appeared as if he was simply following the media, rather than taking the initiative. Dodd concludes that:

The lack of a real sense of urgency was only corrected when the media and the massive response to the DEC appeal actually pushed Oxfam into action … Oxfam failed to approach the deepening crisis in a systematic manner, but allowed itself to be pushed into action, first by the media and then by public concern …

Having been pushed into action, Oxfam then responded with speed, professionalism and panache. A haunting question remains, however. If the media had not moved at that point what would it have taken to have spurred Oxfam into action?

As the report points out, once the head office was alerted to the dire situation, Oxfam sought to remedy its original tardiness. A special assessment was made of the situation when Marcus Thompson and Pat Diskett from Oxfam managed to visit Ethiopia in August 1984. They made the unprecedented and quite dramatic suggestion that Oxfam should use the money from the DEC appeal to charter its own ship filled with grain, not as a solution to the crisis, but to draw attention to the terrible food shortages.[55] In due course the SS *Elpis* left the UK on

11 October with 14,300 tonnes of wheat and eventually berthed in Ethiopia at Assab on 30 October.

Meanwhile a number of journalists were waiting in Addis Ababa to try to reach the famine areas. Once the tenth anniversary celebrations in the capital came to a close, on 3 October 1984, the Politburo finally agreed to give priority to 'the drought' and allow wider media access. The experienced current affairs director Peter Gill and a Thames TV crew, who had been kicking their heels in Addis Ababa, were at last granted permits to travel to the famine areas in the north, in particular to Korem, where famine victims had assembled in makeshift camps and there were Red Cross feeding stations. He was the first foreign journalist to witness the real horror of the widespread starvation. The angle of Gill's film was to contrast the enormous grain surpluses from that year's European harvest, which were rotting in warehouses, with the plight of the starving Ethiopians.[56]

Mohamed Amin, the Visnews cameraman based in Nairobi, had also been trying for weeks to get a visa to return to Ethiopia along with his soundman and Mike Wooldridge. In due course Michael Buerk, from his base in South Africa, had heard about their plans. Paddy Coulter, the head of press for Oxfam, had been urging Buerk to visit the north of Ethiopia. In any case the BBC Foreign News desk was interested in a follow-up piece by Buerk to his July item on Ethiopia. Since there had been such a generous response to the DEC appeal, they decided it would be worth doing an update story for the news on the food problems and to report on how the money raised in the UK was being spent. When Amin was eventually granted a visa in October, Buerk persuaded him to ask for an extra place on the trip so that he could fly up from South Africa and accompany them. Amin agreed to try to persuade the Ethiopian authorities, and after a couple of days' delay he succeeded. As a result, Buerk was allowed to join the other three, and after further complicated negotiations with the Relief and Rehabilitation Commission once they reached Addis Ababa, they were eventually granted permission to visit both Korem and Mekele in Tigray.[57] The problem then was to find transport, as no commercial airliner was prepared to fly to the north because of continued fighting between the Ethiopian government and rebel movements in Eritrea and Tigray. The US-based aid agency World Vision had a Canadian Twin Otter plane and wanted to fly north from Addis to take relief supplies, but had been unable to obtain government permission. Amin negotiated with World Vision to use their aircraft, in exchange for which Amin, using his legendary skills in dealing with recalcitrant officials, obtained a permit from the authorities allowing the NGO workers to travel north as well. As part of the deal Amin agreed to film the World Vision representatives making their own appeal from the famine area—which meant using some of the precious camera batteries, which could not be recharged locally.

Both Michael Buerk and Mohamed Amin have documented their reaction to the mass starvation which they encountered in Mekele and Korem. According to Amin, 'Ethiopia changed me. Until then I had been able to go into any situation, no matter how awful, and switch off. I could remain at a distance from the subject, not get involved. ... But this was different. You can't remain untouched when there are people dying as far as the eye can see.' He went on to describe how he wept when watching the rushes in the edit suite.[58] Buerk described similar reactions. 'It had an emotional impact as well as a professional impact ... we had witnessed something uniquely terrible.'[59] Together they crafted a powerful and moving report.

Fig. 1.1: Michael Buerk and Mohamed Amin filming in Tigray, October 1984. © Camerapix/A24 Media

Yet equally crucial to the impact of their report were the editorial decisions taken by the news desks in London to run the pieces from Ethiopia at length and high up in the bulletins. Buerk had returned to Nairobi and was editing the material in preparation to satellite it when the BBC Foreign News editor Chris Cramer made the unusual decision to bring him back to London overnight on 22 October with his video rushes. This gave him more time to produce a memorable script and enabled the newsroom staff to view the material in greater detail. Buerk describes writing the script on the night flight from Kenya. 'It took half a continent to get the opening right, working and reworking the sentences with the shotlist in front of me but the mind's eye back in Wollo and Tigray. I tried to recapture what it was like to be there.'[60]

The reason why Cramer allowed Buerk this extra time and why the piece eventually ran at an exceptional length was that it felt like a scoop.[61] In fact, the ITV documentary for the *TV Eye* strand, which Peter Gill had been filming, had been due to be transmitted on 18 October, a few days before Buerk's news item, but it was delayed by an Association of Cinematic and Television Technicians (ACTT) strike.

Fig. 1.2: Michael Buerk and Mohamed Amin filming in the compound of the feeding camp at Mekele in Tigray in October 1984. © Camerapix/A24 Media.

The union action, which arose from a pay parity claim for film editors, meant that Independent Television News (ITN) too would be unable to edit and use the ITV footage on their news bulletins. So in a competitive broadcasting environment, this was why Buerk had the luxury of taking more time over his script and travelling back to London before transmission.

This was a huge factor in the way the piece was in the end put together, because rather than shovelling it together and writing the commentary on the back of an envelope in ten minutes, which was what I usually did, I actually edited this piece three times as long as they wanted, because I just felt driven to do that, and got onto the plane and had eight hours on the plane to think about it for once, and think about how it could be written and put together ... which had something to do with the nature of the piece. The second thing was I was able to show it to my bosses in the BBC in the editing rooms, where a couple of them started crying, which was quite extraordinary.[62]

The story led the following day's BBC TV lunchtime news and Ron Neil, editor of the *Six O'Clock News*, used it to lead his bulletin at a highly unusual seven minutes.[63]

Both the BBC news intake and output operations played a key role in the scale and attention which the coverage of the famine received. It was crucial that Chris Cramer as Foreign News editor and in charge of input had commissioned the story and then brought Buerk back to the UK to edit the pictures and dub the commentary. However, equally significant were the decisions of the programme output editors and in particular Ron Neil. He was running a new show, the *Six O'Clock News*, which had been launched on BBC1 with some fanfare earlier in the autumn.[64] Hitherto much of television news on both the BBC and ITV was intended as a form of bulletin of record. The standard bulletin was never more than twenty minutes in length and was designed to cover as many items as possible, but at the expense of doing anything in very much depth. An example of this 'inclusive' approach was the use of HORUS (home round ups) and FORUS (foreign round ups) which were quick surveys of half a dozen stories in a minute, usually with a wipe frame effect between the different subjects. Indeed 'the idea of developing a story or explaining it at two or three minutes length was hardly contemplated.'[65]

The philosophy behind the newly established *Six O'Clock News* programme was to blend the best of the BBC News with the TV current affairs department and its greater emphasis upon high production values.

The bulletin was expanded to half an hour and the idea was that this would enable certain stories to be told at greater length using the skills of current affairs producers to explain and illustrate items in more depth. It was to be a 'current affairs decorated news programme', as one manager described it.[66] Bill Cotton as managing director of television and Michael Grade as Controller of BBC1 had been struggling with the problem of the early evening schedules on BBC1. The establishment of the *Six O'Clock News* in 1984 was part of their strategy to address this problem, along with the planned imminent launch of the new soap opera *East-Enders*.[67] Money and resources had been diverted for the new show, including the key innovation of new electronic graphics; other news programmes at this time were still relying on the old cardboard graphics. The pilots for the *Six O'Clock News* programme had invented the concept of a BEXPO—the 'brief exposition' on a story which might take a minute or so to explain with imaginative graphics instead of the standard ten second in-vision introduction. This deliberate 'news plus analysis remit' meant that 'in a sense the programme was Birtist before Birt'.[68]

The first big challenge facing the new programme had been the bomb explosion at Mrs Thatcher's hotel in Brighton at the Tory party conference, which it had covered well, and overall it was felt to be establishing itself successfully by the end of October. An enormous amount hung on this new programme as it was the second attempt in three years to sort out the early evening BBC1 schedule. Less than a year before the long running *Nationwide* news programme had been axed, amid considerable internal controversy, and replaced with *Sixty Minutes*, another version of teatime news and current affairs. Yet within months that was seen as a failure and was duly taken off the air. In 1984 the *Six O'Clock News* programme, representing a considerable new investment, was the latest high profile effort to reinvent news and factual output for the early evening audience.

Ron Neil arrived at Television Centre as usual at 7am on Tuesday 23 October and bumped into Michael Buerk who had come directly from Heathrow, carrying an onion bag full of video cassettes. Later in the day when he saw the rough cut of the famine story Neil had no doubts about running it at length. There had already been a significant response from the public who had seen the story on the lunchtime news.

It was the combination of Amin's pictures and Buerk's voice which, together, made it such an extraordinary piece of television … we had all seen pictures of famine but these images were different, so haunting and powerful, the whole wide angled landscape of distress combined with wonderfully sparse but powerful commentary made it such a memorable piece of television. Because we were the new programme and we believed in giving good stories proper air time we ran it at length ... When there was a good story we wanted to give the audience a greater sense of the scale of the story, rather than swiping it past them in a few seconds.[69]

Ron Neil had no doubt that it was the right thing to do because it also reflected the values of the new programme, which was at that time regularly getting substantial audiences of 8 million viewers or more.[70] Surprisingly the Michael Buerk coverage on Ethiopia did not lead the 9pm news bulletin that night, which had instead some relatively insignificant development in the ongoing miners' strike as its top story, followed by coverage of a state visit to the UK by President Mitterrand of France. The generous resources which had been lavished on the new *Six O'Clock* programme had led to prevailing resentments between the two programmes which may have gone some way to explain the decision by the evening bulletin to run with a different lead story.[71] Chris Cramer, who was in no doubt about the remarkable qualities of the famine report, was outraged that Mike Broadbent, the editor of the *Nine O'Clock News*, refused to run it as his lead. Reflecting upon this Cramer said, 'It was quite the most absurd decision I have heard in thirty years in television ... as a result of this we had a noisy and lengthy row which lasted for many years after that.' Cramer is aware that the decision was probably prompted by institutional rivalries between the programmes and made a wide ranging observation about the perceptions of competition: 'These things are often driven by programme rivalries and we forget that the competition is outside the organisation with different sets of initials rather than the one inside, with the same sets of initials.' However, the famine item still ran at a remarkable 6 minutes further down the bulletin. The next day, 24 October 1984, Buerk had cut a second piece which also ran at length on each of the three main BBC TV bulletins[72] and was picked up by numerous other BBC outlets in the UK and abroad.

The opposition, meanwhile, was scuppered by the ITV technicians' strike. Alan Sapper, the general secretary of the ACTT union, refused to make an exception for the Thames TV film 'Bitter Harvest', despite its heartrending subject matter. However, after the BBC news item was

Fig. 1.3: 'Ethiopia' by Cam Cardow.

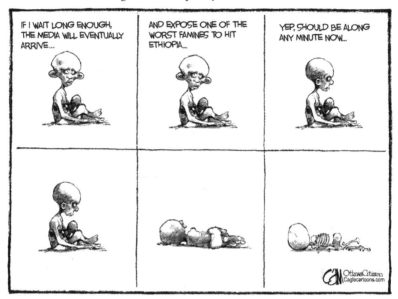

Source: 'Ethiopia' by Cam Cardow. © Cam Cardow / Ottawa Citizen (caglecartoons.com). The Ottawa Citizen, Ottawa (May 16, 2003).

shown and an *Evening Standard* headline described Sapper's decision as 'heartless', he quickly changed his mind and 'volunteers' were allowed to edit the film, which was then eventually transmitted by Thames TV on 25 October.[73] Yet the ACTT still prevented any clips of the story being shown on any of the ITN news bulletins, so it remained exclusive to BBC News.

Unprecedented impact

Disasters have happened throughout history, and plenty of them in the twentieth century, which resulted in more deaths and more devastation than the Ethiopian famine of 1984, yet the media focus on this tragedy was unprecedented. Peter Cutler, who was working for the British based Food Emergencies Research Unit during that period (on a project that was funded by the Overseas Development Administration), had been utterly frustrated by the lack of government reaction to the growing crisis. He recalled coming back again to Ethiopia in September 1984 'and literally giving up. We were just banging our heads against a brick wall. I'd tried all the donor agencies and the media. People were sick of my going on about it. Then along came BBC Television and everything changed overnight.'[74]

There is no question that the BBC television pictures triggered an extraordinary response. Dawit Wolde Giorgis poses the question in his own memoir; he cannot understand why, when as early as the spring of 1983 efforts had been made to attract attention and the R&RC had issued early warnings, the Western governments had not responded and the media had remained silent until the story broke like a dam in October 1984.

To this day it is unfathomable to me why, on that particular date, that particular film created a world wide sensation. The scenes televised nightly by World Vision in the US were just as horrible, 'Seeds of Despair' was just as shocking …perhaps we will never understand the reason. We only know that the result was unprecedented in world history. The magnitude of our tragedy was suddenly matched by an outpouring of sympathy from every corner of the world … was the world simply ready for another drama, another thrilling real-life tragedy?[75]

Giorgis goes on to marvel at the fact that there was even an impromptu collection in the BBC newsroom, after the news transmission, which produced £200 to feed the starving—a pretty unusual response amongst hard-bitten journalists.

The apparent serendipity of news is so often a puzzling conundrum. Those who operate outside the newsroom will marvel that on one day a story is given extensive coverage and taken seriously but on another day an item on the same topic is dropped altogether from a bulletin. Obviously there are all kinds of accidental reasons such as the opinions of individual news editors, the relative merits of various stories on a particular day, but arising out of this there are also a number of more fundamental processes at work. It may be an accident that a particular story is covered and given widespread attention but the processes that lead to such a focus of attention are not accidental. The literature on news values outlines the nature of the overall principles and constraints that underlie news judgements.[76] This helps to throw at least some light on why it was that this particular tragedy at this particular time captured such extraordinary media attention, and what the implications of such powerful exposure were.

Inevitably there is the eternal news syndrome of timing and newsroom judgements. Crucially, this was a 'quiet' period for news. Moreover, news values are always a relative and not an absolute matter. As news editors sometimes comment, timing is to news what location is to estate agents. It is generally the case that 'people in the north only pay attention to crises affecting distant people on a cyclical basis and rarely have the appetite for more than one at a time'.[77] If there had been another major foreign story at the time—greater unrest in South Africa or a war in the Middle East—then neither the resources nor the bulletin space would have been available for Ethiopia. Closely linked to the issue of timing is that of cultural proximity. There is always significant weighting given to a story in proportion to how close to home it happens.[78] In order for a faraway story to make the headlines, at the very least an awful lot of people have to die. Yet sometimes this rule can be broken or at least adjusted. Usually that depends upon a specific human-interest angle, for example where the fate of a single child victim becomes a major news story, but on this occasion, in addition to the wide scale volume of death, the overall tragedy captured the newsroom imagination.

What really enhanced the appeal of this particular famine story was a very particular angle available during that period: the record European grain surpluses, rotting in warehouses owing to the Common Agricultural Policy of the European Community. In the autumn of 1984 the tales of European excess gave an added dimension to the images of starvation a thousand miles further south.[79] This dramatic contrast between the two was the central theme of Peter Gill's film *Bitter Harvest*, and was then repeatedly picked up in follow-up news pieces to great effect.[80] It was no longer just a story of hungry millions, but also of the ridiculous imbalances of Western food policies, and in particular the EEC diktats on agriculture and food storage.

Beyond the news angle, another key reason for the exceptional prominence given to this report was the combination of Mo Amin's dramatic pictures and Buerk's highly effective script writing, which combined to make what Ron Neil as editor of the *Six O'Clock News* described as 'an exceptionally well-crafted report.'[81] Over the coming months these reports went on to win BBC News a collection of prestigious international awards.[82]

By the late twentieth century it was inconceivable that a story could be taken seriously by the rest of the world if there were no pictures.

During the Chinese famine in 1959–61 an estimated thirty to forty million people died.[83] Yet there were never news pictures of this tragedy (which the Communist regime sought to hide completely) and this was part of the reason why it did not become a major story, either at the time or in subsequent years. The most devastating war since 1945 in which around five million died took place in the aftermath of the Rwandan genocide in the Democratic Republic of Congo. But even in an environment of increasingly global media this was a tragedy largely without pictures in its worst phase, and so it barely penetrated the consciousness of the outside world. This apparently arbitrary way in which some faraway stories are covered and others are ignored is a persistent theme in news coverage. Jonathan Benthall in his study of disasters and the media observes that 'the vast majority of natural disasters such as floods and earthquakes are not reported at all in the international media. Some cases of warfare and civil strife might be happening on the dark side of the moon for all we read or hear about them.'[84] The former EU commissioner for humanitarian affairs, Emma Bonino, once posed the question:

What does it take for a humanitarian crisis to make it into prime time slots on radio or television? Deaths are essential, preferably hundreds of them in places that have not captured media attention before. News is by definition new … I became aware that for every humanitarian crisis that made it into the headlines, there were dozens that went unnoticed.[85]

The Ethiopian famine could have become one of those countless international news stories that went unnoticed, which never made the mainstream news. Yet in 1984, thanks to Mo Amin's tenacious attitude towards the Ethiopian authorities and his skilled camerawork, there were powerful pictures to show the world. However, because of the wider issues surrounding news values and timing, dramatic pictures of large numbers of foreigners dying in faraway places are only *a necessary and not always a sufficient* condition for widespread exposure and attention. Michael Buerk then wrote a memorable script to complement Amin's images. He considered it crucial that he had more time than is normal in a regular satellite transmission to work on his script. The removal of the worry of having to 'beat' ITV—because of the ACTT strike—meant that Buerk was given an extra day to come back to London and to craft a much more polished item than if he had been trying to meet a nightly satellite deadline in Nairobi. And it meant he was able to negotiate in person with his editors, rather than down a crackling phone line.

Ron Neil, the editor of the *Six O'Clock News* who took the decision to run the story at length and at the top of the programme, is adamant that the quality of the product was paramount in his decision.

It sprang to the surface and hit the public consciousness for one reason only. It was a remarkable story, yet the same story filmed by a different cameraman and voiced by a different reporter would have ended up half way down the bulletin. Famine is famine—they come and go and it takes a lot to heave our consciousness up.[86]

This comment about the significance of the choice of correspondent for a story is reinforced by several experienced newsroom observers. Both the late Brian Hanrahan[87] and also Nik Gowing,[88] who between them covered numerous foreign stories for BBC News for many years, believe that Michael Buerk's voice and script were crucial to the way that this particular story was received.

What was evident from the remarkable images captured by Amin was the scale and visibility of the crisis: part of the reason why the pictures worked so well is that they conveyed such an overwhelming image of tragedy, referred to by Buerk as 'biblical'. The populations facing hunger had migrated onto the spinal road that runs north and had gathered in huge numbers, 85,000 outside Mekele and 40,000 on the plain of Korem, both of which featured in the news report. It was the long panning shot across the camp in Korem, which opened the report on 23 October, that became the recurring image of the famine. Although it is easier to distribute food if people congregate together, such mass influxes also increase the dangers of disease. Wherever possible food and aid agencies now try to avoid such mass migrations, but such was the desperation in 1984 that it was impossible to stop the movement into the camps, and that gave the pictures an added drama and a greater visibility to the tragedy. Other catastrophes might be just as devastating but they do not create the same visual shock. In a subsequent African crisis, HIV-AIDS victims die singly in their homes or in small groups in hospital wards, and because there is no comparable pattern of wholesale migration there is not the same sense of a mass tragedy with its correspondingly greater visual impact.[89]

It is also important to understand the role of the senior editorial staff in BBC news in the prominence of this story. Both intense competition between broadcasting organizations and the unique structures of the BBC were significant in giving the Ethiopian story such impact. The news bosses took the unusual decision to run a foreign story from an obscure part of the world at great length and high up the domestic news bulletin. Having given this exposure on two days running, the structures of the BBC could reinforce an exclusive story, the 'discovery' of a famine, across the corporation with its multiple and varied outlets. It is conceivable that the ACTT strike helped to make the story bigger in two ways. As it was an exclusive to BBC News, this meant that they were inclined to run it at greater length and high up in the bulletin, in the knowledge that it was unavailable to ITN. Moreover, if the famine report had gone out first as a Thames TV documentary—to a much smaller audience than BBC news—then the competitive pressures would have meant that this story would have rated far less coverage on the BBC. However, because it 'broke' first on the news, when the ITV documentary with its more detailed explanation and its emphasis upon the European surpluses appeared, it served very effectively to reinforce the original drama of the news coverage. Peter Gill, who made the *TV Eye* programme, commented:

I think the current affairs piece that we ran did perform the role of current affairs, which was to provide a measure of analysis to complement and to go with the news ... current affairs can make a solid political point, sustain a political thesis—ours was that here was this grotesque imbalance between the grain mountain of Europe and starvation in Africa.[90]

The issue of competition both within and between outlets is something that journalists are often reluctant to talk about. Michael Buerk, for example, was coy about the BBC's attempt to beat the original Charles Stewart documentary on the famine in July 1984. In the face of disasters where thousands are dying, it is tasteless to talk about the competitive dramas between different TV teams. Nevertheless, as Buerk admits, there was a competitive element. Similarly, Ron Neil admits that he would have felt satisfaction in beating ITN to the famine story: 'Stealing a lead on ITN—the idea of rubbing salt into the wound (due to their problems with the technicians strike) would have been a great pleasure.'[91] Chris Cramer echoes the same sentiment: 'There was fierce rivalry between ITN and BBC news—especially with a new BBC news management and a new editor of the *Six O'Clock News*—they must have choked on our exclusive.'[92] In subsequent years the scope and influence of ITN as a news organization able to rival the BBC has substantially declined, as the ITV system was deregulated and then became less inclined to finance an expensive foreign news operation at ITN. However, in 1984 ITN was still well funded and a world regarded news operation which could challenge and not infrequently beat the BBC with its huge resources. In Africa during this period there was often intense competition between the two.[93] The television coverage of the Biafra story in 1968/69 had originally been a scoop by ITN and the news coverage of the Ethiopian famine coverage in 1973 had also been an ITV/ITN exclusive.[94]

It was not only external competitive pressures that were important in the decision making over the famine news item, but also internal developments within the BBC news operation. This was still a period when television news was restricted to three bulletins a day and nothing else. There were no news channels or 24 hour coverage, let alone online news or social media. An important development during this period was the availability of a new BBC TV outlet for news coverage, the *Six O'Clock News* programme. Chris Cramer stresses the significance of this in the production of the famine broadcast:

A number of unusual circumstances surrounded this coverage. First was a new piece of TV programming on the block and a desire by the people who produce the content to produce good material for that programme. Sometimes input and output are in conflict and there are professional rivalries, but in this case even the die-hard TV news hands, as I would describe myself, could see that the new current affairs hands had got the relationship with the audience. If you put a charismatic editor in charge of a very important programme then everyone wants to please and everyone wants to work together. In my mind here was a marvellous new shop window—and so this item will not go the way of many pieces of memorable television, which is all over in two minutes and onto something else. It won't go that way ... as we are all bought into this programme as the most important programme at that time on this channel (BBC1).[95]

Another significant issue in the positioning of the Ethiopian story is the enduring pattern in news coverage of sudden unforeseen, events taking precedence over longer-term processes. Michael Schudson presents an interesting discussion of this imbalance and the way that the news room journalists 'find their joy and their identity in the adrenaline rush that comes from ... the unplanned and unanticipated.'[96] Clearly famine is not a sudden disaster like an earthquake. It takes place slowly over many months and years. Yet the way the famine was characterized in 1984 (albeit incorrectly) was as an unexpected and newly discovered event.[97] The enforced news blackout in the months before October 1984, on account of the Derg's tenth anniversary celebrations, exacerbated this sense of a totally new and sudden story, thereby enhancing its journalistic appeal. Aid agencies too are well aware of this unfair calculus where the sudden takes precedence over the chronic in terms of attracting assistance. Lloyd Timberlake, in his analysis of disasters for the NGO Earthscan, concluded that 'Disasters that kill a few quickly get more relief than those that grind people down slowly.'[98]

In addition to the virtue of being perceived as a sudden, unforeseen event the Ethiopian famine was also characterized—once again incorrectly—as a sudden event (famine) which had a specific and easily explicable cause (drought). This straightforward explanation was appealing to television as well as later on to tabloid journalists. As Jackie Harrison points out, 'News items of an extremely complex ambiguous or abstract nature cannot easily fit the format of TV news.'[99] Evan Davis, an experienced and thoughtful broadcaster, is one of many journalists who has spoken, with some frustration, about the tendency of television news to 'shy away from complexity'.[100] He concludes that the culture of TV journalism is resistant to ambiguity or uncertainty and likes a clear answer to the question of 'Who is to blame?' The way in which the initial story about the Ethiopian famine was told fitted that pattern well.

TV news bulletins in the 1980s existed in a very different media landscape from the twenty-first century. TV news audiences in 1984 were far higher than in the succeeding multi-channel age. According to Michael Buerk:

The items ran at about three or four times the length of a normal news piece and on the one, six and nine o'clock bulletins over two days. You have to realise that the audiences for those programmes were double, or even triple, what they are today; so you had perhaps 10 million people watching the nine o'clock news, 8 million people watching the six o'clock news and 5 million people watching the one o'clock news ... You are lucky if you get 5 million people watching the ten o'clock news now ... so over two days, two thirds of the population of the United Kingdom actually saw those pieces in a way that could never happen again today.[101]

Buerk draws a contrast about who was actually watching the news bulletins, referring to the impact that the famine report had upon the rock star Bob Geldof. 'There was more of a culture of watching television news, so you even had the pop singers of the day watching it. I doubt you would see *Coldplay* and *The Darkness* watching the ten o'clock news or Newsnight today.'[102] Moreover, the total volume of news in a day was far less in 1984 than in the digital age. In 1981 all the national news from one day could be read, watched or listened to in 24 hours, whereas twenty years later, monitoring a day's news took two and half weeks (leaving aside the internet),which is a 1,800 per cent increase.[103]

However, there was also another crucial aspect to timing: the proximity to Christmas. The previous Ethiopian appeal had been in July 1984 when it is much harder to interest the public and editors in this kind of issue, even though it had raised substantial sums. It is a universal truth of journalism that stories with a charitable dimension fare much better in the season of goodwill, and the Geldof/Bandaid angle on the story with the famous single 'Do They Know It's Christmas?' followed by the US single 'We are the World' gave the famine coverage a huge boost. The charitable effort became a major story in itself. As soon as the original item was transmitted on the BBC112.30 lunchtime news bulletin on 23 October 1984, the phones began to ring in the various overseas aid agencies.[104] By the *Six O'Clock News* the response of the public and the charities to the news of the famine already merited its own slot in the running order.[105] Over the coming weeks in the run up to Christmas, as Bob Geldof became involved and Band Aid was launched, there were other dimensions to the story which prolonged the life of the original coverage. The intervention of the tabloids gave a whole additional impetus to the famine and so there were continually new angles and fresh coverage for several months as streams of celebrities and famous faces, from Mother Teresa and Bob Maxwell to Senator Edward Kennedy (and his family), Cardinal Hume and even Charlton Heston, made the trek to the camps in northern Ethiopia.[106] The proximity to Christmas and the charitable impulse were among the main reasons that the story had this continuing momentum. As Michael Schudson describes it, 'a story with legs strikes journalists as a palpable force with a momentum of its own that will generate follow-up stories.'[107] In these terms the Ethiopian famine was a textbook case study.

It may have been arbitrary that the story was covered in the first place, and the circumstances that enabled Buerk and Amin to reach Korem in October 1984 were pretty random. The greater significance of chance is generally more common in the case of foreign news stories. Invariably there are a huge number of possible stories, including plenty of 'event based disasters', and, partly for reasons of resources and logistics, only a small number of them will ever be covered. However, once an item has been shot and edited, there are a number of fairly predictable processes which explain its impact: the influence of competition between media outlets and the impact of the strike, the timing and absence of alternative foreign news items, the characterization of the famine as a 'sudden unforeseen event', and the contemporary structures within the BBC. The decisions behind news coverage may appear to be capricious, yet often this capriciousness operates within a series of underlying parameters which help to explain why this story about a faraway place took on such momentum and the news item itself gained such an iconic status.

2

GLOBAL STORY

NATIONAL RESPONSE

'I pay tribute to the honourable role played up to now in this crisis by a number of journalists. In spite of the presence in Ethiopia of innumerable humanitarian organisations and agencies, the requests for massive assistance by the Relief and Rehabilitation Commission to these agencies throughout the year, it needed the horrifying pictures of death and starvation shown on the television screens in North America and Europe to galvanise the world into taking notice of what was happening in Ethiopia ...'

Extract from Speech by Ethiopian relief and rehabilitation commissioner Dawit Wolde Giorgis to Donor conference in Addis Ababa, December 1984[1]

'News coverage does not, in itself, determine policy, despite what proponents of the "CNN effect" might content. But it does wield influence in the democratic interaction between public and government.'

Philip Seib, *The Global Journalist*[2]

'It was only when the donor community began to see the effects of the famine for themselves principally through the media, in particular colour television pictures, that actions really began to be taken.'

Famine in Africa, House of Commons Foreign Affairs Select Committee report, 1985.

41

The reaction to the broadcast

Famine in Ethiopia had been a serious problem since 1982, but for two years it remained a story that the international media were not really interested in covering. The BBC TV reporting of the famine in October 1984 broke through this attention barrier. The plight of the starving in Ethiopia developed into a significant news story which suddenly attracted worldwide interest. The news broadcast received unparalleled attention, first in the UK and then throughout the world as the story grew and grew. Once the world had become aware of the crisis, as a result of the extensive television coverage, this extraordinary media profile had a number of distinct effects all over the Western world. Stephen Garrett commented in *Doing Good and Doing Well* that:

the BBC produced a documentary with such power that it fundamentally altered the Western attitude about giving food relief even to this rather repulsive regime, which was at the time a virtual international pariah ... the pictures led to a quadrupling of US aid ... individual officials and the public reaction combined to change policy.[3]

Yet what makes the media coverage of the famine so significant is the effect it had upon public policy. This can operate in two ways—both directly on those involved in the policy making process and also through the lever of public opinion, which itself reacts to the media coverage. When public opinion is exercised in a democracy this in turn may exert pressure upon official government policy, in particular pressure for a humanitarian intervention and the echoing demand that 'something must be done'. The contemporary documents illuminate the way that this process developed in 1984. They clearly demonstrate the swift manner in which government reacted to the media coverage of a crisis, even though it was already well aware of the situation beforehand. They also give an indication of how much was really being done to respond to the famine and to what extent this was more a response to domestic political pressure—reacting to media coverage—rather than a straightforward response to foreign suffering.

Of course, it was not just a matter of how the media coverage affected policy. The second major effect of the famine coverage was the long-term impact it had upon attitudes towards charitable giving, private philanthropy and the aid business within Western countries. The media story generated what became, at that time, 'an unprecedented surge of humanitarian concern and popular mobilisation.'[4] And both the timing and the nature of this outpouring of generosity by the public arose in reaction to the media coverage of the disaster.

Widening media attention

The scope of the media attention and reaction can be measured by the extent to which the original Visnews/BBC story about the famine was eventually picked up in the UK press and by television stations across the world. This in turn provoked a public reaction, which in turn influenced public policy as well as the response encountered by charities and NGOs. One clear indicator of press attention was the amount of space given to the Ethiopian famine before and after 23 October 1984. There was a tenfold increase in coverage by the quality press. On 26 October *The Times'* first leader began, 'British drawing rooms have been invaded by pictures of children dying of starvation in Ethiopia' and spoke of 'a disaster whose coming has been predicted by aid workers for years ... (yet) the present shock is a tribute to the emotive power of television pictures'.

The degree to which the popular press took up the story after the TV news items was even more dramatic. Coverage of the famine in the tabloid newspapers went from 50 column inches in the first three weeks of October to nearly 1,200 column inches in the last ten days of the month, accompanied naturally by full page colour photos (see fig.).[5] In the preceding months there had been almost no interest demonstrated in the build-up of famine in Africa in the popular tabloid press. On the day that the Amin/Buerk item was shown Chris Cramer, as BBC TV foreign news editor, offered a full set of pictures to the *Sun*. The response was: 'We're actually not interested in famine'. Yet just a few days later the *Sun's* front page headline in letters two inches high was 'Race to Save the Babies'. Once the story broke on TV the *Sun* totally changed its mind and was even sending its own reporters and photographers out to Ethiopia.[6]

The original BBC broadcast and the media's 'discovery' of the famine turned it into a worldwide event. Fred O'Donovan, chairman of RTE in Ireland, wrote to the BBC chairman, Stuart Young, on 9 November 1984, 'I congratulate you all on a truly wonderful piece of professional television that has inspired the greatest co-operation of various countries

Fig. 2.1: Quality Vs. Popular Press: Column Inches of Copy Devoted to Ethiopian Famine Coverage' in Mary Kay Magistad, 'The Ethiopian Bandwagon:
The Relationship between News Media Coverage and British Foreign Policy
towards the 1984–5 Ethiopian Famine' (Unpublished Master's thesis, University of Sussex, 1985).

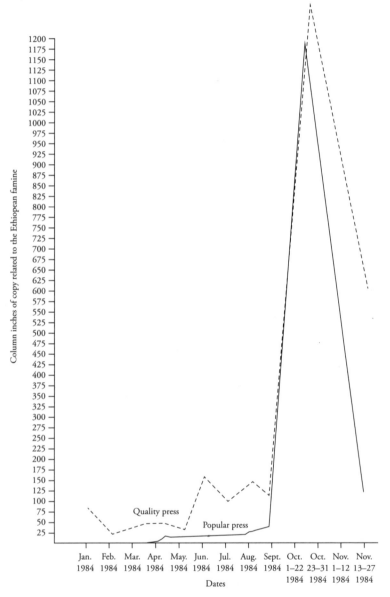

since World War Two. When the history of this tragic famine is written it must never be forgotten that Michael Buerk's documentary started all the effort to help'.[7]

It was apparent from this observation that it was television pictures that 'sold' the story. Radio no longer had the same impact. Mike Wooldridge, the BBC East Africa correspondent, had filed his first radio report on the famine already upon his return to Addis Ababa from the north of Ethiopia, with Buerk and Amin. He had to use the old method of unscrewing the telephone receiver and connecting his Uher tape recorder to the phone with crocodile clips.[8] He was interviewed over a muffled line by Sue MacGregor on the *Today* programme on the morning of Monday 22 October 1984,[9] but it was only when the television pictures were seen on the following day that the impact of the story was felt worldwide. It was a clear indication that television was now the primary medium for news and that television pictures were a necessary, if not always sufficient, criteria for a disaster to be taken seriously by the rest of the globe.

The news story shot by Mohamed Amin and reported by Michael Buerk, broadcast on 23 October 1984, was eventually transmitted in some form by 425 of the world's broadcasting organizations and was seen by an estimated audience of 470 million.[10] Yet one of the most significant of all news stations almost did not broadcast it. The American network NBC was offered the material prior to transmission, because NBC and BBC had a news exchange relationship at that time. This meant that they would co-operate by sharing material between them. Chris Cramer recalls how:

We had very good relations with NBC—our partners in America—the bureau chief in London was Frieda Morris with whom I had a good professional relationship and I knew she adored the work of Michael Buerk—so we invited them to come to Television Centre and watch the material as we viewed it … not as we transmitted it … and shared with them our excitement about it.[11]

In spite of the enthusiasm within the BBC about the Ethiopian report, Joseph Angotti, the NBC European news director, had turned it down when he saw it listed on the 'news prospects' for that day. However, Frieda Morris, having viewed the piece with the BBC team at Television Centre in West London, defied her bosses, and even though they said they did not want it, she sent the material on the feed to New York anyway, in exactly the form it had been edited by the BBC.

Once the item had gone out on the BBC later that day, NBC changed its mind and Angotti asked if it might use the story after all. However, the New York office was still reluctant as it was preoccupied with the forthcoming US elections, but when the pictures were viewed as they came into the NBC Newsroom in New York, there was a stunned reaction and the anchor Tom Brokaw, who also played an important editorial role, argued strongly in favour of showing them.[12] Two news items were dropped from the running order and the Ethiopian story was broadcast on NBC at three minutes—which counted as a long report by normal American standards. What was even more unusual was that the report was transmitted with the original commentary voice—which was of course Michael Buerk's British accent. This is very rare indeed on a network US news programme. Indeed Chris Cramer, who had worked so hard to persuade NBC to see the material in the first place, believes that 'it was a first and a last that a BBC news item was transmitted untouched like that by a US network ... not just as part of another package, as they did for example with the famous Princess Diana interview.'[13]

NBC then went on to place an advert about its famine coverage in the *New York Times*, which was somewhat ironic considering their initial reluctance to take the story. At a subsequent BBC news and current affairs meeting on 20 November 1984 the assistant director general, Alan Protheroe, wryly drew attention to this:

Nothing is so indicative of the difference between British and American news values as the fact that whereas the BBC cleared as much as possible from its news programmes to make way for the film on Ethiopia, the NBC advertisement ringingly proclaimed: 'Last Tuesday the NBC Nightly News showed the kind of pictures that grab the emotions ... Tom Brokaw, anchor of the Nightly News said the pictures had to go out that night. Two stories were pulled to make way for a three-minute piece that ended the broadcast ...'[14]

Eleven years earlier the American networks had declined altogether to show the Jonathan Dimbleby report on the 1973 Ethiopian famine. It was considered to be 'too downbeat'.[15] The drama of Watergate was filling the airwaves at that time and as a result this particular famine, whilst it had a considerable impact in Europe, never became a story in the US. A paltry $1.5m was collected in the US for the famine victims in 1973/74, only a small fraction of the charity donations amassed for the same cause in Europe. In 1984 things were different. America responded wholeheartedly, even if the story still only merited three minutes on US Television.

GLOBAL STORY: NATIONAL RESPONSE

Triggering a response—echoes of Biafra

Sixteen years before the Ethiopian crisis there had been a similar turning point in media coverage of a humanitarian crisis in the developing world when the story first broke of the Biafran crisis. A civil war between Nigeria and the breakaway state of Biafra had led to famine conditions within the mainly Igbo rebel state. On that occasion it had been the tabloid press which had taken the lead in making the Biafran war and starvation a major story (although eventually ITN also played a role), but in 1984 the mantle had convincingly passed to television. In each case the media played a vital role and galvanized opinion in a dramatic way. In 1968/69 the tabloid press highlighted the story of the starving children on the rebel side and Peregrine Worsthorne, who was then the deputy editor of the *Daily Telegraph*, commented that 'If the Sun and the Sketch hadn't succeeded in reporting the Biafran famine there would be NO Biafran crisis today so far as the British public is concerned ... they created the crisis or created our awareness of the crisis.'[16] As would happen later in 1984, the coverage of the Biafran cause inspired public pressure and led to a change in aid priorities. The images of starvation famously led to the American president Lyndon Johnson screaming at his staff 'Get those f.... black babies off my screen'—in other words, do something that stops these images.

At the end of the Biafran war when the Nigerians had triumphed, the Biafran rebellion was judged to have been a hopeless cause; but such was the effect of the black and white newspaper pictures of the starving that the doomed rebel regime was effectively propped up by aid agencies for probably a year or so longer than it would have otherwise survived. The veteran Africa correspondent Colin Legum, who covered the story for the *Observer*, noted, 'Your heart was bleeding, but your head was telling you something different.'[17] As the regime became more and more isolated, eventually a major source, possibly the sole source of foreign exchange for the regime of Colonel Ojukwu (the Igbo rebel leader) was derived from the aid agency presence in his territory. He imposed an absurd local exchange rate and from the spending of the expatriate workers and payment of fees for landing rights for relief aircraft he managed to extract foreign currency to buy arms, thereby prolonging the war and delaying the inevitable Nigerian victory.[18]

In retrospect, the conclusion amongst many of those who have studied this famine and its reporting was that the rebellion would have ended earlier with relatively less suffering if there had not been such dramatic intervention by the aid world.[19] And the humanitarian intervention itself was attributed to the powerful media coverage. Indeed the first photos of starvation splashed by the *Daily Express* were dismissed as 'mere Oxfam posters'.[20] Much of the sympathetic media coverage of the Biafran cause was galvanized by the BBC defector, Freddie Forsyth (later the best selling thriller writer), who focused the world's attention on the suffering civilians in the rebel areas. Forsyth disappeared from his post as a correspondent reporting on the war for the BBC, to the horror of his bosses, and threw his energies into promoting the cause of the rebellion.[21] A highly sophisticated media operation inspired the Western public to donate and enabled the aid agencies to organize a dramatic relief operation, principally through airlifting supplies into Biafra during the night. In the public imagination this is how the disaster is remembered. It was only after the crisis was over that there was a growing realization within the aid community that the whole operation, partly through the influential media role, had been somewhat misconceived. In many ways this was to be a forerunner of the Ethiopian coverage in 1984, where shocking pictures of starving victims prompted a worldwide desire to assist. Yet in retrospect Biafra, like Ethiopia, was also an example of misunderstanding the story and somewhat misguided intervention.[22]

It was during the crisis in the Nigerian civil war that the young doctor Bernard Kouchner first identified the relationship between the media and aid. He was working for the French Red Cross, but he became increasingly disillusioned with the international role of the Red Cross and its insistence upon neutrality and dealing only through official government channels. As a result of what he experienced in Biafra, he helped to found Médecins Sans Frontières (and later also Médecins du Monde), both charities that, in contrast to traditional practices, took a radically different approach both to the provision of aid and to the question of media profile.[23] Kouchner (who would later become the foreign minister of France) was highly critical of the confidentiality espoused by the Red Cross, believing in the vital role of the media in drawing attention to humanitarian crises. Indeed, Kouchner commented that 'MSF were the children of journalism and of medicine'.[24]

Kouchner's most famous doctrine was the 'right to intervene' when he highlighted the role of the media in stimulating a public response. (In the post-Cold War period this became of course a much wider rallying cry against tyranny.) And what Kouchner commented so memorably was that 'where there is no camera, there is no humanitarian intervention.'[25] So not only are the pictures critical in the story gaining a wide exposure, they are also crucial in provoking a response to the story. The manner in which the Biafra story suddenly came to world attention via the media highlights the arbitrariness in the way that disasters are covered, which in turn affects the nature of the response. In observing the Biafran crisis Colin Seymour-Ure commented that; 'For every Igbo baby fed on the funds collected after media coverage of the Nigerian civil war, some other child in a part of the world untouched by the zoom lens of TV war reportage starved.'[26]

Foreshadowing the CNN effect

Many years later, with the emergence of 24-hour TV news channels, this pattern of media coverage that apparently triggers a political or humanitarian response was identified as the 'CNN effect'. This was a description first coined during the first Gulf War in 1991 and it was a 'generic term for the ability of real time communications technology via the news media to provoke major response from domestic audiences and political elites to both global and national events'.[27] The Ethiopian coverage was considered to be a prime example of what subsequently became known as the CNN effect, and the Biafran coverage too fell into this category. Even though the famine broadcasts from Biafra and Ethiopia happened some years before the term was invented they were a classic case of this 'something must be done' scenario. There was an overwhelming response to the pictures of foreign catastrophe which led to a widespread reaction among the public, expressing an urge both to do something themselves and to press authorities to act.

In his study of the CNN effect, Piers Robinson tests the link between pictures and action and distinguishes what he calls 'empathy framed coverage'. Looking back to 1984 he concludes that the Ethiopian famine was a seminal instance of a Western response to a humanitarian crisis and was an example of a strong CNN effect. The story was about suffering individual victims in need of outside help, with only occasional mentions of the political dimension of their struggle.[28] In some ways the effect of this coverage was unequivocal. For example, a detailed Human

Rights Watch report on Ethiopia records how 'the publicity given to the famine represented an earthquake in the relief world.' The figures for official aid certainly support that and are the clearest indication of a rapid change in attitude towards Ethiopia. USAID donations in the financial year 1983 were $11 million, rising to $23 million in 1984 and to a staggering $350 million in 1985. Similarly, EEC donations went from $111 million in 1983 to $213 million in 1984 and $325 million in 1985. Overall aid to Ethiopia was $361 million in 1983, $417 million in 1984 and $784 million in 1985.[29] So, in terms of raising awareness and humanitarian relief, there is no doubt that the media had a substantial effect. However. it is necessary to look at two quite distinct ways in which this operated—both the direction of official public policy, including decisions on aid, and then the area of voluntary, private philanthropic effort.

Public opinion and the policy process

If the Ethiopian famine is conventionally regarded as a well-defined case of a CNN effect where governments were influenced by media coverage to send aid, then how did that process happen in the UK, and was it quite as clear-cut as has been assumed? The serendipitous media 'discovery' of the famine produced for a few weeks throughout the Western world an exceptional public interest and involvement in the subject of poverty and starvation in the horn of Africa.[30] The reaction of the public throughout the UK on this occasion to development issues and aid was a clear manifestation of the wider impact of the coverage. According to the papers from the former Overseas Development Agency (ODA) and from the Cabinet Office[31] the public outcry played a significant role in galvanizing government reaction to the famine, because of the pressure from public opinion on policy makers to 'do something'. The documents demonstrate the direct impact of the public outcry on ministers' and officials' agendas. Departmental memos and internal briefings in the files relating to the famine support this pattern of government reacting to public opinion influenced by media coverage. For example, in a confidential policy paper for the Overseas Development Administration minister, Timothy Raison, immediately after the TV coverage of the famine in July 1984, one official wrote that 'there is widespread public concern in the wake of the recent ITV programme on the drought in

Ethiopia. So far the Government has not been seriously criticized for not doing enough, but reactions are beginning to come through in this sense.'[32] It is apparent that the levers of public opinion, which were reacting to the media coverage, then in turn affected the way that policy makers handled the crisis. Yet for government purposes the coverage was saying little new.

In a statement to the House reporting on famine relief for Ethiopia Raison remarked in 1985 that 'the great international relief effort in which both the British Government and people have played an important part has indeed alleviated much of the suffering which we saw on our television screens in the latter part of 1984.'[33] What he did not indicate was that the government, as is clear from the ongoing embassy briefings and internal discussions, had already been well aware of the scale of suffering long before it was on the TV screens, but had not been inclined to do much to respond to it. It was evident from the urgent concern which Malcolm Rifkind expressed as a junior Foreign Office minister in several letters and memos that there was plenty of evidence available to the UK government of the scale of the famine in 1983/84.[34] Rifkind, who was the Foreign Office minister with responsibility for Africa, recalls noticing the various reports from the embassy in Ethiopia and from others such as NGOs which indicated a mounting crisis, and feeling that he needed to try and push the humanitarian situation into the political spotlight.[35] It is clear from these assessments on the ground that the scale of the crisis was well known to the government departments concerned.[36] The point is that despite the memos which Rifkind produced, the authorities seem to have been resistant to doing very much about it until the fourth week in October 1984 when the scale and nature of their response dramatically changed.

Swift change of heart

One of the irrefutable pieces of evidence indicating the scale of the famine was the research which had been done in Ethiopia by the Food Emergencies Research Unit, based at the London School of Hygiene and Tropical Medicine. Peter Cutler, who was involved in this project, voiced his frustrations[37] that no one would take any notice of the results of the research which predicted widespread starvation. An article arising from the research on famine forecasting had appeared in the publication

Disasters, concluding that 'the logical outcome of the analysis developed here is that we should expect worse famine conditions during 1984 than during 1982–3'[38] and pointing out that 'the need for forward relief planning is demonstrably urgent'. This research was actually sponsored and funded by the ODA, to whom Cutler acknowledges a debt of gratitude. However, it appears not to have had much impact there. In fact a memo from Timothy Raison's private secretary in December 1984 observed that:

In the course of preparing for the Minister's appearance at the Foreign Affairs Committee (giving evidence on the Ethiopian famine) and in following up a letter in the *Times* by Peter Cutler, we happened upon the fact that the ODA has been sponsoring research into the use of economic and social information in famine prediction ... the Minister would be grateful for a note which shows what use has been made of the findings of the research ... within and without the ODA, and indeed how widely its existence was known within the office.[39]

So the research on famine in Ethiopia was funded by the ODA, and presumably the ODA officials who were commissioning it knew about its findings, but the details of this were apparently not then passed on to the minister until after the media had independently highlighted the issue.

Even if they were not paying attention to work on famine predictions supported by their own department, then the civil servants could certainly not avoid repeated warnings of the scale of the famine from the NGOs. Indeed, in his internal letters and memos urging further help for Ethiopia, Malcolm Rifkind refers to the repeated assessments by agencies such as Save the Children on the scale of the famine.[40] In the formal evidence to the House of Commons Foreign Affairs Select Committee investigation into the famine, Colonel Hugh MacKay, overseas director of the Save the Children Fund (SCF), later made an outspoken attack on the way that the government had failed to react to successive warnings about impending famine.[41] The committee's report was subsequently to criticize the government for its 'sluggish response' in spite of having been aware of the disaster for two years.[42]

The committee's observations underline the key role of television coverage and emphasize that the official response to the various pleas for help was pretty limited until the dramatic change brought about by the TV pictures. For example, there was a meeting on 5 October 1984 between ODA officials and the SCF where there was a request for urgent aid to Ethiopia, but the response from the head of the Disaster Unit was that they were already overspent on Ethiopia and could offer little help.[43] Two weeks later, following the media coverage, the attitude had completely changed, even though the facts, as understood by the ODA, were no different. An ODA press release stated that 'The British Government has responded swiftly to the urgent need for further humanitarian assistance to help the victims of famine in Ethiopia.'[44] On 24 October, the day after Michael Buerk's first report on BBC TV news, Sir Geoffrey Howe, the foreign secretary, told the House of Commons that the government was pledging an extra £5 million towards drought affected areas in Africa including Ethiopia and 6,500 tonnes of food aid for people facing starvation in Ethiopia. Five days later, after high level ministerial discussions about the famine, Timothy Raison announced the offer of two RAF Hercules planes to assist in the emergency relief effort for an initial three months.

One example of the dramatic change of heart, even though the facts were already well known, was that early in October there was a long report from the British ambassador including his observation that 'the UK has played our part fully in contributing to the international famine relief effort, although the situation has deteriorated so dramatically in recent months that enormously more is going to be needed if a massive human disaster is to be averted or controlled.'[45] He went on to urge that someone from London should come to Ethiopia and assess the problem. A few days later another telegram from Addis Ababa expressed 'disappointment that no one will visit Ethiopia before February 1985 ... we hope you can reconsider your travel programme to include us ... it would be timely and useful for you to visit us in October or November and look at the famine relief situation.'[46]

A senior ODA official wrote in an internal response to these requests that 'The ambassador is still pressing for East African Department (EAD) to make a visit, but they have my full support in refusing to give this priority over more urgent work for their other clients'.[47] However, after the BBC coverage, the attitude within the department completely changed and civil servants and politicians were suddenly falling over themselves to travel to Ethiopia (including Mr Buist, the author of the memo dismissing the idea of a visit). During the subsequent weeks there were continual visits by the ODA, the Foreign Office and a range of politicians, including several ministers. Indeed, ironically the embassy sent a telegram in December saying that it was unable to cope with the level of visitors which was 'imposing impossible burdens on all concerned'[48] and urging various officials and politicians, who had requested to visit Ethiopia and view the relief effort, to reconsider whether they really needed to come.

The internal official documents demonstrate that the ODA and the Foreign Office clearly had a pretty good idea of the scale of the food shortages well before the autumn of 1984, through aid agencies, embassy communications and independent reports. Yet the whole scale and method of their reaction to the crisis completely changed in the period following the media publicity about the famine. There was of course, at the same time, widespread popular demand for the government to act, especially in view of the European food surpluses. Tim Eggar, MP, parliamentary secretary at the ODA, admitted quite candidly in retrospect that:

We knew of the famine problem obviously before it broke, I think it would be fair to say we had not quite realised the impact it would have on public opinion once the pictures came through. That of course influenced government policy. It would be silly to pretend that it didn't. With the news coverage the famine became a domestic political issue to which we felt we had to respond.[49]

On 22 November, during the debate on aid in the House of Commons, the Liberal Democrat MP Russell Johnston commented that 'The entire aid world has been screaming from the rooftops for the last 18 months that what has happened in Ethiopia was about to occur, yet it was only when we saw it in colour on the screens in our living rooms that the government acted.'[50]

So it appears that although the government was reacting to the circumstances of the famine, it was in fact responding to domestic reactions to media coverage of the famine.

Inside the Foreign Office there was a complete change in pace in reaction to the widening media coverage of the famine from the last few days of October 1984. The two BBC reports were transmitted on 23 and 24 October. On 25 October an Ethiopian Drought Group was established within the Foreign Office with daily meetings scheduled at 10am. It was allocated to the office of Dr Denis Osborne, head of the East and West Africa Department, but 'was hoping to find a larger room soon'; the function of the group was 'giving advice on policy, briefing, correspondence aid administration etc. ... we have many MPs' letters and fear a well-meaning public may send many more.' Meanwhile an

Ethiopian Drought Distribution was set up to circulate material and 'links were strengthened with the Prime Minster's office and the Ministry of Defence.'[51] Another memo a few days later confirms the setting up of a special 'Ethiopia Section' within the ODA to 'deal with the substantial increase in work relating to the famine in that country.'[52]

Sir Crispin Tickell, the permanent secretary at the ODA, also established a daily 9.30am meeting on Ethiopia, and at 6pm each night a report had to be submitted to the minister on the day's developments on the Ethiopian question, cleared by the permanent secretary. The urgency of the proceedings is highlighted in a minute from Dr Osborne to his Drought Group on 3 November on how to present submissions to Sir Crispin Tickell on the famine.

Sir Crispin abhors abbreviation (and in our haste we have been slow to learn this lesson, unthinkingly incorporating drafts from the diplomatic wing or other ODA departments in which abbreviations have been used.) Oxfam is allowed but CAFOD and SCF are not. NGO is unacceptable ... I am copying this minute to those who receive the Ethiopia Drought Group papers so that we can help each other not to fall into one or more of these traps for the unwary ...[53]

Clearly the pressure was mounting over this period as the prime minister's office became involved in reacting to the famine. By 3 November letters from the public were running at 200 per day.[54] Another internal note on 6 November referred to 'the seemingly infinite number of members of the public writing about Ethiopia'.[55] In addition to dealing with letters to MPs the members of the Ethiopia Drought Group were involved in the briefing of ministers for broadcasts and parliamentary appearances. Dr Osborne observed that 'there has been unprecedented parliamentary interest on foreign aid—I estimate 80–100 Members rose to speak after Mr Raison's statement on 30th October.'[56]

Send for the RAF

Six days after the BBC News report on the famine there was a meeting of ministers at 10 Downing St to decide what should be done. This was very clearly a reaction to the media coverage since until then there had been no interest shown in the Ethiopian famine at such high levels. Charles Powell, the prime minister's private secretary for foreign affairs, confirmed in a crisp summary letter following that meeting that there would be an RAF deployment to transport relief around Ethiopia. 'The Prime Minister held a meeting this morning to consider further the Government's response to the famine in Ethiopia … with Ministers from the ODA, Foreign Office and Treasury …' Charles Powell noted, adding that the:

Prime Minster had agreed to provide two RAF Hercules aircraft for three months in the first instance. The MOD and ODA must settle between them how the costs were to be borne. The Government's response should be presented positively in Parliament, with a full account of what had been done, what was in the pipeline and what new steps the Government now envisaged …The uncooperative and surly attitude of the Ethiopian Government should not be concealed.[57]

The government's decision to use the RAF was a highly symbolic and effective way of highlighting the urgency of their concern. Yet airlifts of food are generally impractical as a means of real help. In the aid world they are regarded as the 'last bastion of unprofessionalism',[58] and in the language of some aid workers, 'when you see C130 Hercules flying you know that someone has badly goofed.'[59] Frederick Cuny analyzes just how unrealistic dropping food from the air is as an effective way to help. Every ten tons of food requires ten tons of fuel. At 1980s prices an agency could have bought a truck for every 500 mile flight of a C130. And on a longer flight the cargo has to be further reduced so the plane can take more fuel. As a means of delivery it is uneconomic and impractical.[60] Yet for a politician who wants to be seen to be doing something, this kind of high profile aid can be very successful. Timothy Raison, the overseas development minister, observed that, despite Mrs Thatcher's reservations about the unpleasant Marxist regime in Ethiopia, the RAF airlift was the one thing in this whole process that she was particularly enthusiastic about.[61] Dramatic interventions like this reap more domestic political rewards than the slow, long-term business of development aid which both the Thatcher and Reagan governments were so resistant to,[62] especially in countries they found politically distasteful.

Fighting the Cold War

The Cold War dimension played a crucial role in the way that the government responded to the crisis in Ethiopia. It provided an added strategic bonus to the policy of emergency relief aid, which was being seen to be caring and kind at the expense of the Soviet bloc, which had apparently failed to look after the needs of its client state. This was continually emphasized both in internal Foreign Office briefings and in press interviews and public statements. Mrs Thatcher gave an interview to BBC TV journalist John Simpson in which she remarked:

I saw the television pictures … of children in Ethiopia—I think they were some of the worst pictures of children I have ever seen … it seemed absurd for us to have surpluses of grain while they are needing food and so I raised the question whether we could send some of these surpluses to help Ethiopia and those children …

She goes on to talk about the arms that the Soviet Union was supplying to Ethiopia: 'You see we provide help in terms of food. You can never look to Russia for that kind of food support …'[63]

The same message was also being reinforced internally within the government. The confidential FCO briefing paper for ministers following the BBC broadcasts in October 1984, 'The Ethiopian Famine: Policy Problems', stated as the first long-term policy objective 'to supplant Soviet with Western influence in the Horn, especially Ethiopia.' Similarly, in the report on joint Anglo-German talks held on 14 November 1984 where the discussions covered the Ethiopian famine, the UK representative made the point that 'the UK found the regime inimical … Ethiopia had been a greater prize for the Soviet Union than Angola … the West must attempt to wean them (the Ethiopians) away from Moscow. The enhanced contacts now being made as a result of the famine offered an opportunity to extend Western influence.'[64]

Meanwhile a confidential briefing note for the minister before a Commons appearance is full of hints of how to score points on the Cold War: '(If chance arises) Pity that Soviet assistance to Ethiopia is mainly military: their contribution to famine relief so far sadly inadequate. They must play their part, not least because Ethiopia professes to be a Marxist government.'[65]

Naturally the antipathy was a mutual one. This is evident in a telegram from the UK Moscow embassy reporting on an article by Andrei Gromyko (the veteran Soviet foreign minister) where he blamed the 'current famine conditions on neo-colonialism' and referring to other articles in *Pravda* blaming the West for Africa's problems, saying that their so-called 'aid' was used 'to preserve the conditions for the exploitation of manpower and natural resources.'[66]

On the ground in Ethiopia there were continuing Cold War tussles. So when the Eastern Bloc was apparently unforthcoming on aid and more concerned with military hardware there were criticisms from the West. Yet when the Bulgarians announced at the end of October 1984 that they and a number of Eastern Bloc countries were intending to supply equipment to assist in famine relief, there were complaints that this would mean the Western aid would be hampered if 'as must be likely the Eastern Europeans get automatic priority in an already over-loaded Ethiopian machine'.[67] A couple of weeks later there was an upbeat telegram from the ambassador, Brian Barder, reporting on the triumphal arrival in Addis Ababa of the RAF detachment Operation Bushell, after various bureaucratic problems. However, this too had clear references to Cold War rivalry. According to the report, the RAF received:

[an] enthusiastic welcome from international press (including Mr Maxwell)[68] and Ethiopian airport workers. ... there was vigorous activity by over 50 RAF officers, almost the entire embassy staff, embassy vehicles and swarming press with cameras and microphones, made immense and (in recent years) unprece-dented impact. In Addis rumour among locals is already circulating that Soviet aircraft have been pushed out to make way for RAF. Some resulting euphoria ('The British are back') will be cooled when waves of Soviet Antonovs start arriving at Bole (airport) on Tuesday. But we have made our point simply by being first in.[69]

It subsequently transpired that the arrival of the Soviet Antonovs was brought forward, apparently to coincide with the RAF 'in the hope of beating the RAF to the draw or at any rate of stealing their thunder',[70] and their arrival then led the television news in Ethiopia, relegating the RAF to third place, much to the ambassador's annoyance.

It is clear from these despatches that it was not just the local media that the ambassador was concerned about. In another telegram discuss-ing where the RAF detachment should be based for the duration, there was a suggestion that for operational reasons it should be moved to Djibouti. The ambassador argued strongly against on the grounds that 'Addis is where the media reps are. We will get little attention if not visible.'[71] This last remark hinted that there may have been political motives behind choosing to send the RAF Hercules, rather than other means of transport for relief.

GLOBAL STORY: NATIONAL RESPONSE

Long-term/short-term

The apparent shift in policy with the sudden reaction to the famine in October 1984 was against the background of a Conservative government for which foreign aid had a low priority. Aid was administered by the Overseas Development Administration, a department of the Foreign Office, which was itself not one of Mrs Thatcher's favourite ministries; according to her biographer Hugo Young she saw it as 'bastion of complacency' which was ripe for 'the full Thatcher treatment'.[72] In any case, the concept of foreign aid, especially to unpleasant Marxist regimes and without valuable trade strings attached, was not a popular cause amongst government supporters. According to John Campbell, another of Mrs Thatcher's biographers, 'her attitude to aid mirrored on a global scale her suspicion of the welfare state at home.'[73]

Prior to 1984, Western assistance to Ethiopia was minimal and there was strong pressure against the provision of any kind of development aid (as opposed to emergency aid) to a country firmly within the Soviet bloc. A policy paper, written in the immediate aftermath of the famine coverage, spells out the various policy shifts:[74] 'Revulsion at the Mengistu regime's methods ... led us to reduce and finally cut off development aid to Ethiopia.'

The reluctance to provide development aid was part of a wider political response, and there was a decline in overall spending on overseas aid throughout the period that the Thatcher government was in power. During the 1980s Britain's aid budget fell in real terms by over 7 per cent. As a proportion of GDP it dropped from 0.52 per cent in 1979 to only 0.31 per cent in 1989 (this was against an international target of 0.7 per cent).[75] In fact, in the weeks after the first BBC report on the Ethiopian famine the Conservative government had been scheduled to make a 6 per cent reduction in its foreign aid budget. An *Observer* editorial on 18 November 1984 commented that:

the aid cuts now being contemplated by the government demonstrate how far out of touch it can be with public sentiment. It takes a special degree of ineptitude or insensitivity to consider taking millions of pounds off the government's aid budget at the very time when the public ... is flooding the relief agencies with notes and cheques to save lives in Ethiopia.[76]

In the end widespread public opposition against the background of the Ethiopian crisis eventually led to a significant Tory back bench revolt on the issue (from a party with a majority of over 140 seats), so that the proposed reduction did not take place as anticipated. In the parliamentary vote on 22 November 1984 the aid budget escaped cuts (instead money was taken from the budgets allocated to the BBC World Service). Aware of the political insensitivity which had been displayed, the foreign secretary, Sir Geoffrey Howe, later commented that there had been a misunderstanding all along about ever wanting to cut aid in the first place.[77]

This resistance to spending on long-term development aid was in fact consistent with a wider trend evident throughout this period towards spending on emergency relief at the expense of the more politically contentious development aid. This tension between focusing on development assistance (which involved sustained long-term involvement) and providing quick fix but high profile emergency aid also reflected the ongoing discussions within NGOs, and these debates were evident in the Oxfam reports on the way the famine was handled.[78] There were similar questions raised within government. At the start of the 1980s the percentage of the ODA budget spent on emergency relief was 2 per cent. By 1987 it had risen to 11 per cent and it doubled again within the next fifteen years, reaching 23 per cent by 1993.[79] As a result, within the aid world 'the impression that short-term relief assistance was becoming a substitute for foreign policy in Africa among some northern countries was profound.'[80] This was part of a long-term and ongoing policy debate; for example, a decade later a retrospective evaluation of the crisis in Rwanda made the same observation about the limitations of relief aid. 'The use of short-term relief as a substitute for any real political commitment on the part of the North reduces interventions to technical fixes and detracted from a search for a long-term solution.'[81]

Already in 1976 Henry Kissinger had observed how significant emergency relief was to Western governments, when he commented that 'Disaster Relief is becoming increasingly a major instrument of our foreign policy.'[82] In the wake of the Ethiopian famine Alex de Waal put this rather more bluntly: 'For Western governments the political priority became to avoid embarrassment at the hands of figures like Bob Geldof. Aid became a strategic alibi'.[83] There was a memorable piece of TV news footage soon after the release of the Band Aid record.[84] The news cameras caught live footage of Bob Geldof as he cornered Mrs Thatcher at a reception before the *Daily Star* awards lunch and relentlessly pressed her about the inadequacy of European efforts to donate food aid from the large surpluses available. They had a public argument about butter mountains and the possibility of providing butter oil as food relief. She replied through clenched teeth. The climax came when Mrs Thatcher said, 'Mr Geldof, it is not as simple as that', to which he replied, 'No Prime Minister, nothing is really as simple as dying, is it?' Coincidentally this footage was originally seen as a filmed news insert in a BBC bulletin presented from the studio by Michael Buerk. He commented with some amusement, at the end of the item showing the confrontation between Mrs Thatcher and Bob Geldof, that 'It was difficult to decide who was lecturing whom!' This is a classic example of the kind of confrontation that de Waal is referring to, which politicians were keen to avoid.

New money?

The decision to respond to the 'humanitarian emergency' by the government was a response to the television pictures. Moreover, the nature of the response was one of immediate (and in the case of the RAF, highly visual) assistance. It did not indicate a change in long-term policy. It now seems clear that despite appearances, the extent of any 'CNN effect' was indeed very limited. In fact, it is evident from the documents that, despite appearances, at the time there was not really any 'new money' directed by the government towards Ethiopia. Subsequent analysis of the funding of the relief operations demonstrated that despite the extreme generosity by the public and despite government pronouncements, hardly any new money was made available by the British government for what they considered a distasteful regime.[85] In retrospect it appears that existing ODA budgets (partly intended for long-term development projects) were moved around into emergency aid. The letter to the Foreign Office from Charles Powell summarizing the ministerial meeting deciding on action on Ethiopia, chaired by the prime minister, makes this quite clear.

In discussion it was noted that both the MOD and the ODA would have difficulty in absorbing the costs. The ODA were already having to find the additional £5 million promised by Sir Geoffrey Howe and would have to find a further £4.5 million for the UK share of the Community's additional help. The Economic Secretary said that no funds were available from the Contingency Reserve.[86]

This remained the government's position.

The media exposure of the famine prompted the House of Commons Foreign Affairs Select Committee to hold a high profile inquiry into Famine in Africa.[87] It took evidence from civil servants, academics, NGOs and the ODA minister, Timothy Raison. The Report appeared the following April and it was unequivocally critical of the fact that the government, despite all the hype, had actually not given any additional support:

What has taken place is a diversion of resources towards the African crisis from within the aid budget not the making available of new money ... as a matter of principle it has been suggested that where the public has been prepared to regard the crisis as an appropriate cause in which to give over £67m of voluntary donations then the government should also give additional funds. The generosity of the British people has not been matched by the British Government ... the aid budget is anyway not designed to cope with relief of this scale ... danger is that unless new money is provided the emergency effort will detract from development work.[88]

The report reached further critical conclusions which were all the more significant since the committee had a Conservative chairman and a Conservative majority:

We consider it is not acceptable that almost the entire costs of the UK response to the crisis should fall on the previously agreed ODA budget. The emergency is of such a degree that it must be regarded as a new situation and substantial new money should be provided to help with it. The committee believe that the ODA budget should be increased to accommodate the exceptional expenditure involved so that funds are not diverted from longer-term development work.

Not surprisingly, in its response to the Select Committee report the government did not take up the challenge. It merely referred to 'the overall constraints on public expenditure'.[89]

The fact that the ODA and the Ministry of Defence (MOD) were left to pick up the costs from existing budgets led to a serious Whitehall disagreement between the departments, which is clear both from internal memos and from a bad tempered exchange of letters between private secretaries. Naturally the two departments had difficulties heeding Charles Powell's instruction to 'settle the costs between them'. At one point there was an angry letter from Timothy Raison's private secretary to the private secretary of Lord Trefgarne at the MOD, concluding that 'there can be no question of the ODA meeting the costs of this operation. Had there been any ambiguity about this at the time Mr Raison would not have agreed to the airlift proceeding.'[90] This argument continued over the following months. On a wholly exceptional basis the MOD had agreed to bear the entire costs of the airlift (£1.5 million per month) until the start of February, but from then onwards it was split evenly between the departments, despite the mutual discontent.

At the end of November 1984 an internal briefing memo for the minister about ongoing and future aid to Ethiopia pointed out that in fact, according to the agencies on the ground, the prime need in Ethiopia was for trucks (not planes), a point which had also been reinforced at the hearings on famine before the Foreign Affairs Select Committee. However, the memo observes that despite this request for an alternative type of support 'the political pressure to keep the Hercules in Ethiopia will be strong.' There was also a reference to the ongoing argument between the MOD and ODA about having to pay for the airlift, with the observation by the ODA official that 'civilian aircraft would be far cheaper', he estimated by as much as 50 per cent.[91] The clear implication is that regardless of what was needed or requested the government was following its own priorities. It was keen on dramatic images of Hercules aircraft swooping down low over the dusty plain to discharge their precious loads to the desperate victims.

According to the evidence it appears that the government was also deliberately opaque about the fact that no new funding was to be allocated to the famine relief. As a consequence both backbench MPs and the public seem to have picked up a different message—that the government was providing 'new' money to help the famine victims, both by financing the airlift and by the aid programme. It was only after a number of Parliamentary Questions[92] challenged the government on this issue that ministers made the admission that in fact the money allocated was from funds for emergencies already within the ODA (with the implication that it would be diverted from other relief causes). It was a case of that all too familiar government technique of double counting. As a result the minister had to apologize to Sir Anthony Kershaw, MP, who had queried an announcement about relief aid to Chad and Sudan. Raison 'clarified the point' that a press notice about this aid was in effect referring once again to the same funding already announced by the foreign secretary on 24 October (that is, the same £5 million announced the day after the first BBC Ethiopian famine broadcast). Timothy Raison concluded that 'this notice was thus about further allocations rather than further commitments', adding, 'I am sorry if this was not as clear as it might have been.'[93] It appeared to be a case of the familiar political trick, used by successive governments, of announcing the same funding several times over, to make it look like something new. A few months later the *Observer* journalist Geoffrey Lean, in a story called 'The Meanest Giver', eventually exposed just how very little Britain had given, despite claims by politicians and officials.[94]

Another Parliamentary Question by Stuart Randall raised the question about making funding available for longer-term development to Ethiopia rather than the immediate humanitarian relief.[95] This was obviously a live issue within the government as a number of documents discuss the issue of longer-term and development aid to Ethiopia. The head of the East Africa department within the Foreign Office wrote to his superiors that 'If Ministers consider that domestic public and parliamentary opinion requires that we do substantially more for Ethiopia, it will almost certainly be necessary to have recourse to the central contingency reserve …' He went on to observe that 'it might also be necessary to consider the unpleasant trade-off between what is spent on saving lives now and what would help to save lives later; though the latter would tend to draw us into a capital aid programme for Ethiopia of the kind we have on policy grounds hitherto eschewed.'[96]

In the wake of the media exposure of the famine in Ethiopia and the humanitarian response, there were several other internal discussions within the ODA about whether there should be a longer-term response towards helping Ethiopia with development aid. This would have signalled a change from the policy of previous years. A lengthy memo was prepared for the minister and permanent secretary entitled, 'Should we embark on a programme of long-term capital aid to Ethiopia?'[97] It observed that 'the amount spent on disaster relief will have been thrown away unless the chance is taken of improving the production of food and protection of the land'. Yet it concluded, apparently on political grounds, that there was not a sufficient case to provide development aid in view of the fact that 'Mengistu has the best of both worlds, military assistance from the East and humanitarian assistance from the West'. A similar memo in November had made the same assessment that 'The long-term western objective is to get the Russians out of Ethiopia … we also need to discourage the Ethiopians from assuming that they can get large scale western aid indefinitely without making policy adjustments.'[98] So the enormous effort put into emergency humanitarian aid, where public opinion stimulated by the media played such a key role, was not to be followed up by any more long-term development aid.

The Ethiopian response

Dawit Wolde Giorgis, as head of the Ethiopian Relief and Rehabilitation Commission, had his own particular perspective on the response of Western governments to the famine, following the BBC broadcasts. Before his defection to the West in 1985 he was a well positioned member of the Ethiopian political elite. In his account of the famine, Preston King describes Giorgis as 'quick, competent and firm' in contrast to his predecessor Shimelis Adugna, who is characterized as pleasant and well-meaning but 'not overly efficient'.[99] Nevertheless Giorgis needed all his diplomatic and political skills when he arrived in the UK on 28 October 1984 to be met by a blast of press attention. He was called in immediately to meet Timothy Raison who was waiting for him in his office in Whitehall late on a Saturday night to discuss the proposed RAF airlift. In Giorgis' view the RAF activity was more to help UK public opinion, who wanted their government to be seen to do something: 'sending the RAF would do more for Britain's public relations and domestic problems than for starving Ethiopians', he observed later in his memoir.[100] It is interesting to compare the British account of this meeting that Giorgis had with Timothy Raison. According to the private secretary's note which is headed 'Ethiopian Drought—Meeting with DWG', Dawit Wolde Giorgis called on Mr Raison and Lord Trefgarne (the defence minister) at ODA at 9.30pm; there was:

an occasionally sticky meeting with DWG at which Mr Raison and Lord Trefgarne explained what the British Government hoped to do and the commissioner described Ethiopian needs ... DWG expressed deep gratitude at the response of the British public and contrasted this with the slowness and paucity of the Government's response to his own government's earlier appeals ... Referring to the discussion of the airlift ... DWG objected strongly to the idea that the planes should be committed only for a month. He thought this would do little to meet Ethiopia's long term needs and was more in the nature of a publicity stunt to respond to current media interest. Mr Raison firmly rebutted this suggestion but without convincing Dawit.[101]

In his own account Giorgis gives a rather different interpretation. He emphasizes how the British minister and officials were adamant that they wanted to send the military airlift even though he gave them all kinds of suggestions for assistance that would actually be of more use. Giorgis' view was that the government, including the prime minister, was after quick dramatic action, which was why it was so keen on the RAF intervention. 'This proposal was … the reason Mr Raison waited so eagerly to see me. He wanted to tell the British public that very night that immediate action had been taken by the Thatcher cabinet.'[102]

Giorgis also revealed how he had to dissemble when faced with tough press questioning in London and later in the US. The tabloid press were interested in reports about large consignments of whisky that had been flown into Addis Ababa for the Derg's tenth anniversary celebrations whilst millions starved. This was a classic tabloid story and the papers made the most of it. The subject also came up in ministerial briefings for parliamentary appearances, whereupon there was a distinct note of *Schadenfreude*. Ministers were advised to say. 'it is up to the Ethiopian government to explain the whisky consignments'.[103] Giorgis admitted later that he had had to lie about the whisky story in order not to discourage aid and not to be imprisoned himself upon his return. Meanwhile he wrote that Colonel Mengistu was furious when he heard about the plans for the RAF airlift, complaining about a 'NATO invasion.' Giorgis, as he toured Western capitals at the end of October 1984, complained about the 'press jamboree … there were no quiet, private talks or agreements, it was all done with an eye to public opinion',[104] especially as this was in the period immediately prior to a US election. Meanwhile the UK government view of him was equally uncomplimentary. In a letter to Charles Powell (the foreign affairs adviser to the prime minister), headed 'Ethiopia Response to British Relief aid and Eastern Bloc Assistance', Sir Geoffrey Howe's private secretary referred to Dawit's description of the RAF intervention as a publicity stunt—(a phrase subsequently disowned by his own foreign minister) and went on to say that 'Dawit has a well-merited reputation as a prickly xenophobic nationalist … close to Mengistu'. The letter also assesses how little the Eastern bloc was doing and adds, 'depending on what they do in practice we may be able to stick on them the charge of too little too late … the relative performance of West and East will make a real impression on the Ethiopian regime even if it is not reflected in the Ethiopian media.'[105]

Dawit Wolde Giorgis in his memoir was equally scathing about the way in which his own countrymen were dealing with the crisis. He

describes Mengistu's fury at the BBC news items and the way his celebrations and achievements had been ridiculed: 'the Ethiopian people
had never been told the magnitude of the problem; now it was being
told to them by the world'. At a Politburo meeting Mengistu angrily
denounced the RAF, as well as complaining about the presence in Ethiopia of over two hundred journalists as well as 500 expatriates with 48
different voluntary agencies. He wanted to know why the aid was not
being given directly to the Ethiopian government, leaving it to handle
distribution. In his lengthy May Day speech the following year Mengistu made no mention of the generous international response to the
famine, but instead denounced imperialist interference. And as VIPs and
celebrities from around the world came to tour the camps in Tigray and
the north of Ethiopia, according to Giorgis Mengistu himself made only
one visit to the famine affected areas of his country; he spent a total of
thirty minutes there in November 1984.

Media as enabling effect or acting defensively?

In Britain, politicians and civil servants have argued subsequently[106] that
even if they were aware of the situation in Ethiopia they could not have
acted without the media as a catalyst. In other words, it is almost as if
they were relying upon a CNN effect. Some years later this pattern came
to be referred to in the literature as an 'enabling effect'—in situations
where governments were able to act only because they were supported
by media pressure.[107] According to Brian Barder, who was British ambassador to Ethiopia in 1984:

It was essential to have media coverage that alerted public opinion not just in
Britain but throughout the world to what was going on in Ethiopia, not so
much to put pressure on the government, but to enable it to respond in the way
that was necessary. If the government without the media coverage had gone
into action and spent huge amounts of money, sent the RAF without any kind
of public media campaign beforehand everybody would have thought the government had gone mad.[108]

Interestingly, although this was Barder's view twenty years later his
contemporary reports show, at least in private, rather more sensitivity to
the allegation that officials were slow to become aware of the crisis and
only reacted because they were prodded into doing so by media reporting. He wrote a memo to his office in London in December 1984

entitled 'Ethiopia Famine: Were early warnings ignored?' asking to have sight of any 'detailed defensive briefing' which would help refute the idea that there had been plenty of warning and evidence of an imminent famine which Western governments had ignored until finally prodded into action by the media.[109] He was particularly exercised by a Granada TV *World In Action* programme entitled 'The Politics of Hunger', which made a strong case to argue that Western governments failed to heed the warnings of famine given by the various agencies. The next day Barder sent another telegram along the same lines, arguing that the 'idea is gaining currency that detailed warnings since 1982 about a disastrous famine in '84—that Western governments failed to heed warnings or act in time …' asking again for some defensive briefing: 'what I have in mind would be to try to establish—before the allegations being made acquire the status of universally accepted historical truth—the validity or falsehood of the claims.' He also made the point that there should be an examination of the whole system of forward planning with a need to 'discover whether adequate capacity exists in Whitehall or ODA to identify warning signals of approaching disaster in time to contribute to pre-emptive action as distinct from the capacity to respond quickly and effectively to disasters when they have already begun to take place.'[110]

This was clearly a sensitive topic, and the response from officials in London was that they really did not want to carry out such an exercise, although there is an admission that there were certain warnings and allegations of neglect by the West which 'may have to be met'. Their conclusion in response to Barder's request is that even if they were to carry out such an exercise 'there is no guarantee that the end result (if objective) would necessarily paint as positive a picture as Mr Barder may hope'.[111] Interestingly, there is no mention of the research on famine prediction in Ethiopia by Peter Cutler that the department had actually been sponsoring.

Similarly the minister for overseas development, Timothy Raison, in retrospect, points out that the media coverage was important as a mechanism to enable government to act:

It's absolutely unquestionable that the impact of Michael Buerk's film was very considerable. It certainly had an impact on me, the media stir up public opinion, but I think they forget that their films are actually seen by Ministers who, believe it or not, may be human beings … and some of them do watch these films and they are moved by it. You cannot not be moved by it and you say well there are things we must do about it.[112]

At the time Raison was rather more sensitive to the criticism that the government was only inclined to give aid because the media had alerted, and even shamed, them into doing so. It is evident from the briefing notes to the parliamentary occasions where Mr Raison spoke on the famine, and the briefings for his various broadcast appearances during this period, that this failure to act before the media highlighted that the crisis was a sensitive matter for the minister and officials.[113] For example, in a breakfast television interview he had an uncomfortable time fielding questions both from the presenters Ann Diamond and Henry Kelly as well as from the other guest, Jonathan Dimbleby, with his experience of reporting the earlier Ethiopian famine. The minister's response was defensive—having admitted that the government did indeed know of the famine well before the media coverage he then had a hard time explaining why there was such a limited response.[114] The same defensive tone reacting to criticism of 'too little too late' is evident in the various ministerial briefings for the Commons debates on Ethiopia in November and December 1984.

It is apparent that in retrospect both politicians and officials were able to say that the media coverage gave them an impetus to act and had an 'enabling effect'. They were comfortable in arguing that they needed the media in order to take large scale action. However, it appears that they would not have been able to make such a comment at the time. When challenged in 1984 that they were just responding to media coverage, they were defensive and argued that they had reacted to the crisis quite independently of the media.

How much did policy really change?

It is clear that the political imperative (responding to the media pressure) was for a high profile, quick and visible, intervention in Ethiopia. As far as the government was concerned this was fulfilled by the RAF airlift and the emergency aid both from the UK and via the European Budget. The question of longer-term aid to prevent further famine was discussed within government and subsequently rejected. Policy towards Ethiopia remained firmly within the parameters of the Cold War. Moreover, although this was not made explicit at the time, there was an insistence from within government that any aid to Ethiopia should be paid for by rearranging existing budgets earmarked for development, not by any new money from the Central Contingency Fund. This was in sharp contrast to the 'new money' raised by voluntary charitable organizations. As a result one of the principal effects as far as the government was concerned was the tilting towards short-term emergency relief at the expense of longer-term development aid. Timothy Raison[115] agrees that popular pressure caused by media exposure during this period led to a longer-term shift in the redistribution towards emergency aid at the expense of development aid from within his departmental budget.

Despite superficial appearances, not really that much changed as a result of the government reaction to the media coverage of Ethiopia. There was a substantial reaction in the short-term but what the government did was in response to domestic public opinion, which was reacting to the media coverage. It is apparent that the facts about the famine were well known within government long before the autumn of 1984. However, once there was a public reaction to the sudden media coverage this made officials and politicians want to be seen to care. So in this case it appears that although there was a CNN effect which might have prompted humanitarian action by government, it was primarily for short-term domestic political effect, in response to public opinion within Western countries. At this point in the Cold War, and under a Conservative government in the UK and a Republican administration in the US, there was a strong strategic direction to politics, which meant that policy decisions were far less likely to change or be influenced by media coverage.

Thus we can see that the ability of news coverage to push policy was far less substantial than may have appeared. The government did react to domestic public opinion because that was aroused by the media coverage, but its main objective was to find a way to satisfy these immediate concerns. This analysis indicates that when, in successive discussions, the Ethiopian famine is considered historically as a case of a 'strong CNN effect', that is not strictly speaking true. Public policy did not shift as a result of powerful media coverage of suffering. Official humanitarian assistance was severely limited and there was no change of heart about development aid. However, there were on the other hand, long-term shifts arising from the media coverage in other institutions—in particular the private charitable world.

3

A REVOLUTION IN GIVING

'Live Aid *began with Bob Geldof watching a television programme, and ended up with him making one.*'

David Edgar, *Marxism Today*, September 1985

'*What USA for Africa did and what Band Aid did in England is to make compassion hip. If all that comes out of this is the perceived attitude that it's fashionable to care, then it's worth it, time and time again.*'

Bob Geldof.[1]

It was not only the original news reporting of the famine that became iconic; the media coverage which it inspired would also become a significant moment in the history of television. Western governments were persuaded by the public response to the media images to do something to help the famine victims in Ethiopia, or at least be *seen* to be doing something. The ultimate effect of the television coverage of the famine upon public policy in the UK and other Western countries was, as we have seen, in fact modified and constrained by political factors arising from wider government priorities. However, the media *did* have an indisputable effect upon another part of public life. This was its impact on private philanthropy, aid agencies and the world of charity fundraising.

The media coverage in 1984 stimulated charitable efforts and ultimately changed the long-term nature of charitable institutions and

71

fundraising, especially in the field of foreign aid. Ultimately, its effect was to change the terms of trade between the media and charities. This precipitated both dramatic immediate innovations in charitable fundraising and also long-term structural changes in the relationship between the media and the world of foreign aid.

Celebrity endorsement: The Band Aid story

The news pictures of suffering in Ethiopia as they were transmitted worldwide in October 1984 triggered an unprecedented reaction amongst viewers. Within a day the scale of the response from the public to the reporting of the famine was in itself a big news story, as aid agencies were overwhelmed with donations and the phone lines in the television offices as well as aid agency headquarters were buzzing with offers of help. Crucially, the story and the issue were given a far longer media span by the involvement of Bob Geldof of the Boomtown Rats, and the creation of Band Aid. As Michael Buerk later observed, in the early 1980s even rock stars watched the news[2] and Geldof, having seen the footage from Korem on 23 October 1984, announced that he was determined to try to do something to help the starving. Although he was at this point in 1984 a self-confessed fading rock star, Geldof was to demonstrate a formidable talent as a pop music entrepreneur. He managed to galvanize the great and the good of the rock world into recording a Christmas single, 'Do They Know it's Christmas?' which raised unexpected sums. Geldof had originally assumed the yield from sales of the record would be around £70,000, but in the end the total was £8 million. When it was released it went straight to the top of the hit parade. It remained there for five weeks and sold more copies than any record that had ever been released in Britain.[3]

Geldof had managed to break through hitherto impenetrable legal and bureaucratic obstacles to produce the record and bring it to market in double-quick time by 15 December and then to maximize the exposure and thereby the financial proceeds. He persuaded all those involved, from singers to recording companies to retailers, to waive their fees and profits. He even prevailed upon the Conservative government to waive the VAT on the record sales—as a matter of principle they refused, but then under considerable public pressure agreed to make an equivalent donation to the VAT proceeds into the Band Aid coffers, amounting to half a million pounds. (A newly elected MP, Tony Blair, took up the cause on behalf of Band Aid and appeared on news bulletins calling upon the government to back down on the charging of VAT on the sales of the record). Others were also persuaded to abandon standard procedure in a good cause. Within the BBC there was a rule that a record single which had not yet entered the official chart listings could not be played on *Top of the Pops*, but Geldof knew that exposure on BBC1 as soon as the record was available would be a vital publicity boost in the pre-Christmas period. Michael Hurll, the producer of *Top of the Pops*, declared that the rule could not be broken, so Geldof appealed over his head to Michael Grade, as the Channel Controller, to bend the rules.[4] Grade agreed to make an exception—even clearing five minutes of the schedule prior to *Top of the Pops* to launch the pop video of 'Do They Know it's Christmas?'[5] The broadcast opened with a special introduction by David Bowie, who spoke about the emergency in Ethiopia and asked everyone to buy the record. 'If you cannot afford the money, then club together with someone else to buy it,' he urged. And soon afterwards another song was recorded in the USA in early 1985, entitled 'We are the World'. The recording was masterminded by Harry Belafonte who assembled a group of stars including legends such as Stevie Wonder under the banner 'USA for Africa'. Michael Jackson co-wrote the lyrics and it became the fastest selling pop single in American history, with total global sales of twenty million copies.

This kind of celebrity involvement in charitable causes—especially by the pop world—was something new. It generated substantial publicity which in turn kept the plight of Ethiopia in the headlines. According to a former Oxfam official:

The TV pictures unleashed an unprecedented surge of humanitarian concern and popular mobilisation throughout Europe … the response represented a populist form of anti-establishment politics … Band Aid cut through red tape and chartered its own aircraft, rented its own trucks to distribute food … and thereby shamed donor governments.[6]

Live Aid—new ways to care and give

The staging of the Live Aid concert and eventually Sports Aid, Fashion Aid and similar ventures over the succeeding months and years were to transform the whole nature of charity fund raising. It was not just a matter of money, although the sums raised were beyond all previous records, but what was important was that new participants and new donors were recruited and a new media-friendly way of presenting charitable concerns was born. There was a recognition too that these highly successful campaigns 'were reaching the pockets of people whom aid charities had previously failed to reach, most notably the youth and people in non-professional occupations.'[7]

In the aftermath of the Ethiopia media coverage a report was commissioned by thirteen different aid agencies entitled *Images of Africa*, which sought to analyze the way that the story had developed and its implications for the way that Africa was portrayed. The British report was prepared in association with Oxfam. Amongst their conclusions was the observation that 'post-Live Aid formerly uninterested sections of the media such as teenage music and fashion magazines had covered African stories ... now aid and to a lesser extent development became 'legitimate' areas of concern to the image conscious youth of Britain.'[8]

On 13 July 1985 there were simultaneous marathon rock concerts to raise funds for Ethiopia, at Wembley Stadium in London and the JFK Stadium in Philadelphia, featuring some of the most famous singers in the history of rock and pop music. The media involvement and, in particular, the BBC coverage of the concerts were crucial to the fundraising and the live sixteen-hour TV transmission of the concerts attracted what was claimed as the largest ever TV audience around the world. Originally the organizers had tried to interest the Independent TV channels Tyne Tees television and then Granada in broadcasting the concerts, but both decided the scale of the project was impossible. Then the BBC, with its much larger resources, agreed to take it on—even though it was still a highly ambitious and risky venture. In less than six weeks a small BBC department, Network Features headed by Roger Laughton, planned the biggest rock concert ever seen.

Despite its modest size and finances the Network Features department had established close links with the all-powerful channel controllers because of its role in the regular business of programme transmission. This gave it an ability to punch above its weight, as was the case with Live Aid. Nevertheless one of the senior producers on the show recalls looking around the small and shambolic office and thinking, 'We just can't do this show ... it feels like getting BBC Radio Cambridgeshire to cover the entire General Election.'[9]

A REVOLUTION IN GIVING

The idea of the rock concert was masterminded by Mike Appleton at the BBC, who was also the producer of *The Old Grey Whistle Test*, a late night rock programme, which was produced by the Network Features department. Appleton gives a graphic explanation of what it felt like to be on the inside of an event which was snowballing into something beyond all expectations:

it was planned as limited coverage at Wembley and they would link up with Philadelphia whenever they could. And then gradually it became apparent that it was going to get bigger and bigger. It was an amazing feeling, you were sort of driving a bus and everybody wanted to get on that bus and join and hang on the sides ... it looked like a sort of bus going out of Karachi or something like that. It was just covered with people and when we wanted messages delivered taxi drivers would say well we'll do it for nothing, now that's a pretty rare thing for a taxi driver to do, I think it's probably unique.[10]

Michael Grade as controller of BBC1 had initially been rather wary of the Live Aid concept because it seemed a precarious operation to stage such an ambitious broadcast with so little preparation. However, as it appeared to take off, he agreed that the transmission could switch over to BBC1 when BBC2 had to return to its mandatory Open University schedules during the night-time hours. This was a significant decision in an era before twenty-four-hour scheduling, when there was still an official 'close down' for the evening, and made it possible to cover much of the Philadelphia event as well—because of the time difference with the USA. Live Aid broke the rules of TV in more than just scheduling. Michael Grade recalls watching the show at home on the Saturday afternoon and suffering a 'heart stopping moment' when at 3pm Geldof memorably used the f *** word in making a plea for the audience to donate more money. Grade recalled that it was the first time ever that such an expletive had been used during family viewing time, but amazingly 'no-one complained, neither Mrs Whitehouse [Grade's perennial 'taste and decency' bête-noire from the National Viewers' and Listeners' Association] nor even the BBC governors.'[11]

Despite its unlikely beginnings and the almost impossible planning schedule, the event was an enormous success. It raised over £100 million worldwide.[12] When the BBC TV executives assembled the following week at their Programme Review meeting and discussed the Live Aid broadcast, Roger Laughton congratulated everyone who had been involved and said the whole occasion reminded him of the Children's

Crusade in the thirteenth century![13] The coverage of Live Aid was a classic example of a media event, as characterized by Dayan and Katz,[14] a 'high holiday of communication' transforming daily life into something special and an occasion which indeed electrified a very large audience. They describe the sense in which 'media events go beyond journalism in highlighting charisma and collective action, in defiance of established authority ... the dissatisfaction with official inaction and bureaucratic ritualism, the power of the people to do it themselves, the yearning for leadership of stature.'[15] The whole conception of Live Aid fitted this description well—in particular the way that it conveyed a sense of political action, without recourse to politicians.

The concert was beamed via thirteen satellites to an estimated one hundred and twenty countries. According to BBC research, half the TV sets in Britain tuned in at some point during the transmission, and it has always been claimed that a third of the population on the planet watched Live Aid.[16] There were some shaky moments, for example when

Fig. 3.1: Live Aid. © BBC

Paul McCartney's microphone failed to work or when some of the multiple satellite links went down. There was even a (failed) attempt to broadcast from the flight deck of Concorde as Phil Collins crossed the Atlantic linking the two concerts. Nevertheless the concert was judged an extraordinary success and became a broadcasting legend. Amongst other items the audience saw footage of starving semi-skeletons struggling to stand upright and walk, set to the musical background of the group Cars singing *Drive*. There were sharply divided reactions to this footage. It was shown three times during the broadcast and for some it was the most memorable and moving part of the day; indeed David Bowie even dropped his last number and said instead he wanted the audience to see the Cars sequence again, and the level of donations reached their peak when that song and footage were on the air. However, for others there was a sense that the juxtaposition was in bad taste. One press report criticized 'a video of some of those children dying in Ethiopian refugee camps run to the accompaniment of a top 40 hit of no relevance and less taste.'[17]

The charitable response—broadcasters in a new world

In a world where 'media effects' are dissected minutely, one of the clearest ways to measure the impact of the media is to look at the direct effect upon charitable giving. The overall scale of charitable donations from the public in response to the news coverage of the Ethiopian famine was completely unprecedented. Every major development charity saw a record rise in donations over this period. There had been some concern that Bob Geldof's efforts would divert money from other charitable causes, but as far as raising money for international relief in Ethiopia was concerned there was an overall increase and all the major charities involved saw a sharp rise in funds. For example, in 1983 Oxfam had raised £23.9 million in donations, but in 1984 this figure more than doubled to £51 million and in the following year it still reached £45.2 million.[18] Christian Aid and the Save the Children Fund saw similar increases and all the charities working in this field reported that they were overwhelmed by the scale of the response which started when the phones began to ring on 23 October, the first evening that the original Amin/Buerk item was transmitted on BBC News. Oxfam received over a thousand calls offering help in the first twenty four hours, including three offers of planes. In the US there was a similar overwhelming response—the switchboard at Save the Children Fund USA was jammed with calls, as viewers reacted to the news report from Ethiopia that they had seen on NBC. The UK Disasters Emergency Committee appeal launched the previous July had been due to close in the middle of October but it now remained open, eventually collecting what was at that time a record total of almost £15 million.[19] And all this was separate from the money spinning success of the whole Geldof enterprise, from Band Aid through Live Aid and all the associated events, such as Sports Aid, which themselves raised such remarkable amounts. In the UK alone the Band Aid Trust raised £35 million in 1985.[20]

The Live Aid experience was subsequently described as 'a social movement' because it spawned a whole new means of fundraising on a mass scale. Dayan and Katz describe how, characteristic of a classic media event, Live Aid demonstrated that 'the people can unite to save Africans from starvation … the celebration of voluntarism—the wilful resolve to take direct, simple, spontaneous, ostensibly non-ideological, action'.[21] The Comic Relief enterprises and similar genres developed by Charity Projects over the next few years were direct results of Live Aid. Comic Relief was launched on BBC1 on Christmas Day 1985 with footage from a refugee camp in Sudan. Even the rapid expansion of the annual Children in Need appeal in this period was a sustainable outcome of the 1985 Live Aid experience. In each case these are fundraising mechanisms that rely wholly on the media event.[22]

The staging and televising of such occasions often lead to a blurring of lines because the live television coverage is so integral to the whole enterprise. It is self-evident that if the television cameras were not there the fundraising and mobilizing purpose would be comparatively pointless. As Mark Ellen, one of the original presenters, observed later, 'Live Aid had begun as an event which the cameras covered, but it ultimately became an event staged by the BBC.'[23] This recognition that it was vital to interest television in covering the concert is evident in the way that the negotiations progressed in the period prior to July 1985. It was interesting that the question of who would cover the Philadelphia event developed into a cliff-hanger, as initially none of the three main US TV networks were interested. Without this coverage, the impact of the event would have been minimal by comparison.

This ambiguity about whether the event is for or by television causes some philosophical anxiety within the BBC, which has historically been concerned not to be seen as a campaigner. In later years this same ambiguity occurred with the big fundraising extravaganzas like Comic Relief that were to follow. The coverage of the Live 8 concert organized by Bob Geldof twenty years later in July 2005 still raised the same issue, with the BBC not clear about whether it was involved in staging an event (and thereby endorsing the political message of the occasion) or simply covering at arm's length an event organized by someone else. Two years later in 2007 the BBC was still worrying over the extent to which editorial rules of impartiality had been breached in the way that the whole Live 8 extravaganza was covered. It concluded in a report which dealt with the issue that 'We must not campaign, or allow ourselves to be used to campaign … and we must ensure that our output does not embrace the agenda of any particular campaign group.'[24] Nevertheless the same concerns were raised again just months later both in relation to the staging of an event known as 'Live Earth' and in the sudden cancellation of 'Planet Relief' in 2007, responding to an internal debate about whether the BBC should be associated with a campaign on climate change.[25]

The traditional relationship between charity and the broadcasting of media appeals had been completely overturned by the impact of the fundraising for Ethiopian famine relief. This posed considerable problems for the BBC as it struggled to manage a new phenomenon, and it is clear from the 2007 investigation that the issue was still causing concern many years after the original Live Aid concert. Within the BBC the Central Appeals Advisory Committee (CAAC), established in 1927, was charged with overall responsibility for broadcasting charitable appeals, and the procedure had hitherto been tightly regulated, partly on the grounds that appeals were a form of 'free advertising' which therefore needed very careful supervision.[26] Charities were nominated in turn to benefit from the brief regular broadcasting slots devoted to appeals.[27] This arrangement had historically given the BBC effective control over the charities as far as broadcasting was concerned, but now in the mid-80s the new power of the media to raise money and inspire action overturned all of the BBC's long developed customs and practices. In the wake of the Band Aid/Live Aid phenomenon the CAAC commissioned a report to assess how the landscape had now changed. This described the 'transformation in the image of charitable giving' and noted how

Charity has moved from being worthy, boring and patronising to being news-worthy and exciting—as Geldof has put it, 'making compassion hip.' … with this changed image charity is no longer a filler or something to be put into pre scheduled slots within broadcasting but becomes worthy of news and features attention: charity spills out of its neat boundaries which were easy to maintain all the while charity was worthy but uninteresting.

The CAAC report went on to comment in an unmistakably disapproving way on the new types and attitudes of donors: 'The new image of charities may produce huge discrepancies in income from year to year ... encouraging a new breed of floating givers with no stable allegiances and little understanding of the requirements and achievements of the charities they have supported.'[28]

According to the official appeals policy of the BBC, the point of broadcasting charitable appeals was to provide the viewers and listeners with 'authoritative information and guidance' on deserving causes as well as to raise money. The CAAC 1986 policy paper questioned whether the new style of spontaneous appeals like Live Aid which broke all the traditional boundaries really provided the public with this authoritative information and guidance. This was because they 'took a large part of the decision away from the donor; donors were required only to give and not to decide precisely to what or to whom to give.' In each of these media extravaganzas the public was essentially giving to an umbrella body, such as the Band Aid Trust or later Comic Relief. Viewers were enticed and attracted by the exiting content of the programming—endorsed by their favourite celebrities and pop stars. They were encouraged to give to a particular cause—for example hungry people in Africa, or, in the case of Children in Need, deserving children in the UK. The organization then decided how it would disburse its funds, principally to other charities on the ground or sometimes directly through its own schemes—for example, the Band Aid Trust became involved in a large scale trucking operation taking relief supplies. In the traditional model, funds were generally raised for specific charities directly, which the public were supposed to be informed about. This view is supported by Geldof himself who wrote that it was his impression that people were 'giving money to me and Band Aid in preference to one of the established organisations'.[29] It is clear from the sums raised why the BBC was so concerned to manage and understand this new type of fundraising and to impose some structure. In the whole of 1985 the regular radio appeals broadcast as *The Week's Good Cause* raised £690,456. The total for regular television appeals, including those broadcast in the national regions, was £597,682. Meanwhile the Live Aid concert raised a total of £27 million in the UK alone.[30]

The CAAC report stressed that the effect of Live Aid and this new style of fundraising had overturned the whole mechanism of charitable appeals. Lady Marre, the chair of the CAAC, wrote to Lord Joel Barnett, BBC vice chairman, commenting that 'much of the initiative in appeals broadcasting seems to have passed to programme companies and programme departments responsible for presenting major charitable initiatives such as the 'Live Aid' appeal.'[31] The success of this new style of charity appeal had a widening impact. The Comic Relief enterprise raised over £300 million over the next two decades. Similarly the Children in Need appeal which had been organized by the BBC since 1927 took on a new dimension from this period. In the late 1970s it raised around £70,000 a year. This increased at the start of the 1980s to over half a million as the appeal expanded from a five minute slot to the first use of the 'telethon'. However, in the wake of Live Aid funds raised for Children in Need showed a dramatic rise, so that in 1985 the total doubled to reach £4.4 million.[32]

The BBC board of management, recognizing that this was an entirely different scale of operation, commissioned a report into how Children in Need should henceforth be organized. As well as making a series of recommendations for improving the administration of the appeal and the management of the increased funds, the report noted that 'network programme initiatives e.g. Live Aid and Band Aid have called into question and in some cases contravened the BBC guidelines on Appeals.'[33] It is clear from these reports and discussions that the relationship between broadcasting and charity had undergone a long-term change in 1984–86, which the BBC was seeking to understand and manage.

Change in image

This revolution in charitable images and methods—in particular the association of rock stars and celebrities with charitable causes, leading to a new genre in programming and new scales of fundraising—was a major and long-term effect of the media coverage of the Ethiopian famine. There had been some attempts at this before, for example with 'Rock against Racism',[34] but nothing on an equivalent scale and with this kind of impact. In the years following Band Aid and Live Aid there was a whole succession of similar very large scale media events, involving well known figures in the entertainment world, aimed at raising funds for charity. Midge Ure, once a singer with the band Ultravox, was one of the rock stars who worked alongside Bob Geldof on the production of the Band Aid record and in the subsequent fundraising concerts. Twenty years later he reflected on the overall impact, referring to a young neighbour 'who told me recently that she had learned about us in history ... so I think the legacy of Live Aid is ... that young people's perspective of charity has changed. Twenty years ago charity was something the Women's Institute did. All of a sudden their heroes are up there saying, "I'm involved."'[35] The transformation meant that 'Geldof's bluntness, directness and charm enabled him over a short period to change the face of fundraising, drawing on networks of people who had never before played a major part in charitable giving, and brilliantly exploiting the possibilities of the media on a global scale.'[36]

In 1971 George Harrison had organized a 'Concert for Bangladesh' at Madison Square Gardens in New York. It raised barely a quarter of a million dollars for cyclone victims, as well as leading to protracted legal wrangling and disputes. By the mid-80s, within the rock music world there was an awareness that something had changed. 'Music appeared to have achieved what it had failed to do at the Concert for Bangladesh. It had reached out way beyond its constituency to mobilize those who cared about the famine'. Not everyone was pleased about this: apparently some hard-core rock music types even 'disliked Live Aid because it symbolised the death of rock as a rebel sub-culture. Our music belonged to Fleet Street now, to children and to pensioners, even to the Royal Family.'[37] (A reference to the Prince and Princess of Wales, who had attended the Live Aid concert.)

This highlights the whole nature of change in fundraising images at this time. Bob Geldof positioned himself as outside the charitable establishment and, of course, the official bureaucracy. He offered a 'mission' to feed the starving and appealed directly to the public as a 'voice of the people' and urged them to give. Paddy Coulter, reflecting back on his period with Oxfam as director of communications, observes the change in the nature of raising money as a distinctive outcome of the fundraising prompted by the Ethiopian famine, 'the rise of celebrity that wasn't invented by the Ethiopian crisis, but certainly came to the fore with that phenomenal development of Band Aid, Live Aid, Sport Aid and indeed Comic Relief.' Coulter recalls how he experienced this shift in perceptions:

> I remember at Oxfam a colleague coming up and saying, somebody called Richard Curtis, who I'd never heard of, was coming and he was going to send a comedian to Africa, this was in the context where people were sending their car into Africa, every damn thing, and to send a comedian, that sounded the most ludicrous. "Hang about", I said, "that's quite a good idea, actually that's not bad".

However, he also reflected upon the way that stories had to be refracted through well known faces: 'the rise of celebrity culture demonstrates that it may be a challenge to the British audience in relating to Africa. Somehow this continent seems to need an intermediary.'[38]

Coulter is also identifying a continuing theme concerning the nature of the way Africa is reported, which so often conveys the image of the heart of darkness.[39] His view is that Africa represents so much of 'the other' that a Western audience requires the story to be interpreted to it, preferably by a well-known face. The black comedian Lenny Henry has been instrumental in much of the Comic Relief coverage of Africa. Live Aid began this process which continues to be a theme in the media/fundraising pattern, with celebrities regularly being despatched to report back from grim places. So, for example, the singer Midge Ure was sent by Save the Children to report from Ethiopia twenty years after the famine in 2004. And in the midst of the 2004/5 Darfur crisis, the pop singer Fran Healey (from the group Travis) was despatched to Sudan to make a programme 'Fran in Sudan'[40] which would focus attention on the efforts of charities in that region. There are now countless examples of celebrities from the film and pop world being associated with particular episodes of international suffering, such as Angelina Jolie, George Clooney or Madonna. *Time* magazine referred to this phenomenon as 'charitainment' and celebrity do-gooderism and questioned why we should 'need stars to be our guides?'[41] There was always an additional underlying suspicion that the charitable endeavours were doing more to enhance the image of the celebrity concerned than the other way around. The same questions arose in the wake of the 2005 Live 8 concert also organized by Bob Geldof. The artists who performed at that consciousness raising event saw their sales soar in the following days and weeks. HMV released a Live 8 boost chart and Pink Floyd came top with a 1,343 per cent rise in sales, as a consequence of their participation in the 'charity' concert.[42]

Certainly Bob Geldof's motives were the focus of some suspicion as he rose to worldwide prominence during the mid 1980s. For some he became St Bob[43] (as well as Sir Bob, receiving an honorary knighthood, being an Irish citizen), but others wondered whether his previously faltering career stood to benefit more than the famine stricken peasants of Ethiopia. The anarchist band Chumbawumba even released an album in 1986 entitled 'Pictures of Starving Children Sell Records: Starvation, Charity and Rock and Roll' as a critical response to Live Aid. The Band Aid enterprise, largely because it was such a radical innovation, also led to further controversies and debate. There was a vigorous argument about how Band Aid/Sports Aid as a popular movement fitted into the whole framework of consciousness raising and where it belonged within the political ecology of the left. Martin Jacques and Stuart Hall,[44] writing in *Marxism Today*, argued that it was a turning point in the fortunes of Thatcherism because it dealt a severe blow to the prevailing ideology of selfishness. They praised the capacity of the 'famine movement' to mobilize new forces ... and thereby shift the political centre of gravity', claiming to identify 'a new mood amongst contemporary youth' whereby a 'sea change had taken place'. Jacques and Hall asserted that 'no other cultural form could have played the political role that rock did in the Band Aid/Live Aid phenomenon ... so that when politics makes contact with this culture it finds itself in touch with the cultural language which most authentically expresses how young people experience the world.'

They identify how Geldof was brilliantly able to fuse the two worlds of rock and politics and reinvent the mobilization of the 1960s to forward the cause of aid to the poorest in the world. Equally important, they claim, is the achievement of Sports Aid as a civil society movement encouraging mass participation, combining charity with politics. The generally suspicious and even hostile attitude of the left towards the famine movement they attribute to sour grapes—observing that the 'grudging support and sectarian sniping' was largely due to the left's irritation that the initiative came from new quarters and did not belong to them.

Others on the left felt differently. Robert Allen, writing in *Capital and Class*,[45] disagreed that there had been such a shift in attitude and behav-

Fig. 3.2: A cartoonist's take on the real beneficiaries of Band Aid. © Royston Robertson/cartoonstock.com.

iour within British politics. Whilst agreeing that the famine movement had demonstrated a blow against selfishness and Geldof had achieved a key success by drawing young people 'who had traditionally been loath to get involved' into charitable activity, he totally disagreed about any long-term political change. The popular culture and mobilization which Jacques and Hall were so excited about, he identified instead as a manifestation of consumer culture. According to this interpretation, Geldof's success was in marketing a product and creating the first truly effective version of 'Consumer Aid'. Geldof's campaign was about a packaged disaster and a fast solution, not about engaging seriously with the ongoing problems of Africa. According to other analyses, 'Live Aid was enabling compassion through consumption. People could buy the paraphernalia that denoted they cared ... and watch pictures of themselves or millions like them, caring.'[46] It was a case of 'hedonistic consumption and self delusion.' These events

were not the ingenious outpourings of genuine concern but professionally conceived products...Consumer aid was a substitute for astute political analysis because it offered the public a means through which it could satisfy quickly and with little self reflection, deep seated philanthropic desires.[47]

Allen even went so far as to claim that 'while Geldof's impact on famine itself may be relatively limited and short-term, his efforts may have hampered considerably the ability of others to change things in the future by whatever means.'[48] Twenty years later when Geldof staged the Live 8 concert in 2005, the same arguments about 'Consumer Aid' were still going on.

Real change

In the 1980s other, experienced voices familiar with the issues of development and poverty also realized that Band Aid might be excellent at raising funds and spreading awareness, but that the famine movement would be unable to effect real change until it engaged with politics. Indeed, Geldof himself embarked on a very steep learning curve, so that by 1986 it was apparent that 'storming through political barriers, he has discovered that these problems have only political solutions.'[49] There was a sense that Band Aid had missed the chance to harness all that effort into real change and it had been about short-term crisis management instead of long-term disaster prevention and a genuine change in public thinking.[50]

Interestingly, when Geldof became involved in these issues again at the end of the 1980s and in particular in 2004/5 he took a rather different approach.[51] It was no longer just about inspiring rock fans to care and fundraising but about serious engagement with the political process—although by this time there was a Labour government that was inclined to give positive support and, crucially, had the political will to engage with Africa, unlike the government in the 1980s. By comparison with the previous period, Geldof was now pushing at an open door. In addition there was the advantage for him that, internationally, the issue of aid and dealings with the developing world was no longer frozen in a Cold War stance.

The overwhelming conclusion in 1985/86 with respect to Band Aid was a sense of a missed opportunity to effect a longer-term engagement. At the launch of the new charity One World Action[52] in 1986 Glenys Kinnock, who had been involved in development issues for some time, observed that, 'If the past eighteen months of fundraising and famine films have taught us anything, it is that charity and rock 'n roll are not by themselves going to save the world ... The obvious and trite conclusion is that this demands something more than a sorry shrug and another sponsored walk.'[53]

The former director of Christian Aid, Charles Elliott, put the argument even more bluntly. He observed that,

For most of the time most of us are very adept at ignoring the iceberg of which the Ethiopian tragedy is only the tip. There is a curious, one might say pathological, discontinuity between an intense emotional commitment to a particular dramatic symptom (such as 'famine in Ethiopia') and a continuing neglect of the chronic disease of which the symptom is part.[54]

The resurrection of Band Aid in December 1989 in order to raise awareness of another looming famine in Ethiopia was evidence for those who had been criticizing the short-term and limited analysis.[55] In the end the effect upon the poorest was only a temporary 'band aid', even if the effects upon charitable organization were far more enduring.

It was not only NGO styles of operation, imagery and fundraising techniques that changed; there was a significant long-term institutional impact on NGOs arising from the response to the BBC coverage of the Ethiopian famine.[56] Public opinion, inspired by news coverage, led to the government making high-profile, short-term humanitarian gestures in 1984/85, largely for domestic political reasons, but not much more than that. The media coverage of the famine did not lead to any real long-term policy involvement with the problems of Africa. It inspired a dramatic humanitarian response by individuals, partly manifested by their donations to aid agencies which led to an irreversible growth in size and significance. The short-term effect was one of real euphoria within the charitable world. There was also a change in the nature and style of charitable fundraising which was able to reach out to new kinds of donor. However, in terms of political involvement there was far less impact than might have appeared at the time. A terrible crisis had been identified, major efforts had apparently been made to solve it and the whole operation was perceived as a great success. Yet because all this effort missed the opportunity of any real long-term engagement with the problems, within a couple of years they would recur. Despite all the noise there was ultimately little wider understanding of the fundamental long-term causes and the real nature of the famine.

4

MISUNDERSTANDING THE FAMINE

TELLING THE STORY WRONG

'One of the most written-about famines is also one of the least understood.'

Alex de Waal, *Famine Crimes*[1]

'Certain laws govern the world and they are neither for nor against us. When a storm strikes, you don't blame anyone: you know the thunder is the result of two opposite electrical forces ...'

'But it's not the same thing. What we're going through is down to people and people alone.'

'It only seems like that Jeanne. It all seems caused by this man or that, by one circumstance or another, but it's like in nature: after the calm comes the storm ... It's just been our bad luck to be born in a century full of storms.'

Irène Némirovsky, *Suite Française*[2]

In the popular media memory the Ethiopian famine is remembered as a case of dramatic response to an urgent crisis. Michael Buerk's news coverage and the Live Aid concert combined with the spontaneous charitable responses are key images in the history of the 1980s and indeed in the history of television. The images in turn inspired an outpouring of generosity and concern amongst the populations across the Western world. Yet the real narrative behind the overwhelming media coverage and the subsequent humanitarian reaction is a far more complex and nuanced tale. Moreover, it is also a rather different story from that which has passed into the popular imagination. This makes it crucial to analyze what the coverage of the famine left out, why it produced a misleading message and what were the effects of this distortion. As in many other cases the story of the famine was drastically simplified, which meant that it omitted key issues, and crucially, as with much other reporting of faraway poor countries, the news was depoliticized. And this led to a drastic misinterpretation of both the famine and the causes behind it.

Viewing disasters

A significant reason for the impact of the BBC coverage was the solemn and magisterial manner in which the disaster was characterized. In his report broadcast on 23 October 1984 Michael Buerk memorably used the language of 'a biblical famine now in the twentieth century', conveying the idea that this was a natural catastrophe that had been visited upon the land, like an Act of God. Classically the media, in particular television, prefer an event to a process. Famine is typically a slow burning process but the media reporting characterized it as a sudden event. The news reports told a powerful tale about a suffering population and kept it very straightforward. The complicated political nature of the famine was dropped in favour of a simple story about failing rains and people in terrible distress whom we should help. This is in the nature of television news which prefers a straightforward unambiguous explanation,[3] but it was also very much in accord with the traditional Western discourse where famine is seen as 'simple, huge and apocalyptic, ... a terrible event that descends on particular societies from time to time and yields a number of unfortunate victims ...'[4] It is this perception that underlies the frequent description of famine as a natural disaster.

However, as the literature demonstrates, this received view of famine is an inaccurate and incomplete description. Amartya Sen (and subsequently many others) have pointed out that although we might call famine a disaster it is not a 'natural' disaster. There is always a political and social context. Sen's pioneering work,[5] which began with an analysis of the Bengal famine in 1943, and also the Ethiopian famine of 1973–74, demonstrated that famines tend to occur in societies which are not democratic and where there is no free press. Sen's work is based upon the concept of food entitlements. He demonstrated how famine is caused not by an aggregate decline in food but by a decline in the entitlements of part of the population. It is self-evidently the poorest members of a society whose entitlements are the least secure, but in a free society there are at least mechanisms whereby even those groups will not be allowed to starve. As other members of the society are made aware of the crisis, sufficient pressure will be put upon democratic leaders to increase those entitlements of the very weakest and poorest members. When droughts occur in the American Mid-West the population will not starve because they have, as Sen demonstrates, the entitlements to acquire food from elsewhere. In the USA droughts have not led to a death toll since the 1890s.

In a democracy, the state will receive signals (albeit sometimes weak ones) about their population's chronic unmet needs, and the press and, in turn, public opinion have a vital role to play in this. There is evidence to support this analysis based on entitlements in Ethiopia. During the 1973/74 famine there was no actual Food Availability Decline; indeed the food availability as stated in calories per head of the population was as much as or more than in other years. In other words there were, paradoxically, food supplies present throughout this period in the famine affected areas. Also, food continued to be available in the markets in Wollo and there was no rise in grain prices. Yet crucially, in the midst of this, certain vulnerable groups did not have the entitlements to purchase the food, which is why the situation led to starvation and famine.[6] The famine occurred under the authoritarian rule of Emperor Haile Selassie. The media, in this case aided by the ITV documentary made by Jonathan Dimbleby, eventually played a role in provoking a domestic political reaction to the famine within Ethiopia.[7]

Sen points out that in India, despite recurrent problems with food distribution and malnutrition, there has not been a famine since Independence. A relatively open, democratic society and a free press have been crucial in liberating India from a scourge which it had faced for centuries because 'public pressure facilitated by the publicity offered by a free press induced the state to adopt policies enabling the dispossessed to take up the shortfall in food entitlements.'[8] This does not mean that there have not been chronic food shortages in the period since Independence. Interestingly there was, for example, a drought in the state of

Maharashtra in 1973 that led to great problems with food supply and food riots in the neighbouring state of Gujarat. For a period the Indian government tried to prevent all journalists (domestic and foreign) from visiting the area and the BBC protested against the ban. Eventually Mark Tully, the BBC bureau chief, negotiated access for a BBC News crew, including the correspondent Martin Bell, to report from the area.[9] This is a clear example of the sensitivity that even a democratic government may feel about the publicizing of food shortages.

The worst famine of the twentieth century was in China between 1959 and 1961, which was only publicly acknowledged in the 1980s.[10] Even then it remained a sensitive subject and was still referred to by Chinese officials not as a 'famine' but as 'three difficult years'.[11] Today few young people know much about it, and if they do it is only as a natural disaster.[12] At the time, the information about the famine was completely suppressed and in subsequent years the estimated number of deaths ranged from fifteen million to a staggering forty million.[13] It has since emerged that 'The Chinese famine was at least in part caused by a massive disinformation campaign waged by the government which led the nation to live beyond its means.'[14] Sen's analysis is very illuminating in understanding this calamity. He points out how Mao's belief in agricultural reform as a means of achieving food security for the peasants meant that Communist Party officials assigned to agriculture faced overwhelming incentives to exaggerate performance to their superiors in order to prove that the reforms were working. Neither the press nor the public were free to report on starvation which was happening in remote districts—so the Chinese state, lacking free speech and transparency to the public, did not even know what was going on. A contemporary example of famine is in the secretive and authoritarian country of North Korea, which suffered a severe famine during the 1990s.[15]

Those countries in Africa that have dealt most successfully with food distribution and avoided famine are generally also the more open, democratic and less repressive societies, most notably places such as Botswana. Post-colonial Zimbabwe—the country in which Colonel Mengistu took refuge when he was deposed as the Ethiopian leader in 1991[16]—gives a clear example of the relationship between famine and politics. In the period after 1979, when it had a democratic regime and a free press, Zimbabwe never experienced a famine and was indeed sometimes referred to as 'the granary of Africa' because its record as a food producer was so successful. In subsequent years, as the nature of the regime under Robert Mugabe has changed, including a severe clampdown on democratic opposition and the free press, there have been threats of severe food shortages and many warnings of famine.[17]

From his original pioneering work on the role of entitlements Amartya Sen and his collaborator Jean Drèze went on in *Hunger and Public Action*[18] to develop further these ideas of the role that democratic institutions and in particular a free press play in the prevention of famine. They conclude that 'it is no accident that the countries that have been most successful in famine prevention ... have typically had pluralistic politics with open channels of communication and criticism. A relatively free newspaper system may be the most effective "early warning" system a famine-prone country can rely on.'[19]

A key part of this analysis of the causes of famine is the argument that there is no neat dichotomy between 'man made' and 'natural' disasters. Nature may exacerbate the problem but famine is essentially a social and economic failing[20] and what distinguishes famine from starvation and run of the mill food shortages is that famine is political. 'Famine is more than people dying from starvation. It is an acute breakdown of society that brings turmoil that cannot be ignored.'[21]

Sen also points to an interesting paradox in the relationship between famine, chronic food shortages and a free press. He demonstrates that in India, whilst there have been no famines in modern times, there have been continuing problems of low level malnutrition. China on the other hand has had greater success in feeding its population and ensuring an overall better level of nutrition for the poor; however, there have in the midst of this been 'periodic shocks' leading to catastrophic famine in China. Sen argues that this derives from the nature of the society. A more open liberal society like India will act as a bulwark against extreme starvation, but it has been less successful at general food distribution and allocation. Meanwhile a less free society can, in this case, demonstrate greater efficiency at regular food provision. Yet when things go wrong there is no warning mechanism via free institutions and a free press to alert the authorities to act.

This critical social and political context to famine has been highlighted elsewhere. The philosopher Onora O'Neill points out how misconceived the notion that famine somehow periodically 'breaks out' is. She points to the media accounts and the publicity of NGO famine relief, which depict hunger as 'episodic mass starvation, calling for the same generosity as that of earthquake or flood victims'. Her alternative is that 'famine is like more scattered and less visible hunger, a critical symptom of social and economic structures that leave people in desperate poverty, which cannot be ended without fundamental and long-term change'.[22] This is rather different from the typical media version of famine. Lloyd Timberlake also challenges the notion of emergency relief designed to 'get things back to normal' in a population living anyway in precarious conditions (with minimal entitlements). After all, 'normal was what had led to the disaster in the first place and the status quo may have made people disaster prone'.[23]

A more radical view is that there is no such thing as a 'natural' disaster. All disasters are social and political events which could potentially be prevented, or at least their impact could be dramatically reduced. Floods, droughts and earthquakes in the developed world kill only a tiny of fraction of the numbers of those who die in similar incidents in poorer countries. According to Mike Aaronson, former director of the Save the Children Fund, 'ninety-eight percent of those killed or affected by so called natural disasters come from the developing world. In these poorer nations the average disaster death toll is just over 1,000; in the richer countries it is only 23.'[24] Flood warning systems, stricter building regulations, better planning and infrastructure for rescuing people make all the difference. Earthquakes in developed countries result in far lower death tolls than those in poor parts of the world. After the Asian Tsunami in 2004 there was much criticism that the Indian Ocean, unlike the Pacific, did not have an alert system. Proposals for such a system had previously been rejected on grounds of cost, although after the disaster this decision was quickly reversed. So the implication is that if the Tsunami (on the same scale) had struck in wealthier countries it would not have resulted in the same death toll. The cause of the disaster was a fact of nature, but its implications were very much mitigated by social and human factors.

Missing the point

In 1984/85 the famine in Ethiopia was repeatedly described in the media as a fact of nature, simply a product of the drought. Interestingly, this was also the way it was understood and described within the UK government at that time. The various initiatives in the Overseas Development Agency (ODA) were all concerned with the 'drought', such as the daily meeting of the 'Ethiopian Drought Group' in the autumn of 1984 and the circulation of an 'Ethiopian Drought distribution list' for the various internal documents. The speeches and parliamentary appearances by the ministers concerned also referred repeatedly to the 'problem of drought'. The same description was used by the opposition. Stuart Holland MP, the Labour shadow minister for overseas development, wrote to complain to the director general of the BBC that he had not been asked to appear on programmes opposite Timothy Raison to discuss the 'Ethiopian Drought Crisis'.[25]

This description echoed in turn the official view of the Ethiopian government which, when it did discuss the crisis, only ever referred to the problem of 'drought'. Their spokesmen never used the Amharic word for famine (*rehab*) but only the word for drought (*diriq*), or else referred to the 'natural problem' (*yetefetero chigir*). In this way they were effectively censoring information about the causes of the famine.[26] The Ethiopian Relief and Rehabilitation Commission published a report in 1986 entitled *The Challenges of Drought*, which referred to the (pre-Revolutionary) famine of 1972–74, but only the (post-Revolutionary) drought of 1984–85[27] (even though the latter crisis had a far higher mortality than the earlier one under the reign of Emperor Haile Selassie).

As the theories of Sen and others outline, the Ethiopian crisis, like so many similar ones, was the direct result of social and political factors. Yet as far as the media were concerned they, along with the official authorities, preferred the simple, straightforward, but clearly inaccurate description of the disaster as a food deficiency caused by lack of rain.[28] Indeed, even the dates of the crisis as it was described in the media are misleading, because the famine is commonly supposed to have occurred in 1984–85, whereas there is plenty of evidence to show that famine conditions were already prevalent in 1982, which is the real date of the start of the famine. However, for Western nations the famine only officially began when it was a breaking story featured on TV. So both the official and media versions of the causes of the crisis and its timing were misrepresented.

Soon after the famine finally hit the headlines in 1984—where it was repeatedly described as a dramatic decline in food production as the result of drought—Amartya Sen wrote to *The Times*:

Sir, The appalling famine in Ethiopia calls for international help on a massive scale. It also calls for clearer economic analysis of the causation of such famines, if tragedies of this kind are to be avoided in the future. In particular, it is important that we stop trying to explain famines exclusively in terms of food production per head ... Starvation must be seen as a general economic and political problem and not narrowly as a problem of food production. To see the causation of famines just in terms of a decline in food production per head is a dangerous over-simplification. The Ethiopian famine is no exception.[29]

Sen was clearly fighting an uphill battle against the vast majority of the media that preferred to rely on the familiar if inaccurate descriptions of famine and its causes. A number of subsequent studies of the famine pointed to a rather different picture from the accepted media interpretation. Ondine Barrow, who analyzed the famine in Ethiopia over this period, observed that just as in the 1973/74 famine (which Sen had studied) there were no overall real food shortages and no sharp rise in grain prices in the early 1980s, and concludes that 'if the normal processes of redistribution of food had been allowed to occur there would have been no famine.'[30] In other words, it was once again a matter of entitlements by certain groups which had resulted in famine, not an overall shortage of food. Moreover, Rony Brauman, who was with Médecins Sans Frontières (MSF) in Ethiopia, records that the real drop in precipitation over that period was no more than 20 per cent, which by itself, without the many man-made factors he highlighted, was not enough to cause such widespread devastation.[31]

The subtleties of this debate should not have been lost on the UK government. Towards the end of November 1984 it received a report prepared for the European Council by Jim O'Keefe, the Irish foreign affairs minister and president of the EU council of development ministers, reporting on his visit to Ethiopia and Kenya between 17 and 23 November (Ireland had the EU presidency during this period). O'Keefe made a long, detailed report[32] and observed that neighbouring Kenya had potentially faced the same famine problems as Ethiopia through drought, but its action had averted the worst, so that 'a drought need not become a famine. As was demonstrated in Kenya, prompt action by the government supported by donors ensure that adequate supplies of food were made available and were widely distributed.' He contrasts this with Ethiopia where 'drought became a famine because remedial action was not taken soon enough ... donors did not heed warnings and the

Ethiopian government did not take adequate or timely measures to mobilise its own resources to tackle the famine.'

Famine, democracy and war

As food entitlements among certain groups declined in the early 1980s there were no democratic mechanisms inside Ethiopia which could alert the authorities. Indeed Dawit Wolde Giorgis makes it quite explicit that the highest authorities in the regime were quite indifferent to the starvation, especially in the rebel provinces of Tigray and Eritrea. In his memoir Giorgis talks repeatedly about the callous attitude of the Mengistu regime towards the suffering. In the preface he describes his story as 'that of a regime that instead of saving its people ignored their cries for help and through its unfeeling lethal programs caused suffering and death to a degree no one ever imagined possible.'[33] He observed how the Ethiopian government was hostile to any reminders of the food shortages and, in an authoritarian and tightly controlled dictatorship, there was no question of any domestic press reporting of the imminent famine conditions.

Sen and Drèze[34] emphasize the role of a free press and democracy as a key bulwark against famine. However, this relationship also operates on a wider global level, albeit far less effectively. The worldwide coverage of the Ethiopian famine produced a limited political reaction, in that democratic foreign governments were subject to pressure from public opinion in their own countries to intervene and send aid to Ethiopia. Had there been a democratic regime within Ethiopia itself, according to Sen there would not have been a famine on this scale. However, once the pictures of the famine led to major international media coverage, this had an effect within the donor countries. Governments in these countries were under pressure to send aid (even though the way the famine was being reported and described was only partially true). Clearly this publicity was far less effective than the direct democratic pressure there could have been within Ethiopia, had there been a regime there that took account of popular opinion. The signals there would have been far stronger had there been a free press and a functioning democracy. Interestingly, in the succeeding years the role of good governance and a free press have been regarded as much more significant drivers for development.

The Commission for Africa[35] report in 2005 placed great emphasis upon the need for effective institutional mechanisms—more transparency, less corruption, more accountable governments and a genuinely free press. Hilary Benn, who was at that time secretary of state for international development, regarded it as a key sign of progress when local populations are able to pressure their own governments on matters such as better service delivery:

If we as donors take sole responsibility for delivering ... then the incentive for poor people to demand such services of their own governments would be lost. And it was just these demands that in the rich west made our governments deliver ... it is developing country governments not donors who have to take responsibility for the economic social and political developments of their own people ... It is politics that makes the difference.[36]

Benn's belief in the role of democratic accountability in development also led him to put governance at the heart of his department's White Paper on development in 2006.[37] Yet whilst Western donors may have taken some time to reach this conclusion, for many Africans this rights based analysis is, frustratingly, nothing new. In a publication dealing with human rights in Africa in 1994, Nigerian lawyer and human rights worker, Chidi Anselm Odinkalu, concluded an article by urging that 'Africa needs accountable government more than it needs debt relief and dodgy aid.'[38]

The Ethiopian government in 1984 under Mengistu was an authoritarian regime with no freedom of the press. So the possibility of any kind of local pressure being exerted via the media on the government was completely out of the question. However, there was the far more 'dilute effect' of the global media which covered the famine; but the problem there was that the story told was far from accurate or complete. The vast majority of the reporting of the famine in the international media conveyed the received wisdom in 1984, that what was happening in Ethiopia was a natural disaster and that the famine was an emergency which justified exceptional action. This was part of the overall perception that entered public consciousness at that time. Again and again the explanation for the famine was the lack of rain. Yet this was only one aspect of a more complex story. The crucial part of the explanation, frequently omitted, was that the repressive Ethiopian regime, with substantial Soviet aid, was fighting two long running civil wars in the north against the Eritreans and Tigrayans. Over half of Ethiopia's national budget at this time was spent on the defence forces and the Ethiopian army was larger than any other in sub-Saharan Africa. The battles between the government and the rebels were the biggest in Africa since El Alamein, and yet at the time the war was an official secret. The government referred to dealing with 'bandits'[39] but did not say it was involved in a full scale counterinsurgency operation involving bombing raids and mass infantry offensives.[40] Occasionally information about fighting did emerge, such as when the US Chargé d'Affaires made a protest about the bombing of refugees who were travelling on foot from Tigray towards Sudan.[41] But the war and its key role in precipitating famine were for the most part overlooked and ignored by aid agencies and Western donors.

As far as the Ethiopian government was concerned, starvation had become a weapon of this war, a means of attacking the (predominantly rebel) populations in those areas in order that they would submit. Moreover, the fighting itself was directly causing problems with food supply. Historically the nature of this northern terrain meant huge variations in food production even within small geographical areas. Sometimes neighbouring towns and villages experienced quite different conditions, so that in the same year some had surpluses and others nearby were short of food. In these circumstances frequent trade was very important to even out the imbalance and traditionally there were regular markets and trading operations. The Ethiopian air force was deliberately bombing the markets and the trade convoys in order to disrupt food supplies in Tigray. Detailed accounts of attacks by MiG fighters were conveyed to the UK government in December 1984.[42] There were attempts to hold markets and to transport food at night in order to evade the attacks. On the ground there were army roadblocks, ostensibly for security reasons, but which also had the effect of hampering the transport and distribution of food. There were also reports that the Ethiopian troops were burning food stores in Tigray, attempting to 'starve the population into submission'.[43] This was part of a deliberate strategy of counterinsurgency which involved poisoning wells, destroying livestock and planting mines. Indeed, 'strategies pursued by the Derg were instrumental in setting the famine in train.'[44]

Sen and Drèze stress the frequent relationship between war and famine through a series of factors, including disruption of trade, destruction of crops, deflecting resources to military activity and population displacement. All these conditions that they mention were present in Ethiopia in this period.[45] Just days after the BBC news coverage of the famine, on 27 October 1984 the Ethiopian forces launched a major new air and ground offensive against Tigray. The lack of attention this received in the media led to it being named 'the Silent Offensive'. Yet it was the largest army attack on the rebel areas since the 'Red Star offensive' in 1982, which involved an estimated hundred thousand soldiers.[46] The Red Cross nurse Claire Bertschinger, who featured in Michael Buerk's original television news reports from Tigray, very unexpectedly came across what were clearly wounded soldiers in a hospital in Mekele in late October 1984 and remarked that 'usually these war casualties would have remained hidden from us.'[47] Throughout 1985 the army launched a series of further offensives and the losses were so great that another round of military conscription followed.

A number of detailed studies, often based upon eyewitness accounts, have pointed in retrospect to the diversion of food relief for military ends and widespread brutality against civilians in the rebel areas which were the epicentre of the famine.[48] Barbara Hendrie, later an official with the Department for International Development (DFID), but who in 1984/85 was monitoring food aid in Tigray, wrote that 'the Government's use of counterinsurgency warfare, including direct attacks against the civilian population in rural areas acted as a catalyst for the decline of the countryside to starvation.'[49] She points to the direct role of the fighting in destroying crops, housing and storage facilities, as well as the indirect effects whereby the traditional survival strategies of the peasantry in times of food shortage could no longer operate. Hendrie concludes that 'in a non-war context it is unlikely that drought alone could have produced starvation on the scale that occurred in the famine of 1984/5.'[50] The Africa Watch report on the famine published in 1991 speaks of 'the systematic use and denial of food relief for military ends [which] was the most notable aspect of government strategy that also included extraordinarily sustained and widespread brutality against civilians'.[51] Yet according to the simplified media accounts, the fighting was seen as a diversion. Indeed some journalists reporting on the famine talked of the fighting sometimes hindering the aid operation—except that they crucially omitted to say that the fighting was a substantial *cause* of the need for aid in the first place.[52]

Tony Vaux, who spent many years working for Oxfam, is quite clear that it was not a 'biblical' famine:

Buerk scarcely mentioned the war. The plains of Korem were quiet and peaceful. Buerk did not record the scream of Ethiopia jet fighters that often broke the silence as they flew northwards to bomb the rebels ... He did not swing the camera sideways to show the multiple rocket launchers that also occupied the plains of Korem. Even today, most journalists and aid managers continue to take the view that it was in the greater interest of humanity to keep the issues simple and elicit the largest possible response.[53]

Buerk himself strongly disputes this version: 'I did mention the war, I mentioned the war an enormous amount ... we all know that famines aren't merely caused by drought and harvest failure, famines are caused certainly in Africa by war that prevents any help going through.'[54]

In fact Buerk himself did cover the war in the second of his two reports from Ethiopia, broadcast on 24 October 1984[55] and filmed in Tigray. The problem was that as the story reverberated around the media and was picked up in an increasingly simplistic way, especially by the tabloid press, the subtleties and complexities of what was a complicated war were then left out. Just as the distorting effects of news selection are in some cases accentuated as a story goes up the production chain— what is newsworthy is emphasized and what is not seen as relevant is suppressed—so the same thing happened in this case as the story was taken up by different media outlets. The tabloid press in particular prefers simple, unambiguous explanations. Barbara Hendrie witnessed at first hand the repeated bombing of civilians by the Ethiopian air force and observed later how 'The close connections of war and famine were lost in the ensuing coverage'.[56] Reflecting back on this, she is in no doubt that 'the Ethiopian Government was deliberately bombing victims of famine—out of sight of international cameras.'

Difficult appeals

In 1984 television news characterized the famine in Ethiopia as a sudden and urgent catastrophe. It was reported as a (sudden) event rather than a very slow process. Yet starvation is never an immediate disaster, like an earthquake. It happens very slowly over months if not years. This was the message that some of the aid agencies had been trying to convey throughout 1983. They were trying—without success—to draw attention to a gradual process where conditions were slowly becoming worse. In general earthquakes, landslides and sudden disasters, which are events that kill a number of people quickly, get more media attention and relief than those crises that kill people slowly.[57] This depiction of disasters fits closely with the wider definitions of what makes news. Most natural disasters like earthquakes or volcanoes display many of these key characteristics that are classically associated with news values. They are something that is sudden, unexpected, dramatic, negative and unambiguous.[58] This is why disasters, even though they occur in faraway places, are often highly newsworthy events, provided there is sufficient media access. The Asian Tsunami on 26 December 2004 was a perfect example of this—it was perceived as the ultimate act of nature, where no one was to blame. This, combined with direct Western involvement in the tragedy (tourists on the beaches) and the proximity to Christmas, generated a fast and generous response.

As the donations flowed in early 2005, in response to the media reporting of the Tsunami, there were continual comparisons with the problems of Africa. Every year far more people die in Africa from disease and starvation than were killed in the Tsunami, but it is a continual and 'hidden' problem without the sudden drama of the Tsunami. The chronic and continuing nature of Africa's problems makes them susceptible to 'compassion fatigue'. The Commission for Africa report in 2005 referred to 'a Tsunami every month in Africa. But its deadly tide of disease and hunger steals silently and secretly across the continent. It is not dramatic and its victims rarely make the television news'.[59]

The Asian Tsunami fulfilled a high proportion of the key criteria for news values apparent in disasters because it was sudden, unexpected, dramatic, negative and unambiguous. It was a classic case of a sudden disaster killing people, quickly attracting far more relief than a chronic and less visible crisis that grinds people down slowly. The Tsunami also had one extra factor, which was the involvement of elites. Typically natural disasters occur in poor countries, which might detract from their newsworthiness, but the Tsunami involved a number of Western tourists which gave it an additional dimension. And in many cases, because there were nationals involved, it became a domestic rather than just a foreign story. It is therefore unsurprising that the areas which involved Western tourists, in particular Thailand and Sri Lanka, received far more media attention than those which did not—specifically those parts of Indonesia such as Banda Aceh which were by far the worst affected and had the highest death toll. So there is no relation between the level of coverage and the number of deaths. Instead the presence of Westerners and Western deaths is related to the volume of media stories.

Tsunami death toll

	Dead/Missing	Number of Stories
Indonesia	167,000	343
Sri Lanka	35,000	729
Thailand	8,200	771

Source: UN Office of the Special Envoy for Tsunami Recovery.
Source: Analysis of Lexis Nexis Stories.

In general sudden disasters, once they are known about, will sustain significant media attention, at least for a while, and this helps to generate a humanitarian response, although there are still exceptions.[60] Famine, on the other hand, can never be a sudden event. It is generally a chronic, creeping process that can be complicated to explain. This generally gives it a far lower ranking on the accepted scale of newsworthiness.

Yet in 1984 the characterization of famine as a sudden, urgent problem was significant in the way that it gained major exposure and attention. The Michael Buerk news item which went round the world highlighted the 'discovery' of a famine. Christopher Bosso in his analysis of the impact of the media coverage of the famine makes much of the way it was presented as a 'sudden discovery'.[61] The perception of famine as an act of nature due to failing rains was also important in the scale and generosity of the response in 1984. The distinction between natural disasters (good causes) and man-made disasters (more dubious and complicated causes) prevailed in public perceptions. It had a significant effect on the way the public responded to appeals, because the way in which disasters are characterized within the media is of key importance in fund raising.

The Disasters Emergency Committee

It is not only the media that will tend towards a simple explanation; charitable appeals through the media also prefer an uncomplicated account of why the money is needed. In the UK the key focus of these major broadcast appeals is in the institution of the Disasters Emergency Committee, which brings together the broadcasting organizations and the principal charities involved in overseas relief. It was established to 'meet a new level of response from the British public to the publicity given, through the development of the television medium to any major natural disaster occurring in a country overseas.'[62] The Disasters Emergency Committee is a peculiarly British institution which links co-operative fundraising between the big charities and the broadcasting organizations. Jonathan Benthall describes how this 'preference for solving problems discreetly behind closed doors and a commitment to regulatory authority in broadcasting'[63] characterizes the DEC very much as part of the British establishment. It was set up in 1963 when a cyclone hit Sri Lanka (or Ceylon as it was then known). The Ceylonese high commissioner appeared on television and asked for British citizens who wanted to help to send their donations to the charity War on Want. There was great concern by the broadcasting authorities that rival agencies would object to this and perceive it as unfair publicity for one charity. The solution they devised was to establish a committee of the five leading international agencies[64] and for this to act as a channel to the broadcasters to carry appeals in response to emergencies and to organize a joint collecting arrangement at the banks and the Post Office. It was conceived as a pragmatic way of balancing the various institutional pressures.

The first joint appeal by the DEC was in 1966 in response to the Turkish earthquake, when the BBC appeal was made by the broadcaster Cliff Michelmore. A permanent arrangement was established with the BBC and the Independent Broadcasting Authority (IBA) regarding air time for these exceptional television and radio appeals, which are broadcast during weekday peak time hours (as distinct from regular scheduled charity appeals). The IBA and BBC chairmen (on behalf of the governors) had to approve the emergency appeal, although in practice 'the system puts the agencies in a strong position to exert moral pressure.'[65] This tendency is reflected in some of the internal discussions within the BBC, responding to requests for appeals by the charities via the DEC, where there has sometimes been a sense of great reluctance.[66] There were a number of cases in this period where the broadcasters held lengthy and convoluted debates over the merits of an appeal, although in the end they gave consent.

On average there were one or two appeals a year throughout the 1970s and 1980s. A wide range of well-known figures were chosen to present the appeals, including, for example, the comedian Michael Bentine, who made the appeal following an earthquake in Peru in 1970, or

Dame Margot Fonteyn, the ballerina, who appealed for aid after an earthquake in Nicaragua in December 1972. In the period before the Ethiopian appeal of 1984, the highest amount ever raised by an appeal was £6 million for an African famine appeal in 1980. However, there was a big variation in the results of appeals and the average was in fact much lower, usually no more than a million.

As with other fundraising, the amounts raised were not always in proportion to the need. Once again the dilemma was that the way in which the disaster was perceived was crucial in the level of response. In the DEC handbook in 1981 one of the criteria for allowing an appeal was 'the degree of response which can be expected from the public ... This should be judged as far as possible on the merits of the disaster and not on the publicity or lack of publicity in the press.'[67] Yet in the discussions surrounding one not very successful appeal there was criticism from the board of governors that 'the issue should be brought clearly into the consciousness of the British people before the appeal broadcast was made.' Otherwise there might be a poor result which would call into question the status of emergency appeals generally.[68] Similarly, a board of governors paper discussing appeals policy emphasized that there should be 'a sufficient degree of public awareness of the emergency ...'[69] before a decision could be made to launch an appeal.

This question of media awareness prior to an appeal is something of a chicken and egg conundrum. If agreement to allow an appeal depended upon how much the public knew about a crisis, then it was only disasters that were already reasonably well known that were likely to be permitted a broadcast and thereby have the opportunity to raise large amounts. It begged the question of whether there were other less well known crises that were not being allowed to make an appeal (simply because they were less well known), and reinforced the continuing role that the media have in constructing what we know as a disaster.

Within the BBC at this point there was also a clear sense of a distinction between natural and man-made crises when considering whether to broadcast appeals for particular causes. At the start of 1982 there had been considerable hesitation and anxiety about allowing an emergency appeal for the victims of fighting in Central America. The request was for a special appeal to raise funds to help the victims of civil disturbances in El Salvador, and on this occasion it took a month of prevarication within the BBC before permission was eventually given for the broadcast to take place. Both the BBC appeals secretary and the chair of the Central Appeals Advisory Committee presented arguments against the appeal, citing the overall uncertainty of the situation and the fact that it did not qualify as an 'emergency disaster'.[70] This concern was reflected in press reporting on the merits of the appeal. The *Guardian* reported that 'a Charity appeal for victims of escalating civil strife in Central America has aroused serious concern in the BBC (and the big banks who collect the money) about the political implication of such assistance.'[71] When the matter came up for discussion at the BBC board of management there was a long discussion about the nature of the crisis and suffering in El Salvador and whether an appeal was merited. Dick Francis, the director of news and current affairs (who would later go on to run the British Council), was distinctly sceptical. He said that 'he doubted whether the appeals process should be invoked to deal with problems caused by man's folly, as opposed to natural disasters.'[72] Yet after further lengthy discussion a decision was taken that, provided the aid could be distributed in areas of fighting, then the precedent of an earlier appeal for the Vietnamese boat people in 1979[73] should be followed and the recommendation to the governors was to allow the appeal to go ahead.

At the board of governors meeting which followed some of the governors argued against the appeal on the grounds of the political origins of the crisis. Stuart Young, for example, 'was doubtful of the wisdom of an appeal in what he described as an escalating war situation and felt that the "acts of God" distinction should continue to be made.'[74] Another governor, Alwyn Roberts, disagreed with the relevance of such a distinction on the basis that the 'consequences for the victims were very much the same.' He also argued that the BBC had never previously rejected a request for an appeal and 'such a gesture would be interpreted as a political gesture.' In the end the governors agreed to support the DEC and consent to the appeal. However, as the chairman, George Howard, put it in a letter to the Central Appeals Advisory Committee, 'Our decision to grant an appeal was taken after a good deal of agonising.'[75] Interestingly, one of the caveats that the BBC made on this occasion is that they were not prepared to put someone up (generally a celebrity presenter or actor figure) to make the appeal as had traditionally been the practice. So in the end it was the DEC chairman Lord Hunt of Tanworth (formerly the cabinet secretary) who presented the appeal on the BBC himself. Some weeks later, when the Central American appeal had yielded a rather disappointing total (less than £400,000), Sir John Johnston pointed out at a governors' meeting that 'there was a lesson to be learned from this and if the BBC were ever to be asked to mount an appeal in similar circumstances again it would be able to point to this unhappy experience as a reason for declining to do so.'[76]

Nevertheless the same discussions occurred just a few months later in June 1982, when there was a request for an appeal for those caught up in the fighting in Lebanon. At a Radio Review Board concern was again expressed by Dick Francis, who was now the managing director of radio, about allowing an appeal for refugees from the Lebanon fighting, on the basis that emergency appeals were only permitted for natural disasters. He pointed out that the rule had previously been ignored in the 1970s appeal for the Vietnamese boat people and warned that 'the traditional policy should not be breached unthinkingly lest allowing some appeals would be seen to involve a political stance'.[77] In fact, when the original request came to the BBC for the Lebanon appeal on 15 June 1982 it was rejected on the grounds that it was not a natural but a complicated, political and clearly man-made disaster. The BBC responded to the DEC by saying that 'Manmade disasters with political implications … always fit uneasily into our rules'.[78]

The DEC withdrew its request for Lebanon and negative press reaction followed, accusing the BBC of blocking the appeal.[79] At that time the practice was that the chairman acting on behalf of the board could agree to DEC requests for emergency appeals. Three weeks later there were further discussions and this time the matter was put to the whole board of governors which, after some discussion, eventually agreed—albeit reluctantly—to the appeal. Sue Lawley (a well known presenter of BBC1's *Nationwide* programme) made the appeal in the BBC broadcast on 14 July 1982. Interestingly there were comparisons made during the discussion between the situation in Lebanon in 1982 and that in El Salvador a few months earlier. Two of the governors said that they could not understand why 'publicising relief for the Lebanon was acceptable' whilst requesting 'relief for the victims of violence in El Salvador on a previous occasion was not'.[80] The director of public affairs tried to argue that one case was more complex than the other and it was impossible to make comparisons, but it was clear that this was emerging as a tricky issue to resolve. George Howard, the BBC chairman, urged again at a later meeting that there should be a review of this whole policy and the principles underlying such appeals.[81]

In 1983, following the Central American and Lebanon appeals, the rules for appeals were amended. After considerable discussion and revisions to the guidelines there was now a clear recognition that the DEC could in some circumstances support appeals for victims of 'man made' disasters.[82] In the introduction to the handbook explaining the original establishment of the DEC, the reference was now to 'disasters' instead of 'natural disasters' as in the original text. However, in view of the more tricky and controversial nature of such requests it was decided that whilst the chairman acting alone could still make decisions about whether to proceed with appeals for natural disasters, it was advisable to seek agreement from the whole board of governors in the case of man-made emergencies.[83] Twenty-four years later, in the summer of 2006 there was another war in Lebanon. The DEC request for an emergency appeal was on that occasion turned down by the BBC and other broadcasters on the grounds that 'given the political complexities of the crisis' there was concern whether people would support it.[84] Similarly, in January 2009 in the midst of the war in Gaza, the BBC rejected the request for a DEC appeal on the grounds that it would compromise impartiality.[85] This indicates that the broadcasters still have the same anxieties about what they perceive as 'political' appeals, but also that they are prepared to be more resistant to the wishes of the DEC than they were in the 1980s.

What is notable in the discussions on these matters in the early 1980s is that there was still apparently a belief within the BBC during this period that the two categories of emergency could be neatly classified as distinct and separate. The Ethiopian famine, for example, was unambiguously perceived as a natural disaster,[86] a view which was later on to be radically reinterpreted in some circles. In subsequent years a much more nuanced approach was developed overall in order to classify international crises, with the introduction of the concept of 'complex emergency'.[87] It was gradually being recognized that in many cases there was not a single explanation and that so often in a crisis there was an interaction between climate, conflict, political unrest and other factors. After the disagreements over the two appeals in 1982 discussions had already begun within the BBC about how to define disasters in the future.[88] These debates continued over the years. In January 2001, when the BBC was considering whether to allow an appeal by the DEC for victims of the Gujarat earthquake in north-west India, there was some discussion, amongst those making the decision, of whether the disaster was partly due to flimsy buildings and inadequate building regulation, in which case the merits of an appeal were somewhat removed. However, a decision was taken that whilst this was a possible news angle on the crisis, it should not prevent the BBC from allowing the appeal for the victims of the earthquake.[89] Yet it was now apparent that there was a blurring of the line dividing natural and man-made causes amongst those who were making the decisions.

The request for an appeal for Ethiopia in July 1984 raised other concerns. No one within the BBC disputed at that time whether the famine was a natural disaster, but questions were raised instead as to whether it really counted as an 'emergency'. This again was a matter for continuing internal debate.[90] Within the BBC there was concern in July 1984 to show that the developing famine in Africa merited an emergency appeal for something out of the ordinary, not as support for relief work in an area where there was a continuing problem, which should be using the regular charity appeals system.[91] Questions were also raised as to whether the food crisis demanded more extensive and radical economic measures than humanitarian aid could provide. After some discussion Stuart Young, who was then the chairman of the BBC, decided, despite considerable reservations, that there was a demonstrable humanitarian need and the situation was an emergency, so that an appeal was justified.[92] The same issue had arisen in 1980 over a previous famine appeal for the Horn of Africa. The board of governors discussion reflected that 'The DEC was concerned with emergencies and the usual assumption was that it existed to respond to humanitarian feelings in a British public already alert to a disaster emergency. In this case … there was not a sudden emergency; the suffering had been going on for a long time.'[93] Nevertheless, as in 1984 the governors agreed to the appeal, although they said 'it was approved on the understanding that it was out of the ordinary run.'

In the intervening period since the early 1980s there has been more analysis not just of the interaction of natural and man-made disasters but also of the categories of 'sudden', 'creeping' and 'chronic' disasters.[94] In retrospect Young was indeed correct that the famine was a chronic disaster, not strictly speaking a sudden emergency, and that therefore technically speaking the appeal breached the rules. This was made quite evident when famine continued to recur in Ethiopia throughout the next decade, just as it had done in the period before 1984. Indeed, there were two further DEC appeals for famine in Ethiopia before the end of the decade, indicating that the huge efforts in 1984/85 hardly did anything towards solving the problem. By the time the policies of the DEC were reviewed again in 1992 the broadcasters agreed, after some persuasion, that there should henceforth be a category of what were called 'non-sudden appeals'. A memorandum recognized that there were 'situations involving drought, harvest failure, war and internal conflict where deteriorating conditions lead cumulatively to a life-threatening crisis of widespread proportions calling for urgent aid from the international community.'[95] This change of emphasis indicated that the broadcasters and the charities were now recognizing that disasters were no longer neatly divisible into the two distinct categories of natural and man-made, but were becoming aware of the existence of the 'complex emergency' and the need to recognize the important social and political context of almost all disasters.

In retrospect it is apparent that the Western media reporting did tell a simplified, incomplete and on occasion plainly wrong story about the famine. As the scale of the coverage grew, the story was depoliticized into a tale of bad weather and not enough food to go round. This was reinforced in the way that the broadcast appeals for donations to Ethiopia were made. The Live Aid and Band Aid message was one about sending relief to a hungry population suffering from drought and the DEC appeals on the BBC and ITV were for donations to assist in alleviating a natural disaster. To some extent this was not the fault of the media, since governments both in Ethiopia and in donor countries were also telling a partial story about a famine caused by drought. The complicated facts of warfare and a regime using famine and also aid as a tool in the fighting were largely omitted.

By the time Dawit Wolde Giorgis—who had played a central role in misleading relief appeals—wrote the afterword to his memoir in 1989, he admitted that the wrong story had been told. Referring to another drought and relief appeal by R&RC in 1988, he observed that once again:

Mengistu is blaming as usual the weather ... the truth of the matter is that (once again) drought is not the main cause of the famine; the most immediate cause is the escalating conflict ... the regime allocated more of its resources and funds to the war effort ... villages were burned and peasants forced to flee... land lay fallow and became more of a battle zone.[96]

The inaccurate and limited explanations of the famine, which became so widely accepted, were to a large extent part of a classic problem about reporting Africa, which became a recurrent theme in the late twentieth century. The episodic and out of context way that so much news about Africa is reported makes it possible for this kind of wide scale misapprehension. If there had been more understanding in particular about the political background to the fighting in Ethiopia, then it would not have been possible for such an inaccurate version of the famine and its causes to have taken hold. However, on this occasion, as with other African crises, before and after, the lack of a sustained longer-term understanding meant that such an inaccurate and incomplete version of events became easily accepted. Ethiopia in 1984 was the biggest story out of Black Africa for over a decade, yet for many reasons, the way it was told was inadequate. And equally serious were the misunderstandings and misperceptions of the aid agencies who were also telling a partial story—albeit sometimes with good intentions.

5

THE HUMANITARIAN DILEMMA

'A starving child knows no politics.'

USAID director Peter McPherson 1984[1]

'A hungry child is created by politics.'

Alex de Waal[2]

'The evil that is in the world always comes out of ignorance, and good intentions may do as much harm as malevolence, if they lack understanding.'

Albert Camus, *The Plague*

The media reporting of a sudden, natural disaster which was caused by drought now appears to be both an inaccurate and an inadequate description of the Ethiopian famine. However, it was not only the media that were telling a selective story. Equally, many of the aid agencies were at the very least economical with the truth. The plight of the starving as witnessed on television meant that unprecedented amounts of aid were flowing into Ethiopia from all over the world. Indeed more money was channelled to this disaster than to any previous emergency humanitarian operation.[3] According to their own narrative and the one that was continually being retold in the media both then and subsequently, the NGOs which had been inundated with donations were doing a remarkable job in alleviating the suffering which was caused by the drought. Yet

113

in subsequent years it became apparent that the aid story had been misunderstood at the time and was not a simple one of saving starving famine victims. Despite the way the humanitarian relief effort in Ethiopia was reported, the aid operation was, in fact, highly complicated and problematic, and many now argue that it may have ultimately caused more harm than good. There are a number of institutional reasons why NGOs told a partial story, why they overstated their position in alleviating suffering and, crucially, ignored the messy complexity of what was really happening on the ground.

In the decades since the famine, and in particular since the end of the Cold War, there has been a huge effort to understand the interaction between politics and humanitarian intervention. The 1980s is now considered a 'golden age' of humanitarianism. There was still an attitude that it was possible to help innocent victims of a crisis regardless of the surrounding politics. Aid could somehow operate in a neutral 'politics free' space. Gradually, in the years following the mid-80s, this belief has unravelled. Successive episodes of humanitarian intervention across the world (although primarily in Africa) have demonstrated that there needs to be a far more nuanced understanding of the way in which aid agencies, as growing and increasingly powerful institutions, operate in emergency situations. In particular, there has been a recognition that it may not be possible to intervene satisfactorily without engaging with the political circumstances of the crisis. And crucially this means conveying an accurate and properly informed picture of what is happening. The Ethiopian famine was an important turning point in this understanding. There has also been a developing awareness of the extent to which, in telling a more accurate story, aid agencies should also be accountable—both to those who fund them and to those they are supposed to be helping.

Keeping it simple

As the aid started to arrive in Ethiopia in late 1984 and early 1985 a formidable logistics operation was established. The process was co-ordinated by a special UN office set up in Addis Ababa under Kurt Jansson, who had previously run the operation to deliver aid to Cambodia. The UN Emergency Office for Ethiopia (UNEOE) liaised with the Ethiopian government through its Relief and Rehabilitation Commission.

Just as the media reporting did not emphasize the role of the civil war in creating famine, there was a similar omission in many parts of the aid operation, including the UN. This refusal to acknowledge the role of the fighting in causing starvation—both intentionally and as an unintended side effect—meant that the entire aid operation was distorted. This is because the vast majority of those who were suffering were located within the rebel held areas. The Ethiopian government refused any suggestion of a safe passage of aid into rebel territory. The politics of the UN, which would only deal with sovereign states, therefore refused to acknowledge the need to help beyond the boundaries of territory under the effective control of the Ethiopian regime. As a result it is believed that 90 per cent of the official aid went to the government, whilst only 22 per cent of those who were starving were under their jurisdiction.

The vast majority of those facing starvation received no help from the official aid operation in Ethiopia, because they were located behind rebel lines in Tigray or Eritrea.[4] Alex de Waal estimates that relief programmes on the government side were only reaching 15 per cent of the Tigrayan population. Between April and August 1985 Tigray received barely 5 per cent of the food relief distributed through government channels despite having between 21 and 33 per cent of the needy population, according to different estimates.[5] De Waal and others are extremely critical of the UN operation, which claimed that 75 per cent of those in need were being helped through the official channels.[6] It was equally worrying that because the huge shipments of aid were being distributed via the Ethiopian government, there were other agendas at work besides feeding starving civilians. Just as starvation had been a weapon of war, so aid too became a useful fighting tool. In late 1984 the Ethiopian foreign minister, Goshu Wolde, admitted publicly at a meeting with Western diplomats that 'food is an element in our strategy against the Fronts ...'[7] The aid agencies were either unwilling or unable to acknowledge this.

According to de Waal and others the unwillingness of the principal aid operation to engage with the realities of the war was a consequence of the 'depoliticisation of relief', which meant that a 'natural disaster' model of human suffering prevailed.[8] The blame was put on the weather, so that 'a famine caused in large part by a combination of military strategy and Stalinist social engineering was attributed to drought and ecological crisis.' Alex de Waal believes that even the rainfall statistics were first suppressed and then fiddled. 'Most NGOs swallowed this line. Others went along with this deception believing that to dispute it in public would prevent them feeding the hungry.' The complicated and political nature of famine was quietly dropped in favour of a story about fellow human beings in distress whom we should help. There were many reasons why the aid agencies preferred this narrative. In particular, it simplified their dealings with the Ethiopian authorities. Furthermore, any other story would have been more complicated to explain to potential donors. It would have elicited less compassion and far fewer donations. Once the aid started flowing the story was again a simple one about stalwart agencies performing miracles in difficult conditions.

There were repeated human interest stories about the individuals and agencies working to save the impoverished and starving Ethiopian peasants. Very little attention was given to the majority of the starving who were located in the rebel areas. They were overlooked by most of the agencies and by the majority of the media coverage.[9] A small number of agencies broke ranks and set up a cross-border operation which was based in Sudan, to try and help the populations in Tigray and Eritrea. This was a highly complex arrangement, which involved painstaking and tricky negotiations to deliver aid over the border.[10] However the UN, which controlled the major aid programme and most of the large agencies, had nothing to do with this, largely because it was not prepared to risk the wrath of the Ethiopian government. Jansson was so close to the Ethiopian government that in the book he later produced about the famine, he referred with some warmth to his regular contacts with Mengistu.[11] The UN special office, first under Kurt Jansson and later under Michael Priestly, insisted that it must maintain its policy of only dealing with sovereign governments—not rebel movements—even if a government was not in control where most of the victims were situated. Tony Vaux later criticized this 'exaggerated western respect for the nation state'[12] and objected to an approach 'which put sovereignty above all other issues including humanitarian need and human rights.'

At the time the UN Special Emergency Office was lauded as having been a remarkably successful operation, as Jansson's own account makes clear.[13] Only in subsequent years did it emerge that in fact the UN action was deeply flawed. Jansson's office was unduly complicit with the Derg, which meant that it ignored the needs in rebel areas. It also ignored the misappropriation of aid by the Ethiopian government, and it failed to address the underlying cause of the famine by displaying an attitude of 'Don't mention the war'. The UN was later criticized for concealing disturbing evidence produced by its own monitors with regard to diversion of aid or forcible resettlement.[14] Peter Cutler, writing about the UN Special Emergency Office, described how its main function was to:

act as a 'screening device' giving the appearance of competent action in response to famine, but not compromising its actual position in Addis Ababa by unduly antagonising the host government ... it would have been as embarrassing for the donors who had entrusted resources to the Ethiopian Government as it was for the government itself to have aid misallocation exposed.[15]

Other organizations involved in aid were rather more self-reflective about their role than the UN. Cathy Corcoran was the deputy director of Catholic Agency for Overseas Development (CAFOD) and closely involved in aid to Ethiopia in 1984. She recalls in hindsight:

the tightrope which aid agencies walked in those days. You say Michael Buerk didn't mention the war, but, equally, if we mentioned the war, if we drew attention to the context of the famine, we were putting not ourselves at risk, but our aid operation of reaching the most vulnerable people at risk. And if you went through local organisations, which CAFOD did, you put the people you worked with at risk, so you have to compromise the humanitarian principle.[16]

This same dilemma is summed up well by Jonathan Dimbleby, a veteran of the relationship between media and aid agencies who puts it more bluntly, when referring to those times '... when your "friends" in the aid agencies and embassies are more constrained by the demands of local diplomacy than by the urge to unburden themselves of what they know for the passing camera. They have their own priorities and their own constituencies. And for them, indeed, truth is contingent.'[17]

Diverting aid

The consequence of aid agencies' unwillingness to acknowledge the role of the civil war in the famine had far wider implications. Not only were most of the starving not being reached by the main aid operation; equally disturbing, there is the subsequent evidence that the food aid which was supplied to the Ethiopian Government, was being diverted to uses other than feeding the victims of famine. Alex de Waal gives an uncompromising critique of the aid effort in Ethiopia: 'it is no longer seriously disputed that the massive inflow of aid ... contributed more to the survival of the Ethiopian government—whose army was the main reason for the famine—than the famine-stricken peasantry.'[18] Many years later it was also evident that there had been similar diversion of aid from the less official operations which were supporting the populations in the rebel areas; once again there were allegations that some portion (although there is disagreement how much) was used to fund arms supplies.[19] The Tigrayan rebels who were being supported subsequently became the government of Ethiopia in 1991 under their leader Meles Zenawi.

In retrospect the agencies were inadvertently helping the Ethiopian government (and the rebel forces) to fight their war. Much of the aid intended for the starving victims was diverted and never reached its intended target. On the government side aid was used, for example, to feed the huge armies—indeed some of the fighting units became known as the 'wheat militias' (*Milisha sirnai* in Amharic),[20] as the Ethiopian government appropriated the food aid and used it for their own purposes. Army conscripts were paid in food aid, which was supplied to their families. An international food monitor estimated that these militia men were receiving around 90 kg a month of which they kept about half for consumption and sold the other half for cash. She described how the diversion took place by falsifying the rationing and distribution records.[21] There are other accounts of army garrisons surrendering hurriedly and the rebels, when they then overran the surrendered posts, discovering large amount of supplies which from their labelling and origin were clearly aid donations.

The flow of aid allowed the army to maintain garrisons that would otherwise have surrendered and kept open roads that enabled the military to re-supply its front line. Food aid distributions enticed young men forward who were forcibly conscripted ... most insidiously the aid programmes gave the government spurious humanitarian credentials whilst its soldiers were busy destroying farmers' livelihoods and hence forcing them into relief shelters the government could claim the credit for allowing international agencies to feed these captive peoples.[22]

It is clear from the records that it was not only the food itself that was diverted, but the trucks and equipment which were being supplied specifically to distribute aid also found their way into the wrong hands. There is direct documentary evidence which confirms this diversion.

One very clear example appears in the minutes of the Band Aid Trust (responsible for administering the money raised by Band Aid, Live Aid etc., and including high profile trustees such as Michael Grade), which show that at a meeting on 23 January 1986 there was a report of the seizure of a truck from the ship *Band Aid Express*, when it had docked at the Ethiopian port of Assab in November 1985. The 65-ton trailer truck with markings 'For the people of Tigray from the people of Watford' contained relief food and special educational supplies designed for Tigrayans. £45,000 had been raised by community groups and local businesses in Watford through the local Hungry for Change project, in order to help famine victims in Tigray, but the truck and its contents were seized and re-consigned to the Ethiopian government. According to the Relief Society for Tigray (REST) this was not the first time that relief supplies intended by donors to help the famine affected population in Tigray had been diverted by the authorities. The Band Aid Trust acknowledged this and wrote to REST regretting the incident and offering to replace the truck and its contents.[23] The notes indicate that this was only one incident of many where the Ethiopian government seized aid donations and used them for its own, often military, purposes.

There is also evidence from the Foreign Office and Overseas Development Agency (ODA) files indicating that there were a number of reports of aid being misappropriated and diverted to the Ethiopian army. For example, a telegram from Dr Denis Osborne, head of the East and West Africa department in ODA, describes 'the sadness and anger of the RAF crew who flew their supplies to Alamata only to find them left on the tarmac and then carried off in a Russian army lorry without any evidence of supervision by the voluntary agencies.'[24] On 3 December 1984 Malcolm Rifkind queried a *Spectator* article entitled 'The Mengistu Famine' by George Galloway making allegations about diversion of aid.[25] In a reply to Mr Rifkind, his private secretary confirms that 'There is little doubt that a small proportion of Western aid is falling into the wrong hands';[26] however, he concluded that the West had little influence over the Ethiopian government, so that there was not much it could do. As the allegations of diversion arose there were some formal enquiries by the various donor governments and agencies. Their representatives and ambassadors were variously taken on tours to 'prove' that the accusations were unfounded—but it is clear in hindsight how easy it was in a tightly controlled environment to fool such official delegations. Only years later was it understood just how much aid was being channelled away. Once again Dawit Wolde Giorgis, who was an insider in the Ethiopian government, confirms in retrospect that as a matter of course aid was frequently diverted and resources were transferred to the war effort. Nearly two decades later he confirmed that 'Millions remained hungry in the midst of one of the greatest ever relief efforts.'[27]

Years later, when Meles Zenawi was prime minister of Ethiopia, UN Under-Secretary General for Humanitarian Affairs John Holmes recalls trying to persuade him to allow aid convoys to assist the suffering population in the Ogaden, where there was also a rebel movement: the Ogaden National Liberation Front (ONLF). Meles objected, saying that as a former guerrilla leader of the TPLF he knew only too well how easy it had been fool the aid agencies and divert aid for other purposes.[28]

Jason Clay and Bonnie Holcomb were amongst those most acutely aware of the political dimensions of the aid operations. They concluded that 'the provision of "humanitarian assistance" with no questions asked helped the Ethiopian government get away with murder'.[29] According to Fredrik Erikson, an economist who has specialized in this area, 'aid became a cause of famine and helped Mengistu to intensify the suffering':[30] in other words, the aid operation in Ethiopia exacerbated the fighting, which precipitated further famine and suffering over that period. Jason Clay talks of 'the role that western humanitarian agencies played ... both in intensifying and extending the famine.'[31] This is a radically different interpretation from the popular account of how aid saved the starving in Ethiopia. In subsequent years an equivalence was drawn between the role of the aid agencies in Cambodia and in Ethiopia. In both cases the aid operation was perceived to have prolonged the suffering.

William Shawcross, who also examined the parallels between Cambodia in the late 1970s and Ethiopia, describes how poor the food position was in Ethiopia in mid-1985. Despite all the donations and the millions of tons that had arrived in the ports, the death rate of children in the famine areas was higher in May 1985 than in December 1984. Food had been diverted and, vitally, trucks and transport had been requisitioned so that the aid could not be distributed to the areas that needed it.[32] Meanwhile the rebels were using aid to finance purchases of arms. Many of those resources provided through the generosity of donors all over the world did not find their way to help the starving. And crucially, it appears that 'aid was being used to prolong rather than end the disaster.'[33]

120

THE HUMANITARIAN DILEMMA

The resettlement controversy

In 1984/85, even when the international food aid was being used to feed starving civilians, it was manipulated by the Ethiopians. The most notorious example was in the so-called resettlement and villagization programmes intended to remove populations in the famine areas and transport them to settlements in the south of the country. The official justification was to help vulnerable farmers transfer to more fertile parts of the country. The suspected underlying purpose was to remove civilians who might be inclined to support the rebels, and aid was used as a deliberate enticement. Although Giorgis at the time supported the scheme, in retrospect he gives a horrific account about what actually happened during the resettlement process. He is also explicit that one of the rationales was 'to depopulate rebel areas in order to deprive the guerrillas of support'.[34] Special feeding stations were set up using donated aid in order to attract the hungry who would then be rounded up for resettlement. So the centres run by aid agencies became magnets with which to draw unsuspecting people who were then whisked off to the resettlement camps hundreds of miles from their homes.

In their publication *Politics and the Ethiopian Famine*, Jason Clay and Bonnie Holcomb made one of the most detailed studies of the methods and impact of resettlement by interviewing refugees who entered Sudan.[35] Such was the fear and resentment of what was going on at the relief camps that a large number of Ethiopians chose instead to walk for weeks under appalling conditions into refugee camps in Sudan, as an alternative to the nearby but dubious 'government feeding centres' from which others had been forcibly transported.[36] Clay and Holcomb, in their project which interviewed 277 refugees, uncovered evidence of terrible conditions and manipulation against the peasants, who as a result were choosing to cross the border rather than enter the so-called relief camps, because they knew they would face coercion. The interviews indicated that many of the early 'volunteers' amongst the starving were deceived by party officials about conditions they would find in their new location. Upon arrival they discovered malarial and even crocodile infested swamps in place of the splendid new villages they had been promised.

Clay and Holcomb were extremely critical of the narrow media explanation of the famine which referred only to failure of rain and described the war as an impediment to delivery of aid—rather than a cause of famine.

Information from affected people themselves appeared only as a quotation or two intended to provide human interest, an embellishment to a story whose main point lay elsewhere. The experience of someone standing in a food line or waiting in a clinic was adduced to confirm the rain shortage, lack of harvest and subsequent sale of animal. People were not asked what had brought them to the point of starvation. It was not possible to understand what had happened in the lives of peasant producers to bring about such disaster. In short the victims remained bellies; they did not have brains.[37]

In subsequent years, Clay and Holcomb's conclusions that the death rates attributable to resettlement reached 100,000 have been widely quoted.

Resettlement became a highly controversial issue from 1985. It led to fierce arguments between those who believed that removing people from the highland areas to the lower plains was the only viable long-term solution to famine and those who characterized it as a brutal abuse of human rights, implemented for political reasons, which had appalling consequences for the families who were transported. Based on his observations of the Ethiopian famine, Graham Hancock, who was with the *Economist* and wrote *The Challenge of Hunger*,[38] was a strong supporter of the concept of moving populations away from the areas of Tigray and Wollo. He argued that the land was over-farmed and deforested and suffered from erosion. Others such as Lloyd Timberlake of the agency Earthscan agreed. The problem was the manner in which the resettlement was conducted. Germaine Greer too visited Ethiopia and (never one to shy from controversy) wrote in favour of the resettlement programme.[39] So did Alula Pankhurst, the grandson of Sylvia Pankhurst and son of Richard Pankhurst, one of the foremost international scholars of Ethiopian history. Alula had been brought up in Ethiopia and went on to publish a controversial book[40] based on fieldwork in newly resettled areas, which was broadly supportive of the resettlement schemes. Mother Teresa too, who had visited Ethiopia at the height of the famine publicity, went on record to support the Ethiopian government in its resettlement policy and urge Western donors to support the plan by 'adopting' resettlement sites.[41]

However, the far more common view was vehement opposition to resettlement and in particular the way in which it was implemented.[42]

There were stories and even (secretly filmed) pictures of peasants forced at gunpoint into unpressurized Antonov cargo planes, supplied by the Soviets, and terrible reports of the conditions that faced them on arrival in the new areas. Even more credence was given to these stories when the former relief and rehabilitation commissioner, Dawit Wolde Giorgis, published his memoir *Red Tears*. His account of what had been going on within the party and the government at this time left no doubt about the abuses involved.[43] He described resettlement as 'a spontaneous act designed to take political advantage of the people's suffering ... an exercise in utter hypocrisy', and told how the programme became an obsession for Mengistu and the Politburo. Ludicrous resettlement targets of up to 300,000 families a year were set and the entire government machinery was contorted in order to try and fulfil them. Those who tried to escape resettlement were executed and Giorgis estimates that at least 500 were killed in this way. He describes the pressures to fulfil quotas and the coercion and misery involved as families were separated and officials used 'calculated brutality', referring to what one of his assistants called a 'genocide of helpless people'. And not only were the peasants involved deliberately misled, so were outsiders. Giorgis describes how party cadres were dressed up and disguised as peasants in some of the new settlements in order to give interviews to visiting foreign journalists and VIPs praising their new homes and the way in which they had been brought there. As a consequence 'They found the 'peasants' cheerful, willing and in excellent health.'[44] This puts a rather different gloss on the interviews and evidence which Greer and others were reporting in support of resettlement!

According to the documentary record, during the RAF airlift operation in Ethiopia the UK government was repeatedly asked by the Ethiopians if the British planes could also be used to transport people from the highlands. There were some internal discussions amongst ministers and officials on the matter, but in the end permission to use the aircraft in this way was always refused. This was in spite of all kinds of reassurances and even after the scheme was rebranded by the Ethiopians as 'rehabilitation' for victims of famine.[45] It was also in contradiction to the views of the UN special representative in Ethiopia. Kurt Jansson at his farewell press conference in 1985 appealed publicly to Western donor governments to help Ethiopia with its resettlement programme.

The role of relief agencies and NGOs in this saga was an uncomfortable one. Some agencies actively helped in the resettlement programme, supporting the Ethiopian government and agreeing with the UN representative. The Irish charity Concern was active in the resettlement camps, and so indeed was Band Aid. At one point a Band Aid Trust meeting discussed the dilemma of whether to allow its resources to assist in resettlement. After some consideration it was decided on balance that the organization should continue to maintain its presence in the resettlement camps. The meeting, which was discussing project funding, acknowledged, according to the minutes, that:

Despite some of the Ethiopian government's policies such as resettlement and 'villagisation' which the committee felt were rather controversial, it was agreed that since a decision had already been made to fund Ethiopia, BA should carry through this policy. It should attempt to help the local population as best it can given all the constraints present, rather than wasting energy trying to change the system.[46]

This was typical of the 'let's cut the red tape and get on quickly with the job' attitude which Band Aid championed. Yet it is a classic case of where a rather more nuanced and sophisticated understanding of the surrounding politics could have yielded a better outcome. David Rieff describes how donors may have saved lives but 'even more may have been lost in Live Aid's unwitting support of a Stalinist-style resettlement project.'[47]

Other charities found that—in spite of their grave reservations—they were unintentionally helping the cause of resettlement. Oxfam discovered, to the intense anger of several local staff, that some of its equipment had appeared in the resettlement camps.[48] And in other cases relief and supplies from aid agencies were being used as an enticement to unknowing populations. Hungry peasants were encouraged to visit feeding centres and then taken—occasionally at gunpoint—directly onto the trucks and planes to be resettled elsewhere. One important agency, Médecins Sans Frontières, made a protest about the human rights abuses, publishing a paper entitled 'Mass Deportations in Ethiopia', demanding an independent inquiry into the conditions of resettlement. Their outrage was inspired by a policy that in some relief centres the Ethiopian government did not allow children to receive food from Western agencies until their parents agreed to be resettled. Médecins Sans Frontières (MSF) protested after an estimated 3,000 children died in a camp where they had ensured there was adequate material for assistance, but were then not allowed to distribute it because, according to government officials, a sufficient number of adults had not agreed to be resettled.[49] As a result of its protests MSF was expelled from Ethiopia in December 1985. MSF subsequently expressed disgust at the resettlement programme and at the UN's and other agencies' connivance with the government, a position it continues to emphasize today. Rony Brauman, who was in Ethiopia for MSF, later wrote about 'misguided humanitarian action doing more harm than good' and spoke of a 'reign of terror in which NGOs played an essential role'. He considered that the NGO involvement in resettlement (which was itself modelled on Stalin's policy of collectivization in the 1930s) was a case of 'tangible proof that humanitarian assistance could be turned against its supposed beneficiaries'.[50] Meanwhile Michael Priestly, Jansson's successor,[51] argued that MSF was just seeking publicity in antagonizing the government and it was better to work quietly behind the scenes.[52] The ethical and practical arguments behind this action by MSF in Ethiopia were still being discussed many years afterwards.[53]

Do no harm

The civil war against the Eritreans and the Tigrayan rebels continued throughout the 1980s. Famine too resurfaced in Ethiopia, with two further disaster emergency appeals launched in 1987 and 1989,[54] only highlighting the fact that the aid effort in 1984/85 had no lasting effect. Eventually in 1991 the Tigrayan rebels of the Tigrayan Peoples Liberation Front (TPLF) went on to conquer Addis Ababa and defeat the Derg, and Mengistu fled into exile in Zimbabwe. The TPLF—which had once declared its support for the views of Enver Hoxha, the hardline communist dictator of Albania![55]—was led by Meles Zenawi, who eventually became prime minister of Ethiopia and in 2005 was a member of the Commission for Africa, established under Tony Blair. Coincidentally, both Michael Buerk and his cameraman, Mo Amin, were back in Addis Ababa to report for the BBC on the final battle in 1991—in which Amin was badly injured and their sound man was killed.

In retrospect it is certainly arguable that the scale of the aid effort in the mid-1980s—because food and trucks and other aid were so widely and regularly diverted—helped to prop up the regime of the Derg and assist the Tigrayan rebels, so making the war and the suffering of civilians last longer than it otherwise would have done. The foreign currency brought in by the aid organizations was also useful to the regime in assisting the war effort. They were obliged to convert their dollars to the local currency at a rate favourable to the government, and the Derg is estimated to have tripled its foreign currency reserves in 1985.[56] So the fighting continued and with it the famine. This was the same verdict that had once been passed on the Biafran aid operation in 1968/69. The media account of the crisis focused upon a terrible famine. The aid agencies which helped the Biafrans were seen as angels of mercy aiding the starving victims. Then it later emerged that they were helping to feed the rebel troops, providing a valuable source of foreign currency and thereby propping up a doomed regime and causing the war and thereby the suffering to the civilian population to be prolonged.[57]

This is a bitter pill for aid agencies and, indeed, for those who donate to them. The superficial media story is saying one thing, but the messy reality of operating within a 'complex emergency' results in a quite different outcome from that which is intended and that which is being written about. Since the 1980s there have been further occasions when this conflation of war, famine and aid has led to similar confused outcomes. Michael Maren, a former aid worker who has since written a harsh attack on the whole aid industry, describes in stark terms what he called the 'template for famine reporting'.[58] He outlines five steps ranging from the first 'early predictor story', through the process where a few local relief agencies persuade one or two journalists to describe the problem, after which the journalists report a 'discovery of famine'. As the momentum gathers pace the story is taken up by more news organizations which 'expose' the suffering, and the story now becomes simplified. Then there is a key moment where the 'famine fires its booster rockets' and becomes a major media event. Most famines in Africa never get beyond step one, but if and when step five is reached the crisis has become a cause and the international public is mobilized. Critically, Maren points out that 'as press coverage of a particular famine reached step three and beyond, it typically has gathered such momentum as to be impervious to facts that do not fit the popular story line.' So not only does the reporting need to be better informed, but those operating on the ground in relief agencies need also to be more aware of the wider political implications of what is really happening. As one Red Cross official, Urs Boegli,[59] observed:

Far too many disasters with political causes and for which there can only be political solutions are today labelled 'humanitarian crises' ... After all, rape is rape ... no one would describe it as a 'gynaecological disaster.' Yet conflicts which are referred to as 'humanitarian disasters' are often much more than that. This steers the international response in the wrong direction, towards purely humanitarian action in cases where political action is required.

Boegli connects the presence of graphic and instant television pictures as a reason for politicians to shy away from hard decisions in such crises and prefer humanitarian action which has 'little political cost. It is duly filmed and shown to an admiring public. And the reality behind the "event" is thereby distorted.'

In Ethiopia misinformed reporting was precipitated by the regime because, as Rony Brauman of MSF observes, the disaster was a useful bargaining chip in its relations with the international community. 'The victims were a valuable resource in terms of funds in hard currency and a propaganda tool because the famine was presented as a natural disaster.' Brauman points out how surprising it was that no one bothered to challenge this version of the facts although the reality was clearly very different:

The drought played a considerable part in the appearance of food shortage, but the cataclysmic extent of the famine [just as under Stalin and Mao] was due to very human reasons: ... land collectivisations, nationalisation of agricultural production and marketing and irrational taxation systems, as well as the war and repression in the north. ... an additional factor ... was the bureaucratic compartmentalisation of the country which prevented the exchange between regions enjoying surpluses with those with shortages.[60]

These were the background reasons why a moderate drop in rainfall, no more than 20 per cent compared with the average of previous years, should have had such terrible effects. However, this story was not being told either within the media or in most of the aid world. Instead, there was a one-dimensional story of a natural disaster and a straightforward (and successful) aid operation. It was 'a script of apolitical, moral concern'.[61]

This central dilemma has occurred since 1984/85 in different forms all over the world. The ending of the Cold War, which at least gave a straightforward narrative to most crises, has meant that interpreting foreign crises and wars has become even more difficult. The apparently simple process of sending humanitarian assistance in Somalia, Rwanda and Sudan became fraught with difficulty because in certain cases it could end up doing more harm than good.[62] In 2011 the same issues arose with the famine in East Africa, centred on Somalia. The rebel force Shabab in Somalia presented dilemmas for aid agencies, since it maintained control of considerable territory and had little regard for the welfare of those under its control. Of course, the agonizing question then arises, what can be done to help relieve suffering? Mark Duffield makes a brutal assessment that 'the new accommodation is sacrifice lives today on the promise of development tomorrow' because the previous doctrine of 'prophetic, neutral humanitarianism is now seen as naïve'.[63]

The position of the aid agencies in the relief effort in Ethiopia in the 1980s was a watershed in the issue of so-called neutral humanitarian assistance. There had always been a widespread assumption that the role of relief was neutral intervention to help the victims. This was derived from the historic position of the Red Cross as an independent, honest broker between warring factions. However, the paradox which Biafra, and to some extent Cambodia, had already shown is that in some situations it is not possible to find a neutral space and ignore the surrounding politics. Any intervention invariably helps one side or the other and, however well intentioned, may have an overall detrimental outcome. The role of the relief effort in Ethiopia demonstrated this on a much larger scale. Whereas the popular perception, and that of many agencies and donors, remained one that 'a starving child has no politics',[64] it was becoming clearer that it was impossible to operate without political awareness no matter how needy the victims; in other words, 'a starving child knows only politics'. Yet it was only in hindsight that much of this became clear.

Tricia Feeny, who was a senior policy adviser with Oxfam, speaking on a radio retrospective ten years after the Ethiopian famine, was aware that only afterwards did the agencies realize the underlying political factors and become able to confront the 'readiness of such regimes to manipulate famine and abuse aid'.[65] Alex de Waal in the same programme went further and spoke of situations like Ethiopia where political leaders 'use the humanitarian imperative for their own ends ... deliberately cultivating starving children ... in order to attract aid ... which can be used to feed their soldiers or further war aims.'[66] In this kind of scenario naive agencies which just 'want to help and not get involved in politics'[67] are bound to find themselves outmanoeuvred.

Since the mid-1990s an extensive literature on the problems of humanitarian intervention in what are now referred to as 'complex emergencies' has emerged. Although in 1984/85 the term had not been invented, it does appear in retrospect that Ethiopia had more or less all the elements that are recognized today as components of complex emergencies:

the exploitation of existing differences within the civil society; the disputed legitimacy of the host authorities; famine; a tidal wave of journalistic interest that turned a far-away political conflict into a tangible human disaster 'story'; the likelihood of assistance being manipulated by warring factions to obtain military or diplomatic advantage; and the division of the international relief community.[68]

At the time MSF was probably the first agency to articulate the paradoxes and dangers faced by those trying to do good in such situations. Brauman observed that intervening under such circumstances was 'no longer a choice between a political position and a neutral position but between two political positions.'[69] And typically, MSF was also well aware of the media dimension which acted as a vital catalyst, where 'the humanitarian boom was amplified and accelerated by the existence of television.' Brauman, with his highly developed awareness of the political aspect of aid, was, of course, highly critical of Band Aid's attitude towards Ethiopian government policy and its unwillingness to confront the political realities in dealing with a regime which had entirely different motives from helping hungry victims. He scathingly described Bob Geldof as 'the best spokesman of the Derg'.[70]

Band Aid at the time became the symbol of media-inspired, pure humanitarian intervention. The simple message of starving victims of drought was given huge media exposure. The solution too was a simple one—if the public donated money then aid would be sent, the hungry would be fed and the problem would be solved. All the complicated issues of the surrounding politics and the long-term nature of development and operating in a conflict zone where it was not clear who should be helped were left aside. In retrospect it is clear that delivering aid in a highly charged situation is problematic, as scenarios such as the East African famine in 2011 have demonstrated. But at that time, as the Ethiopian crisis unfolded, according to Ondine Barrow 'the rules governing humanitarian action in complex emergencies were only gradually and painfully being worked out'. She goes on to argue that 'Indeed, to a large extent these rules were worked out as a result of this particular emergency.'[71]

In view of what was to come, Barrow's view is probably unduly optimistic. Although the difficult issues were clearly highlighted in the way that the media and the agencies dealt with the Ethiopian famine, the same paradoxes were exposed and the same mistakes continued to be made in subsequent crises.[72] For over the years the same pattern reasserted itself; media depict terrible emergency in stark and simple terms, public donates money and agencies rush in without necessarily knowing how and whom to help, because there is a complicated background which mostly the agencies are unaware of or unwilling to confront. One of the worst examples of this pattern was the aftermath of the Rwandan genocide in 1994.[73] There was an extraordinary media and aid operation in eastern Congo amidst the camps for Rwandan refugees. As a response to the worldwide dramatic television coverage of refugees fleeing Rwanda, millions were raised to support the aid effort. Over two hundred different agencies[74] turned up to help and were operating in places like Goma and also vying for media exposure. Paddy Coulter described the multiple logos of the agencies on display in the camp as something 'like walking down Oxford Street'.[75]

However, the Western media had paid very little attention to the genocide which immediately preceded the refugee crisis, when Hutu extremists slaughtered an estimated 800,000 Tutsis and moderate Hutus in less than three months. It only emerged later that the Hutu refugees now being helped by the NGOs in the camps included many people fleeing possible arrest; the notorious Interahamwe who had been responsible for the genocide in the first place, now escaping with their families. David Rieff makes a chilling comparison; 'It is as if two hundred thousand SS soldiers had taken their families out of Nazi Europe as it fell to the Allies, to somewhere they could hope to be sheltered from retribution, by sympathetic NGOs.'[76] The agencies with all their humanitarian intentions were actually helping the killers and their hangers-on. Mark Duffield observes that 'The aid agencies response to the Hutu refugees crystallised everything that was wrong with humanitarian assistance. By helping to feed and shelter refugees ... the NGOs and the UN were also supporting the vicious killers that lived among them', and he concludes that 'If the sentiments that lay behind the formation of Band Aid coalesced in the arid highlands of Ethiopia, in a little over a decade they unravelled in the rainforests of the Congo.'[77]

It was not just the media reporting, starting with the BBC news broadcast, that was telling an inaccurate story about Ethiopia. Furthermore, it was not all the media uniformly that failed to grasp and convey the implications of the story. Aid agencies, international agencies and governments were also at fault in conveying a partial and misinformed account of the crisis. The overall effect of the coverage was to produce a distorted and misleading impression in the way it characterized the famine, how it explained the causes of famine and reported the relief efforts. And this was a pattern familiar from other crises, most of them on the African continent. There were several reasons for this. Partly the problem was due to the overall way that Africa has been covered by the press and television, and the lack, in so many parts of the media, of an ongoing engagement with the problems facing countries like Ethiopia. The news was reported in such a way that it seemed as if it had appeared out of nowhere. Crucially, there was very little long-term context. The effect of this lack of background understanding was to depoliticize the story. This turned it into a narrative of failing rains and then wonderful relief efforts which solved the problem.

Another significant factor was the lack of accountability amongst aid agencies. The benefits which NGOs gain from being outside the government sphere do not give them immunity from the mistakes which governments make, yet historically aid agencies retain the status of a sacred cow—beyond reproach. David Rieff laments 'a narcissistic conflation of the sincerity of our good intentions and the effects of those intentions',[78] and Barrow writes of the 'failure of humanitarianism, as constituted in the 1980s and 1990s, to analyse power and to maintain any meaningful sense of accountability', pointing out that:

the massive NGO participation in all aspects of development and relief work is a testament to the humanity of those involved—yet the charitable impulse all too often has been channelled through organisations that are not accountable to their beneficiaries and only a limited extent accountable to their benefactors.[79]

To a great extent this problem still exists today. Ed Miliband, when he was minister for the Third Sector, made a speech drawing attention to the huge and paradoxical contrast in accountability expected on the one hand from a political party and, on the other, from a large development NGO, reliant on voluntary donations. He marvelled at the way that charities still retain such reservoirs of trust—especially about the way that money is raised and spent.[80] This absence of expectations with regard to accountability from charities was even more apparent in the mid-1980s when NGOs were rapidly expanding in size and importance. And underlying both the inadequacies in reporting and the gap in accountability is the ongoing and not always satisfactory relationship between the media and the aid world.

6

TOO TIGHT AN EMBRACE?

THE AGENCIES AND THE MEDIA

'In the past decade I have watched the emergency aid business from the famine in Ethiopia … grow from a small element in the larger package of 'development' into a giant global unregulated industry worth £2,500 million a year.'

Lindsay Hilsum, *The Guardian*, 31 December 1995

'The belief that the objectives of the media on the one hand are the same as those of the human rights and the aid communities on the other contributes to the failings of both.'

Timothy Weaver, freelance cameraman/journalist[1]

The coverage of the Ethiopian famine and its aftermath was a key moment in the whole relationship between the aid agencies and the media. Fifteen years earlier, following the Biafra crisis, Bernard Kouchner, in founding Médecins Sans Frontières (MSF), had been instrumental in developing a new compact between the role of media and the provision of aid in emergency situations. However, Ethiopia proved a turning point. As the agencies and the local aid workers on the ground struggled to focus international attention on the food shortages in Ethiopia during 1983/84, they were only too aware of the need to attract media and preferably television attention. This was proved so very clearly by the transformation which the BBC report eventually brought. The famine coverage inspired new ways of charitable fundraising, but it was also a crucial milestone in the overall growth and significance of non-governmental organizations in the world of aid and development. This rapid and sudden expansion as a result of the famine led to an important transformation of aid agencies as institutions. But as the charities working in relief and development grew in size and importance, so their dealings with the media became both more crucial and sometimes problematic. In this way the Ethiopian crisis was a milestone in the ongoing understanding between aid agencies and the media.

Disasters and growth

The most obvious effect of the famine upon Western charities was the overwhelming and sudden growth in funding, whereby many of the existing aid agencies doubled their annual income from donations almost overnight.[2]

This huge rise in income given directly from the public was only one factor in the dramatic expansion of the existing agencies. In addition there was all the funding that came into the voluntary sector from the newly established Band Aid and Live Aid enterprises. Thirdly there were the donations to the NGOs from governments and official agencies, which were starting to see the Third Sector as a way of reaching their goals. The rise in overall income from these various sources eventually translated into institutional growth. For example, Oxfam's staff numbered 480 in 1983. Two years later the number had shot up to 726, and by the end of the decade it had reached over eleven hundred.[3]

International development and aid charities generally do well from disasters. Hilary Blume of the Charity Advisory Trust observed this process during the 2004 Asian Tsunami disaster:

I watched the BBC TV coverage with increasing distaste as the spokesmen from the large aid charities relished their 15 minutes of fame and got their fund raising campaigns under way. I was reminded of working for a UK aid charity 35 years before when the management hoped for a disaster to secure their finances.[4]

The incremental and frequently unsung world of development assistance does not often attract sudden or vast donations—except for special cases such as the Microsoft billionaire Bill Gates. Emergencies on the other hand, if they capture the media, can bring in enormous funds quite rapidly. The refugee crisis during August 1994 in Goma in the wake of the Rwandan genocide precipitated a 500 per cent increase in NGO income over that period. Michael Maren describes with some cynicism the way that NGOs seize upon 'growth opportunities' when disaster strikes.[5]

In the wake of the Asian Tsunami in late 2004 there was considerable discussion about the disparity in the fundraising, which raised hitherto unprecedented levels—the DEC appeal for the Tsunami reached almost £400 million, a huge amount compared with the sums raised for so many other, less well-publicized but deserving causes. There was even a concern that the Tsunami had raised 'too much money'[6] and MSF very unusually told its supporters that it had raised enough and they should divert their generosity towards other causes. This outpouring of donations led to some odd outcomes. For example, in 2005 the few thousand Somalis who live in the coastal region that was (not especially seriously) affected by the Tsunami received a 'Rolls Royce service'[7] of aid convoys, but meanwhile the far larger numbers of starving Somalis located in the interior of the country were entitled to none of it. This highlights a perennial problem within the charitable world—they need to balance integrity towards donors and yet to direct funds to where they are most needed. Often there are less overt or popular causes which are deserving but overlooked. The role of the media in sometimes arbitrarily highlighting certain causes at the expense of others is highly problematic.

Tony Vaux's concern is that 'you either have an aid bonanza or you have nothing' and he compares the distribution of fundraising to a 'roulette wheel … suddenly a particular number comes up and there is wide scale media exposure and the disaster will become high profile and a money spinner.' This is the result of what is known in the aid community as a 'noisy emergency', the crises which 'attract a storm of media attention, a high proportion of official donors funds, generous private donations which leave … so many 'silent emergencies' and the millions trying to survive them, in the shadows.'[8]

Originally, what have now become the major aid and development charities were each founded in response to a particular emergency, which was able to attract a large influx of funding. The Red Cross was a product of the humanitarian crisis arising from the wars of Italian unification, Save the Children was founded by Eglantyne Jebb to deal with the famine and refugee crises in the wake of the First World War, Oxfam started in response to the Greek famine in 1942. World Vision was founded from the refugee crisis in the Korean War, MSF began in response to the Biafran crisis and Concern began in the wake of the upheaval surrounding the founding of Bangladesh in 1971.[9]

The Ethiopian crisis not only prompted a new charity and new ways of raising funds, it also gave a huge and sudden boost to existing agencies. In the wake of this growth there was no turning back. Like all businesses, the charities adjusted to new levels of income and overheads and sought to build on that growth in the years that followed. This sudden expansion had a substantial impact on charities as institutions. In particular, fundraising faced enormous challenges in order to sustain and maintain the sudden expansion. An interview with a Charity Projects fundraiser in the late 1980s indicates the scale of the pressures they were experiencing and still continue to face:

A big organisation like Oxfam or Save the Children now has an annual requirement of fifty or sixty million pounds a year. That's a million pounds a week they have got to make … divide it by seven and every morning their fundraising department has got to come up with one hundred and eighty thousand pounds … just to meet commitments, that's a hell of a lot of money. So the pressure on fundraisers is extreme … they can't let the side down because what suffers is the fieldwork.[10]

By the mid-1980s the fundraising and the marketing of charitable objectives were entering a completely different era. And this growth led to a very different mindset. 'Charity is no longer philanthropy; it has emerged from its cocoon as a vast multi-layered and multifaceted global business.'[11]

Beware the hand that feeds …

The rapid and sudden growth of development NGOs in the mid-1980s coincided with other important institutional shifts. In fact, the continuing growth in size and importance of NGOs over the past thirty years would probably have happened at some point in any case as governments sought to outsource some of their involvement in this field.[12] Ethiopia and the media coverage which was such a bonanza for the charities acted as a catalyst for this growth and became a tipping point in their expansion. As the Cold War was winding down then there was less reason for governments to keep such direct control over foreign aid distribution. In Ethiopia, in particular, official donors, both countries and international institutions, preferred increasingly to channel their assistance through NGOs. 'The international relief efforts of 1984/5 relied to an unprecedented degree upon NGOs as channels for the provision and distribution of relief assistance.'[13] The reasons for this were both convenience, to keep a distasteful regime at arm's length, and trying to ensure greater accountability for the money. This has continued to be the practice where donor governments, when faced with unpalatable regimes, seek to channel aid into the Third Sector.

Between 1977 and 1988 the British government, and in particular the Overseas Development Administration, increased its annual support of NGOs from £5 million to £42 million.[14] This increase in official funding, as a result of changing overall policy, which occurred especially during the period following the Ethiopian famine, was another key factor in the rapid expansion in the operation of voluntary agencies, in addition to the big increase in private donations.

Peter Gill describes how 'as the famine crisis became the focus of public concern the ODA made more and more of a virtue of its association with the voluntary agencies … many of the funds from the ODA Disaster Unit were funnelled through the charities.' Meanwhile the World Bank too was seeking to engage with the 'vol ags', as they were known, and set up a special unit to liaise with them. 'Senior officials from its Paris office were seen dining Oxfam and others in some of London's better restaurants in 1985.'[15] In the years since the Ethiopian famine the relationship between multilateral institutions like the World Bank and NGOs through whom they channel funds has become a significant issue.[16]

The trade-off for NGOs when they accept official funding became, and has continued to be, a tricky dilemma and the cause of much anguish within the voluntary sector.[17] As a result many agencies seek a 'balanced portfolio' and aim to set a ceiling on the proportions of official donations in order to avoid becoming too beholden to government. Yet already in 1985 Michael Harris, Oxfam's retiring overseas director (when the amounts were first starting to increase), was voicing anxieties about the compromises that accepting official aid might entail. These same concerns were expressed by Susan George, a development economist, speaking at a conference for voluntary agencies held at Dakar in

Senegal in May 1985:[18] 'Beware the agency that has so much money that you and the people you want to help could easily drown in it'; she went on to accuse governments of wanting 'to spend infinitely less on overseas aid than they did before, but to get enormous public credit by giving whatever tiny sums remained to the NGOs ... I implore you to guard your independence ... Just remember if somebody still dislikes you, you must be doing something right.'[19]

This very rapid growth of the main aid agencies and their ability to attract official funding also took place against a background where charities as a key part of the voluntary sector were gradually becoming more important across public life. The ethos of the Thatcher and Reagan years was one of distrusting the state and favouring the charitable sector, as an alternative to big government.[20] In recent years initiatives such as David Cameron's 'Big Society' have built upon the same ethos. Charities were increasingly entering the mainstream of public debate, growing in recognition and often rebranding themselves. Organizations concerned with foreign aid had an additional advantage in a political environment that was inclined towards a Victorian view of 'deserving poor' and 'undeserving poor'. Whilst domestic victims might be complicit in their fate, impoverished foreigners and in particular victims of famine were unquestionably pure. This was even more the case when they were suffering at the hands of an evil communist regime.

In the 1980s international aid charities retained the romance of 'the other', and crucially, they appeared less political. This was important to a government which was hostile to the politicization that conflated social issues and charitable causes. Although Oxfam did eventually get into trouble for encroaching too far into political waters, in general foreign charities were on safer and more neutral ground. There was a public perception of overseas aid as emotionally stimulating and susceptible to immediate positive consequences—the issues appeared simpler and less ambiguous. Indeed, as the foreign aid charities began to grow so dramatically there was some resentment and jealousy on the part of domestic charities at the effect of the television images in catapulting this dramatic expansion.[21]

After the Labour government came to power in 1997 in the UK the pendulum then swung somewhat in the official attitude towards aid charities. Clare Short as the first Labour secretary of state for international development had a tense relationship with the world of development aid agencies. She argued that governments, which unlike the aid bureaucracy were elected, were often able to help more effectively,[22] and she later went on to question the rather random nature of media mobilization in taking up certain charitable causes. The view of the Department for International Development (DFID) was moving towards questioning the need for the 'NGO middleman'.[23] This was in direct contrast to the culture of the preceding government in which aid, just like so much else, was subject to privatization. 'In an era where the dominant ethos was the repudiation of government, private agencies were thought to be more efficient, more accountable and more appropriate conduits for the West's largesse.'[24]

Increasing competition

Charities, in this period of rapid growth from the mid-1980s, were developing into large and self-perpetuating big businesses, so that competing for market share and the way they publicly presented themselves to their donors was becoming increasingly important. Against the background of general expansion in the voluntary sector, the response to the images of the famine was an additional boost to sudden and irreversible growth for development charities. This was to continue throughout the succeeding decade. The existing agencies grew bigger and plenty of new ones entered the field. In 1985 there were around sixty agencies in Ethiopia involved in the famine crisis.[25] Not surprisingly there were organizational complications and wasted effort, which arose because of the numbers of different agencies. Yet ten years later, in the wake of the Rwandan genocide, there were up to two hundred different NGOs[26] present in the refugee camps in the Great Lakes region—all wanting to be seen to be doing something useful. It was without doubt a growth industry. And fifteen years later when an earthquake hit Haiti in 2010, there were many thousands of NGOs large and small, all competing to help.[27] With the growth came more competitive positioning between organizations, each keen to safeguard its position. In this environment, dealings with the media became increasingly significant, as a means of raising funds and also to maintain market share.

In his critique of humanitarian relief and NGOs, Alex de Waal considers that the true legacy of Band Aid was in the domestic politics of aid in Western countries. 'It had the effect of intensifying competition among NGOs with a greater scramble for media exposure and endorsement from stars'. He called it another stage in 'humanitarian deregulation'.[28] According to one NGO official reflecting on the impact of the coverage of the Ethiopian famine in 1985, 'competition rocketed ... there was a mad scramble for public attention' amidst the higher profile NGOs. They all 'had to be seen to be doing something', which led to a general expansion of their work, and then 'financial requirements had to keep up with the expansion.'[29] According to another former aid worker, 'With a plethora of new organisations entering the lists, profile is all and accentuating the positive a must ... especially for those agencies dependent upon government funding—since governments want to support organisations doing highly visible work'.[30]

Even the semi-official history of Oxfam, which gives a generally upbeat view of the aid world, observes this process with some candour.

In the 1960s the television camera became part of the dynamics of disaster relief. For the first time, people in the West were confronted with images in their homes of other peoples, many in traumatic crisis right before their eyes. The effect upon the viewing public was an outpouring of compassion in the form of cash donations for disaster relief and demands that the Government rush to give aid. In the capacity of angels of mercy the charities were part of the news event, both as purveyors of help and as anguished critics of the sluggish nature of officialdom's response ... A less fortunate aspect of the media's growing influence was the tendency of charitable emissaries to rush to a scene of devastation and compete for publicity—and the funds it produced—while doing things of dubious usefulness on the ground.[31]

As the sums of money and the numbers of people and organizations involved grew, these observations rang ever more true. It was not just those within the aid world but also outsiders who were aware of the intensified rivalry between agencies, each seeking to position itself. Bob Geldof, when he became involved in raising money for Ethiopia in 1985, observed 'the rivalry ridden world of the voluntary agencies'.[32] This is rather different from the popular view of the charitable agencies as just there to make the world a better place. Those who were closer to the ground, as Geldof had become, were seeing a different slant. Government officials at that time were also aware of the competitive positioning of the NGOs. In October 1984, in response to a request from Oxfam, the head of the East Africa Department in the Foreign Office wrote in a memo to ministers, 'We should be cautious about endorsing a specific Oxfam initiative in a situation where there is a good deal of infighting between the voluntary agencies and competitive attempts to obtain public endorsement of the individual agency's efforts.'[33] And clearly the media played a role in this infighting. 'Increasingly relief organisations find themselves competing between themselves or with others for public support. Motivated by the best of intentions they fight for the attention of the press and of the public.'[34]

A symbiotic relationship

As agencies were growing they were increasingly aware of the need for wider exposure and liaison with international media, not least because this was vital in the promotion of an agency and the crucial business of raising funds. Yet at the most fundamental level the media were so crucial in focusing attention upon a crisis in the first place—even prior to their role in raising funds and ensuring a profile for the various NGOs. As Randolph Kent observes, 'the media has become the Fourth Estate of the International Relief network ... the media in all its forms is the mobiliser.'[35] Both Tony Vaux and Earthscan observed ruefully, in their assessments of the Ethiopian famine, how the agencies were dependent upon media exposure of the crisis; no matter how much they continued to inform those in authority about the crisis, there was no demonstrable will to act until the media were involved.[36] As a result, 'humanitarian relief workers consistently report [that] the presence or absence of media attention may mean life or death for affected populations. The media do not change the importance of humanitarian crises, but they significantly affect their impact.'[37]

The same observations were still being made in the aftermath of the 2011 East African famine. 'Die First Aid Later' was the grim title of a report on the attitudes towards relief in the aftermath of the starvation. Oxfam and Save the Children criticized the attitudes of donors wanting to see proof of extreme hunger before they would agree to large scale aid.[38] The report quoted Justin Forsyth, Save the Children's chief executive: 'We can no longer allow this grotesque situation to continue; where the world knows an emergency is coming but ignores it until confronted with TV pictures of desperately malnourished children.' This was reference to the same old cycle of reluctance to act until there were the grim pictures.

Philip Seib observes how NGOs have their own strategies for dealing with the news media 'because like governments they are intensely interested in public opinion. NGOs use media coverage to spur government action and stimulate the flow of money from private as well as government sources.'[39] He quotes a media consultant in this field who speaks of 'the formal dance of intricate detail between UN officials, aid workers, reporters and news managers'.[40]

As the complexities of real time media have progressed, these dealings have become ever more involved. Nevertheless, a symbiotic relationship was already developing by the early 1980s between the aid agencies and the media. Newspapers and television stations were cutting back on local correspondents based in developing countries, tending to rely upon flying in 'fireman' reporters from outside. They were likely to be skilled professionals, adept at using the newest technology and turning round a story fast, but without much background knowledge of the area. This made them more dependent upon those with local expertise, frequently NGOs, who could also provide English speaking interviewees for a story. And at a more basic level, in the midst of difficult conditions in a humanitarian crisis the local NGO workers were likely to have the vital access to transport and all the other necessary logistical requirements. So agencies were becoming used to facilitating and helping journalists, in the anticipation that they would receive something in return. In some cases they will even go as far as subsidizing a visit by journalists. A senior media officer in CAFOD is candid about the expectations that then arise:

The aid agencies which facilitate media trips are in very close contact with the journalist ... Journalists are now more dependent on aid agencies than they used to be ... as staff numbers have dropped and budgets have been cut. There is a potential opportunity for even more influence over the journalist. They will feel some level of obligation to the agency who is facilitating or even paying for the trip.[41]

In the 1980s these relationships and trade-offs were starting to become explicit. Oxfam assisted Michael Buerk's visits to Ethiopia in July and October 1984 with information and local help.[42] The Red Cross nurse Claire Bertschinger, based in Tigray,[43] was a valuable interviewee in the BBC TV news item and the agency World Vision gave space to the BBC/Visnews crew on its plane, when it was impossible to find any other means of transport between Addis Ababa and Tigray. But it is clear that the agencies expected a *quid pro quo*. In more recent years there has been much debate about journalists who are embedded with the military in war zones and the compromises this can entail. And there are distinct similarities when journalists are operating in close connection with aid agencies.

Not only do agencies want the media to focus attention on the overall story; in a competitive environment they want to maximize the publicity benefits for their own operations. According to David Styan, who has written on this relationship, 'It is insufficient for NGOs simply to be doing something, they need to be seen to be doing it on prime-time TV.'[44] A clear example of this appeared in the BBC weekly news and current affairs editors meeting on 6 November 1984 in the aftermath of Michael Buerk's reports. The minutes noted that World Vision 'had written to remind the BBC that the agency, which claimed to be the largest one working in Ethiopia, had provided the plane from Addis Ababa which had made Michael Buerk's important visit to Korem and Mekele possible.' World Vision expressed its disappointment that in view of this there had not been due recognition on screen of the charity's contribution.[45] In his capacity as foreign news editor Chris Cramer recalls that there had already been some agonizing in advance amongst senior news room staff about whether Michael Buerk and his crew should accept the use of the World Vision plane.[46] Given that there appeared to be no other way to reach the famine affected areas, there was in fact no other option open to the team. However it is clear that Cramer and others in the newsroom could foresee that there would be consequences from accepting aid agency hospitality.

Over the coming months in late 1984 and through 1985, as the reporting of the famine developed, World Vision continued to prod the BBC into giving it more exposure in various forms. It sponsored an ambitious documentary *African Calvary* about the famine, incorporating interviews and comments from the great and the good, popes and presidents, across the world. This was shot by Mohamed Amin for transmission in April 1985 and was shown on the BBC. Mother Teresa had even suggested the title when she referred to 'an open Calvary ... the passion of Christ being relived again in the bodies of the African people.'[47] Having provided substantial cash and facilities for the project, the World Vision director Peter Searle entered into protracted negotiations with BBC executives about the appropriate credits which should be given to the agency and the wording of an appeal following the broadcast. Both the BBC board of governors and board of management expressed concern about the relationship with World Vision in sponsoring the documentary and then trying to control aspects of its transmission. Ultimately there was a bad tempered exchange of letters after transmission, with World Vision alleging foul play, and at the same time there was much recrimination within the BBC for having ever allowed this project to go ahead in such a form.[48] Even more controversially, around the same time World Vision entered a co-production deal with the BBC current affairs programme *Panorama* in February 1985 on a film about development aid projects in Kenya, contributing £12,000 to a cash budget of £45,000. Once again the agency tried to flex its muscles and reap a worthwhile publicity benefit from its investment. When the relationship inevitably turned sour the producer noted in a memo to his editor that 'World Vision were disappointed by the programme, evidently expecting a 50 minute commercial'.[49]

Of all the agencies, World Vision raised a particular dilemma for the BBC executives who were negotiating the arrangements. There was a widespread belief in this period that the charity was closely connected with the CIA. Germaine Greer, who had observed it operating in Ethiopia, made her own typically caustic assessment:

World Vision is as devoutly anti-communist as they are deeply Christian … they have come to Ethiopia not only to perform the corporal work of mercy of saving lives but the spiritual work of saving souls from dialectical materialism. Some of the other agencies call it Blurred Vision … it is taken as read that World Vision is the spiritual arm of the CIA, a charge the more gung ho workers do not even bother to rebut. Most of the journalists struggling to see anything of Ethiopia are obliged to beg rides on World Vision aircraft, a propaganda opportunity that World Vision would be foolish to waste, for its massive budget $72m to spend in Ethiopia in 1985 alone, must be fuelled by constant fund-raising.[50]

Bill Cotton, as BBC director of television, voiced reservations at the board of governors about the *bona fides* of the organization,[51] and the Rev. Colin Morris (head of religious programmes), speaking at the weekly TV programme review meeting, 'expressed the gravest reservations about the BBC being involved with what he called 'this dubious organisation … which some had suggested was a front for the CIA.'[52] Similarly, at the BBC board of management, the director of public affairs, John Wilkinson, 'registered a warning against the organisation World Vision'.[53] It is clear that whilst World Vision presented a special cause for concern, then at least the BBC internal processes were well tuned to picking up such a problem and articulating the concerns which arose.

On other occasions aid agencies less controversial than World Vision were also involved in tricky negotiations with the broadcasters during this same period. A whole group of second rank aid charities such as Help the Aged and Action Aid were putting pressure on the Disasters Emergency Committee to be allowed into the preferred group of five (CAFOD, Christian Aid, Oxfam, Save the Children and the Red Cross) which benefited from the broadcast emergency appeals that were reaping such enormous sums at this time.[54] And the big, well-established agencies had their own ongoing discussions and disagreements with the BBC. Christian Aid was tipped off about the *Panorama* link with World Vision and immediately wrote to the BBC to voice its concern about the bias in the story and question whether it too should be making 'a budget allocation for such deals with broadcasters'.[55] The BBC crafted a fairly defensive reply concluding that 'The co-production arrangement ... facilitated the making of a significant programme about an important subject without in any way necessitating a departure from the BBC's editorial standards.' It was simply a matter that 'the agency showed an interest in acquiring some of the television rights and a contract was drawn up.'[56] Within the BBC feelings were not quite so sanguine when the matter was raised at the weekly Programme Review.[57] Roger Bolton, a former *Panorama* editor, expressed grave concern that *Panorama* could accept money in such a way and leave itself potentially compromised. Michael Checkland, who was then director of resources for BBC Television (and later deputy director general and director general), recalls that this episode of a current affairs producer doing a deal like this with an agency, which had its own agenda and then expected editorial control, did cause problems for the BBC. In fact, he said later that it contributed to a decision by the BBC to formalize all such co-production arrangements and move them into the specially created Enterprises Department.[58] Obviously for commercial channels and publications, in the UK and the US, the delicacies of these relationships were not so pronounced, but the BBC was obliged to tread very carefully.

The detail of the BBC's dealings with Christian Aid and World Vision give a clear indication of the complicated expectations on both sides in the relationship between the media and the agencies. Derek Warren was a press officer with Oxfam who subsequently moved to the press office at the Department for International Development, thereby gaining wide experience of how the relationship between media and aid agencies functioned. In his view:

The interdependence between the media and aid agencies is unlikely to change. Aid agencies continue to work in situations and places where they are the main source of news to the outside world and there are often vested interests which want to prevent that information getting out, so journalists are very dependent on them to provide information. Similarly, without the input of the media the public profile of the agencies would be, clearly, considerably lower; although most of their work may be in long-term development, in terms of their public profile, and their gaining new supporters, that comes almost entirely through the focus they have at the times of humanitarian emergency, so I think that relationship works both ways and I don't see that changing.[59]

However, in succeeding years there have been occasions where this relationship has soured considerably and at times come close to breaking down. The former Africa correspondent Richard Dowden (currently director of the Royal African Society) is highly critical of journalists who are 'embedded' with aid agencies, whereby in exchange for transport and hospitality the name of the organization will be slipped into the story. He even speaks of a 'pact that has become poisonous'.[60] And David Loyn, as BBC international development correspondent, was wary of accepting any kind of favour from NGOs because of the danger of being 'hijacked by their agenda'.[61] Michael Maren as a disillusioned former aid worker has seen it all from the other side. He comments how the aid agencies are only too happy to help with lifts and logistics. 'The return on investment makes it all worthwhile because NGOs need nothing more than publicity. Their prime interest is in reaching their customers, the donating public.'[62] Nevertheless, the more thoughtful aid workers are aware of what exactly the quality of the exposure may consist of. Urs Boegli of the Red Cross[63] refers to 'Humanitarian workers, often posing with dying babies in their arms' as the prime source of information in the midst of many emergencies, but observes that 'their message has been encapsulated in a few shots and sound bites wedged into a two-minute-thirty second bracket.'

On the one hand, the agencies need media for publicity and for fundraising. On the other, the media need agencies for logistical support and for sources and stories. Yet there are potential difficulties in both directions, beyond the obvious trade-offs. For the agencies there are likely to be compromises about the way stories are distorted in the balance between using images that raise the most funds and telling a responsible story. For the media there are questions of impartiality and giving an independent view that entails real accountability. As Philip Seib observes, 'for reporters, dependence on an NGO carries with it the same risks as overreliance on government sources. The agency may be doing fine work but it may also have its own agenda. Nobility of purpose does not rule out efforts to manipulate the media.'[64] And with the advent of new media and online communication the ability of NGOs to mould their own messages has become ever more sophisticated. Like many other organizations they have sought all kinds of ways to communicate directly using social media, often voicing their frustration with mainstream media.[65]

Getting the message across

On the other side of the divide, journalists may face difficulties because of their relationships with aid agencies. One of these is the problem of simplicity. The journalist is under pressure to tell a clear story and sometimes for the best of motives. The former broadcast journalist Daniel Wolf[66] refers to a discussion he had with Michael Buerk in the late 1990s on the question of why his famine reports did not contain much reference to the civil war and the fighting in Ethiopia:

Buerk still held the view that the wars had 'complicated matters', but he did agree that self-censorship had played a role in his own and others' reportage at the time: 'You've got ... to make a decision: is this side story of any real significance? And also, at the back of your mind is: "if I overemphasise a negative angle to this, I am going to be responsible for ... inhibiting people from coughing up their money?"'[67]

Jonathan Dimbleby is even more candid when he describes the making of his film about the 1973 Ethiopian famine. He speaks of having to 'edit out some key facts' referring to the war with Eritrea. He admits that he consciously did not want to deter his audience from giving money and was concerned that if he described the fighting which was the background to the famine then the reaction would be 'typical Africans are just going to waste the money'.[68]

The relationship with aid agencies does not only mean that journalists are prone to telling a curtailed story in order to maintain fundraising.

There is also the tendency that if a journalist is too closely involved, then the role of the aid agency may be unduly enhanced in the overall scheme of things. A number of development writers have commented on how reporting will over emphasize the role of an outside Northern agency and the expatriate relief workers in alleviating a crisis. Naturally the NGO wants to emphasize how much it is doing, especially when there are so many competitors in the field. Yet on the wider scale this may not be very much. Mark Duffield describes the multiple coping mechanisms which Africans use to deal with food shortages, which are generally overlooked: labour migration, the use of wild foodstuffs, ways of managing resources.[69] The Western media coverage of the famine in Ethiopia, in common with other reporting on humanitarian crises, tended to emphasize the role of outside intervention in solving the crisis. The location interviews were predominantly with white helpers. Claire Bertschinger, the Red Cross nurse based in Mekele and interviewed by Michael Buerk, makes a wry comment about this as she quickly became media savvy: 'My name was the one that was given to the journalists as a contact when they arrived in Addis. I soon understood what they wanted: a picture of a young, English-speaking, white woman working in these terrible conditions, with whom their readers could identify, as well as pictures of starving children.'[70]

Alex de Waal argues that in 1984/5:

the government of Mengistu became a master at managing humanitarian propaganda. It recognised that the international press is more concerned with the marginal contribution made to rural people's survival—overall no more than 10 per cent of the average daily ration—provided by international food aid, than the 90 per cent provided by the people's own efforts. The latter could be destroyed without international protest, neatly providing a captive population for the military and a needy population for the relief agencies.[71]

Cate too refers to the way that relief organizations will 'exaggerate the role of Western aid and overlook the importance of indigenous relief efforts.'[72] Amartya Sen has an amusing angle on this when he describes the pattern of the 'donor's exaggerated perception of its achievements' in alleviating a crisis, and he refers to an Oxfam bulletin which 'had no hesitation in reporting how a poor peasant sighed that the drought "may be too big a problem for God; but perhaps Oxfam can do something."'[73] However, it is not just the peasant but the journalist who may be lured into believing that the aid agency is omnipotent, or at least a lynchpin in the story.

In a wider sense it is not only that the reporting omits unfortunate facts in order to assist fundraising, or exaggerates the role of Western aid agencies; it also suspends normal journalistic instincts.[74] Interestingly, as the NGOs grew in size and significance as institutions, it was a long time before there were calls for any kind of broader accountability or appraisal of their effectiveness. They retained the status of 'sacred cows' because of their ultimate do-gooding mission. It took many more years of expansion before questions started to arise about their accountability to those who had donated and even to those whom they were intending to help.[75] As far as the assessments of the Ethiopian famine were concerned it was several years before there was much discussion about the omissions by aid agencies—the misleading narrative of a natural disaster and unwillingness to confront the real causes of famine. Eventually there were a number of critical appraisals of the way that aid agencies had behaved. Jason Clay for example, who had done the research on the underlying causes of famine and the impact of resettlement, wrote an attack on agencies which had been unwilling to engage with or explain what was really happening on the ground. But many of these arguments are still a long way from the mainstream discourse about aid agencies and in particular the discourse about such iconic events as the Ethiopian famine and its aftermath.

Clay's analysis was particularly withering about World Vision, which had even said it was 'immoral to publish research into the causes of the famine'.[76] Tony Vaux concluded that this experience exposes a fault in the theory that 'everyone involved in aid has a duty to be positive', and said journalists covering the Ethiopian story should have been asking harder questions.[77] And Alex de Waal questioned, in the light of such rapid growth, whether the 'analytical capacity and accountability of these organisations matches their power?', concluding that the 'literature on the last decade of relief operations in Africa contains little true analysis and much hagiography.'[78] Naturally, some journalists have sought to ask difficult questions about the aid industry and call for more accountability, but they are in the minority.[79] The dominant tone of the coverage continues to be about praising the agencies, rather than asking awkward questions.[80] In more recent years there have been some attempts to assert accountability by NGOs in various ways, such as websites dedicated to their performance and encouraging discussion of mistakes and ways to improve.[81] But there is still a long way to go before aid agencies are subject to the same kind of scrutiny as other kinds of institutions in public life and journalists refrain from 'relying heavily and uncritically on aid organisations for statistics, subjects, stories and sources'.[82]

Paradox of images—the worse they are, the better for the NGO …

If the question for journalists is the need for independence and account-ability, one of the principal concerns for foreign aid NGOs in their relationships with the media is the delicate matter of images. The cover-age of the Ethiopian famine and the huge response from donors were, of course, dependent in the first place upon the television reports which featured the iconic pictures of the starving. These images played a crucial role in the whole fundraising effort that was so significant for the aid agencies. Henrietta Lidichi argues that 'Clearly 1984/5 was a crucial moment in the trajectory of NGOs. It brought their work prominence and assured them greater prestige and a much larger income than they had experienced previously. These benefits were achieved by virtue of a hyper-inflation in images of Africa.'[83]

Despite the extraordinary (financial) benefits to the aid agencies there was concern in some quarters about the way that the famine victims had been projected. The criticism emphasized how 'Northern NGOs were dependent upon media exposure which produced typically populist, simplistic and ethnocentric images' of poor Africans waiting to be saved by white outsiders. These concerns eventually precipitated a debate within the world of development charities about the nature of imagery. Henrietta Lidichi concludes that 'as a result of the surfeit of negative imagery that was produced and which prompted previously unthinkable levels of donation in the West, the ethics of representation became a central issue of concern.'[84] There was a clear sense of discomfort that Southern disasters qualified as news only after tragedy had struck and when 'good images' were available, preferably with plenty of emaciated bodies. David Loyn, as BBC International Development Correspon-dent, remarked that it is such a predictable reaction that he characterizes the 'dying baby shots' as a recurring 'journalistic commodity,' even refer-ring to the clichéd way they are used as 'instant coffee journalism'.[85] The author Thomas Keneally, in his account of the famine, describes the process of cameramen in the relief shelters searching 'up and down the rows of famine victims, selecting only the most skeletal for filming and in some cases waiting for them to die before filming', and reflects upon the relief agencies' collusion in this process.[86]

In the years following the Ethiopian famine and Live Aid there was much examination of this dilemma. The 1987 landmark report co-ordinated by Oxfam, *Images of Africa*,[87] was assembled largely as a result of the Ethiopian coverage, which raised all these issues about media reporting of humanitarian crises. A key outcome of this questioning was the publication in 1992 of the Red Cross Code for Conduct in disaster relief, which was signed by several hundred NGOs. Clause 10 of the code covered dealings with the media and referred to the use of pictures in charity publicity material, stating that 'In our information, publicity and advertising activities we shall recognise disaster victims as dignified humans, not hopeless objects …',[88] and in the guidelines for the media, the code stated that agencies should 'not allow external or internal demands for publicity to take precedence over the principle of maximising overall relief assistance …' Internally, too, aid agencies adopted informal codes of conduct which encouraged the 'responsible' use of images. Many relief agencies did try to avoid using iconic images such as the lone malnourished child with the distended stomach. In later years the Voluntary Service Overseas (VSO) also produced its own account of *The Live Aid Legacy*, which questioned the lasting imagery from that period. It highlighted the negative image of helpless, starving Africans, which was contrasted with the stereotype of the beneficent, white, Western helper.[89] The problem is that the same dilemma of negative images enhancing fundraising, which Ethiopia showed to such an extreme extent, is never likely to go away. And over twenty years afterwards there were still ample examples of this in the portrayal of famine victims, notably in the reporting of Niger in 2005 and the East African famine in 2011.

This ongoing tension between the shocking images and telling a responsible, balanced story in which poor people are more than helpless victims is evident within aid agencies as well as between them and the media. There is a kind of centaur effect between the fundraising and the development/educational function of the charity. Paddy Coulter, who was head of communications at Oxfam in the 1980s and was closely involved in the original coverage of Ethiopia, observed in 1989 that 'International aid agencies will have to overhaul their priorities. They have to stop treating fund-raising as the overriding priority and accept some responsibility for public education.'[90] He reported a fundraising official who had said quite openly that 'happier more positive images don't bring in the money'. So if there is already this ambivalence within the agencies it is difficult to criticize the media for using shocking images and trying to tell the most dramatic story.

In 2001 the DEC published an evaluation it had commissioned into the Gujarat earthquake, which again raised many of these same issues.[91] It made the criticism that DEC members were more 'fund driven' than 'need driven' in their response and therefore 'became victims of their organisation's fundraising success'. The report spoke of 'an underlying problem that funds are skewed disproportionately towards situations of high media profile rather than actual need' and questioned 'whether agencies allow the desire for publicity ... to outweigh humanitarian principles.' Four years later the same themes recurred in the initial DEC evaluation of the response to the Asian Tsunami.[92] This was very damning in some places, and in fact the original report was so critical of inter-agency rivalry and unnecessary media profile that it was never made public. BBC *Newsnight* obtained a leaked copy which included references to 'concern about the proliferation of signboards and the tendency to mark every item with the agency's name' and to 'a few cases where relief flights seem to have been used more for public profile than because of real need.'[93]

Emergencies and disasters are the most successful way for charities to fundraise, but this brings the danger of what some aid workers call the 'pornography of poverty': that is, the repeated use of shocking pictures of starving children as a means of raising the most funds. The problem is that those agencies which are savvier in using publicity will prosper at the expense of those which advocate a more measured approach. There is even a kind of 'humanitarian Greshams law'[94] operating, so that there can be a downward spiral in which agencies may seek to grab attention through shocking images and high profile attention-seeking publicity. So another paradox in this relationship is that 'relief organisations have a strong incentive to stress negative news about developing countries.'[95] One journalist familiar with this syndrome observed that 'Agencies which understand the demands of the media can use the situation to run their charity appeals, knowing that if they provide the right 'sound bite', a pithy phrase summing up the horror of the event, they will feature in the news.'[96]

Richard Dowden cites a particular case of this syndrome. In the midst of the Great Lakes refugee crisis in 1994 there were nightly joint press conferences, which reported the scale of the cholera epidemic in the camps. He noted how the large agencies would seek to trump each other in announcing the numbers of deaths[97]—they were competing to outdo each other in ramping up the level of horror in the knowledge that the one who said things were worst of all[98] would be the agency that would duly appear on the television news and in the papers. Aid agency officials have made it their business to know what journalists want (those same criteria originally identified by Galtung and Ruge),[99] which includes a clear story and negativity. A measured and nuanced report that downplays any sensational material will not be so likely to find its way onto mainstream media outlets. Michael Holman was Africa editor for many years at the *Financial Times* and makes the same observation: 'In Africa, the source of the story is so often one of the thousands of NGO workers on the continent, and it takes a brave local NGO rep to admit his ignorance, when he or she knows that a rival NGO rep competing for the publicity that fills the collection box at home, will be all too ready to brief the visiting hack.'[100]

The implication is that the aid agency will attune its remarks to what the media need or want. Urs Boegli as head of the Red Cross Media Services made a speech which issued a warning to aid agency staff, 'Shocking figures will naturally boost your chances of appearing in the evening news ... but think twice or you may end up regretting your lack of circumspection.'[101]

Charles Elliot, a former director of Christian Aid, points out that NGOs are more successful at mobilizing people on the basis of a comprehensible, if simply-packaged, disaster than they are at encouraging themselves to commit to the enormous and complex problem of world poverty 'which is barely within the grasp of the human mind'.[102] And Clare Short, whilst secretary of state at DFID, made a controversial contribution to this debate, criticizing aid agencies for unnecessary fundraising which portrayed developing countries as full of 'constant suffering, failure and famine' and 'blaming an obsession with crisis for deflecting serious debate about longer-term development work.'[103] In general less than ten per cent of aid agency funds are used on development education, but the problem is that this is much harder to fundraise for, even though it is of great importance. Clare Short did ensure that some DFID funds were spent on development education, but that allocation did not last for long, as the UK Treasury preferred money to be spent on items with 'measureable outcomes'. The erstwhile president Nyerere of Tanzania once said he would prefer that NGOs 'should take every penny they have set aside for Tanzania and spend it in the UK explaining to the people the facts of poverty and its causes.'[104] He sensed that a more sophisticated level of understanding within donor countries was a key precursor to really changing things on the ground within Africa. The problem of course is that not only is it a tougher goal for which to raise funds, it is also more complex to campaign for.

Long-term/short-term

In 1984/85 the need for a deeper and better explanation of the famine was prompted in the immediate aftermath of the original Michael Buerk broadcasts. The acting director of Christian Aid, Martin Bax, wrote to the BBC director general Alasdair Milne, recognizing the pivotal role that the news items had played in attracting aid and attention to the problem, but questioning why it was that no one had taken notice of the charities that had repeatedly warned of the crisis in the months and years before. Bax observed that 'it is of life and death importance that we try to find a way of bringing this kind of event to the public attention in a rather more planned manner'. He was also concerned about the implications of the enormous publicity and donations which the broadcasts had inspired. Despite all the sudden media attention:

attempting to inform the public at greater depth of the real underlying reasons for poverty, underdevelopment and starvation, there still remains an enormous gulf of misunderstanding. People still are surprised and feel that something ought to be able to be done rather rapidly. They fail to understand that the present situation in Ethiopia is the legacy of many years of failure on behalf of many people including the Ethiopian Government, Western Governments, Eastern Governments, the charities themselves ...[105]

This highlighted one of the key tensions in the relationship between the agencies and the media. There was frustration that the media were reluctant to cover a situation until it was critical and there were starving, skeletal children to film. The painstaking story leading to the build-up of famine and the wider long-term issues affecting developing countries were not newsworthy. Yet, paradoxically, the agencies also benefited from a more dramatic story. On the one hand the agencies wanted to tell a complicated story about development and to give positive images of people in developing countries. Yet the simple story favoured by the media also reaped the agencies better rewards in terms of publicity and funding. There is a persistent problem in agencies tempted to tell a more shocking story in order to attract more attention for the institutional purposes of building their brand and attracting funds. And in the aftermath of the famine in East Africa in 2011 these very same criticisms recurred. Later evaluations of the situation criticized donors for waiting until the story was one of extreme crisis before taking notice, on the basis of 'Die First, Aid Later'.[106]

The paradox again for aid agencies is that a disaster averted will never hit the headlines in the same way as a major crisis. In the period since 1984 there have been some cases where early warning systems have worked successfully to ward off famine. Fred Cate describes the sequence of famine alerts in 1992 in twelve southern African countries, where there was a worse drought than in 1984/85. However, as a result of the predictions there was a rapid response both by the countries involved and international organizations such as the Food and Agriculture Organization (FAO), which ultimately prevented drought from causing famine. 'The unprecedented early response prevented a famine and as such a major news story ... what went largely unreported, the FAO concluded, was the 'story about millions who could have died but did not.'[107]

Ten years later there was a wide consensus that a potential famine was threatened in sub-Saharan Africa. Dereja Wordofa of Oxfam described how difficult it was to bring the media in early on the story before there were any starving babies: 'The famine threatened in Southern Africa and some of our media and field officers had difficulty in getting the story out, despite the fact that they had a very concrete analysis and data. It was an impending crisis but there was very little interest from the media'. In the end:

because of push and a lot of discussion the media eventually came in to bring the story out ... It was the same story also in Ethiopia where the crisis in 2003 was one of the greatest threats to Ethiopia but the combination of efforts by government and importantly by media actually helped to prevent, or at least substantially limit, famine. Therefore we did not see a catastrophic story.[108]

This was a rare and impressive example where the media took up a story before it became a disaster. It was partly because in Malawi there was a scandalous element to the story. Large grain stores were discovered whilst the population was facing imminent starvation, and the media helped force a public investigation into the story. According to John Seaman, a veteran expert who worked with Save the Children on food security issues, 'It forced a public inquiry into what happened to the grain stocks in Malawi which is probably the first big piece of public democracy Malawi has ever seen.'[109] This is an interesting example of Amartya Sen's thesis in action, even if it was initially difficult to attract attention to the impending problems. It provides a case study illustrating that there is a role for the media to 'help accelerate the shift of the societal emphasis from post-disaster relief towards pre-disaster initiatives'.[110]

Yet it is not only the media that arrive too late. The same paradox comes from those who donate. Invariably disaster 'cure' is more appealing than disaster 'prevention'. The Mozambique floods of 2000 were a clear example of this. About six months before the floods occurred Mozambique had put out an appeal to the international community for $2.7 million for boats, tents and other necessary supplies. It received less than half this amount. However, once the floods materialized—as had been anticipated—then Mozambique received over $100 million in emergency assistance, partly because of the dramatic media coverage. And at a subsequent conference a further $450 million was pledged by the international donor community in rehabilitation costs.[111] If the impact of the flooding had been mitigated by the earlier modest expenditure there may not have been a disaster or at least nothing on such a dramatic scale. In consequence, the huge influx of donations to aid agencies that was prompted by the dramatic pictures of the crisis would never have arrived—so, paradoxically, the NGOs involved who received publicity were ultimately substantial beneficiaries from the floods. At the most cynical level, the worse the story becomes the better for NGO fundraising. Aid agencies are well aware of this dynamic. It is generally in their publicity and financial interests to tell a more dramatic story, even though they may criticize the media for not responding to earlier warnings: hence Clare Short's criticism of the 'mutual parasitism of the media and the fundraiser'.[112]

This focus on the long-term is at the heart of the tensions between media and aid, as outlined in the letter quoted above from Christian Aid to Alasdair Milne. The BBC news coverage of the Ethiopian famine was very unusual in concentrating widespread attention on a problem in a faraway place. After the initial 'discovery' of the famine by the media there was a period of 'euphoric enthusiasm' as the issue of famine in Africa and the efforts to relieve it became a major story.[113] Broadcasting could not sustain the interest it had originally inspired. Having told a series of dramatic stories over 1984/85 it was unable to mobilize support for more fundamental and longer-term change. Ultimately, the famine was part of a long-term process, whereas television in particular is geared towards reporting events. Moreover the nature of television journalism is both to craft a story and then to show how that story develops and ideally resolves itself. As Martin Bax of Christian Aid pointed out, the hugely complex and long-term problem of food insecurity in sub-Saharan Africa was not susceptible to being told as a simple 'story' and certainly not something that could be neatly resolved. Nevertheless this is the way the media reported the Ethiopian famine. It was a story about the 'sudden revelation' of starvation and then the remarkable efforts by Western countries to send aid and thereby solve the problem. In response to the story, the public made its donations, participated in new types of charitable activities and urged humanitarian intervention—and each of these events was extensively covered—but this was not a recipe for any form of real structural change and before long the same problems re-emerged. For the aid agencies this pattern of storytelling worked well. They were repeatedly seen as doing something active, responding to a crisis—which suited their image and expanded their profile.

It is somewhat ironic that exactly two years after the first Buerk broadcast on 23 October 1986 there was a tiny Reuters item about a famine risk in Ethiopia, an appeal for 1.2 million tonnes of food aid to feed an estimated 7 million people who were at risk.[114] On this occasion the famine alert never hit the headlines. Over the next decade there were repeated warnings and dangers of food shortages and starvation in Ethiopia and other places in Africa. In 1987 there was eventually another DEC broadcast appeal for famine relief in Ethiopia which raised reasonable amounts, and a similar appeal followed two years later, but there was by now diminishing interest in the story. There was a sense that Band Aid/Live Aid had been a missed opportunity to harness that effort into changing development education and bring aid agencies together in a way that reduced fundraising competition to achieve a complete change of emphasis.[115] This could have promoted the need for long-term crisis prevention, not short-term crisis management, but it

157

would have required enormous political will, far beyond the craving for instant popularity.

This conflict between the media's need for a good story with a visible resolution, on the one hand, and on the other hand the immense, complicated, long-term question of development was eventually understood by some of those involved in the original euphoria. Bob Geldof himself pointed out in 2005 that returning to Ethiopia twenty years later he found that things were just as bad as ever. Speaking at the 2005 Live 8 concert in Hyde Park Geldof said 'Band Aid was supposed to be just that: a "band aid". And it is a disgrace that twenty years later we should be here today, with half the youngsters in Africa still going to bed hungry.'[116] He says that this was what prompted him to become involved in the Commission for Africa, which was a detailed political process and organization—not just a feelgood fundraising effort.[117]

In a film entitled *Bob Geldof: Saint or Singer?* the pop star Bono, who also became involved on a continuing basis in the issues of African poverty, expressed this distinction well. He mused that making a song about Christmas and organizing a pop concert were very far from giving a voice to the poor people of the world, and that twenty years later really nothing had changed because the structures were the same. Bono, who had travelled the world with Geldof talking to governments, said they had been trying to 'give a real and powerful lobby for the poor and most vulnerable people of the world, like the National Rifle Association or the tobacco lobby in the US, and that is a long way from strumming a guitar and singing "feed the world, do they know it's Christmas?"'[118] Bono and also Bob Geldof clearly made a decision to stick with the problem of Africa for the long-term, and have continued to campaign over the years. But for many of those who were inspired in 1984/85 to donate and participate in events there was a sense that now that the story had been told and plenty of aid was donated, somehow that would solve things for good. In the biography of the cameraman Mohamed Amin there is a tribute to him by the singer Kenny Rogers at a Los Angeles award ceremony, saying, 'He, his gift and his contribution will always be considered the turning point in solving world hunger.'[119] Alas, Amin was certainly instrumental in focusing attention on hunger, but the pictures he filmed did not solve the problem.

As far as the NGOs were concerned there were big institutional changes and certainly new and highly successful ways of raising funds

Fig. 6.1: The Making of St Bob. Geldof, visiting Ethiopia after the success of Band Aid. © Manchester Daily Express / Science & Society Picture Library

which were a direct result of the very high profile media coverage of the Ethiopian famine. There were also serious debates within the charitable world which arose out of the way the media had depicted the famine. And in the years after 1984 engaging with the media was becoming more critical for aid agencies; their communications departments have expanded and grown in sophistication, especially since the explosion in social media from 2008/2009.[120] Yet the overall effect did not change the situation on the ground, particularly in Africa. There was still only a superficial portrayal of famine or, for institutional reasons, not much will to engage with the political context which was behind the suffering. As David Rieff observes, 'there is no necessary connection between caring about the suffering of others and understanding the nature and cause of that suffering'.[121] The complicated background to the 2011 East African famine, in particular the difficulties of dealing with Somalia where there are powerful factions pursuing agendas quite apart from the welfare and nourishment of the wider population, demonstrated once again this ongoing paradox.

As the agencies increased in size so rapidly in the mid-1980s it was apparent that the pressures of fundraising, competition and maintaining a media profile were starting to increase. The new and developing relationships with the media and the dramatic institutional growth of the aid NGOs brought with them a series of contradictions. A key part of this debate was to highlight and emphasize the need for better understanding and reporting on both sides—media and aid agencies. And the inadequate way in which Africa was covered by the media emerged as a crucial part of this discussion.

7

INTERPRETING AFRICA

'There is always something new out of Africa.'

Pliny the Elder.

'Africa was a distant land that never really troubled us.'

Alasdair Milne, BBC director general 1982–87.

The news reporting from Ethiopia in 1984 represented an extraordinary landmark in the way the Western media covered the 'dark continent'. Extensive news coverage about Africa is a rare event, except on those occasions when there is a Western or white angle to the story. As a former newspaper foreign correspondent observed, 'Africa correspondents have a lot to be grumpy about. They go through hell to report African wars, but ultimately the story seems to be framed by domestic politics and celebrity endorsement.'[1] Against this background the scale and extent of the Ethiopian coverage were very unusual.

In the immediate post-colonial period, Africa was still covered in a considered and serious fashion. Most of Fleet Street employed Africa specialists in the 1950s and 1960s. Newspapers had correspondents based in Africa who filed on a regular basis and offered informed comment on African affairs. The fact that newspapers and broadcasters had invested in correspondents meant that they were then inclined to take their material and the story was reported in a steady, incremental way, informed by locally based expertise. In retrospect it appears that Africa was interesting as long as it was perceived as an end of Empire narrative. After decolonization there was a gradual diminishing of interest in most of the continent. One exception to this was the story of Cold War proxy fighting, which continued to merit some coverage.[2]

The overall pattern as described by several studies on the media coverage of Africa is that although the continent was reported by the media during the Cold War, it was mostly discussed through the prism of great power conflict, which severely hampered the way it was covered and perceived.[3] The fall of the Berlin Wall led to some hope of more comprehensive and nuanced reporting of Africa and an expectation that 'the end of the Cold War may ... mean the major western based transnational news agencies will improve their coverage of the developing world—or at least lead them to view a third world crisis as something other than a Cold War related phenomenon.'[4] That optimism was, alas, misplaced. Instead there was a further decline in reporting, on the basis that Africa was no longer of immediate significance to the West (since it had ceased to be the location of proxy wars). In fact the reporting of wars in Africa in successive years resorted to narrow 'ethnic' descriptions with the general presumption that these were now incomprehensible conflicts between warring tribes.[5] Evidence of the lack of understanding and serious explanation of Africa has been highlighted many times over the past decades, from the ongoing unrest in the Congo to the reporting of the crisis in the Darfur region of Sudan[6] or the unrest in Kenya after the disputed elections in 2007/8. Whatever the circumstances, the same standard stereotypes have prevailed throughout in the way much of the mainstream media deals with Africa.

The frame of superpower rivals using African nations as a setting for their conflicts had a familiar appeal to editors.[7] Otherwise, for many years the overwhelming trend of the coverage, for the purposes of Western media, was a narrow focus on the move away from white rule, whether that was in Kenya, Rhodesia/Zimbabwe or, more recently, South Africa. In other cases news interest in sub-Saharan Africa was for the most part very limited. As a rule, European countries (in particular Britain, France, Belgium and Portugal) were interested in news about their own colonies, and when these countries became independent the interest gradually waned, but as a rule they still report their ex-colonies more than the rest of the continent.[8] So, for example, when there was a coup, attempted secession and then a refugee crisis in Mali during 2012 it was given reasonable coverage in the Francophone press. Yet even though this was a significant story, the reporting in the English language press was minimal.[9]

John Seaman spent many years as an African expert for Save the Children Fund. He is critical of the level of political analysis given to Africa over the years since decolonization.

It should be much higher than it is. I have the sense that when I watch the media in the Middle East, with all its limitations, I get some detailed analysis. The people talking to camera know something about the region ... whereas Africa gets rather slight coverage. It is intermittent, without permanent representation and internationally Africa is not taken seriously. It is like the old joke: if somebody towed Africa off into the Atlantic and sank it, nobody in Europe would notice for a week. It has no ... political effect.[10]

Or, according to another observer, 'Africa is no longer politically fashionable, instead the continent presents a repetitive litany of coups, corruption and famine', concluding that 'the media view of Africa (in the 1980s) was of a vast black hole fringed by South Africa and Libya.'[11]

This absence of sustained interest by the media in the developing world, and Africa in particular, has been a subject of regular concern and fits into an overall pattern. The problem is a recurrent one: where poorer, developing countries are concerned, the news coverage is generally episodic stories about war and disaster (with the exception of royal or celebrity visits). As for serious factual (current affairs and documentary) programming on developing countries, this has now become a disappearing genre, at least on mainstream terrestrial TV.[12] Television news bulletins report stories about disasters in the developing world, but there is often no interest in the longer-term issues behind the immediate breaking news and what can be done about them. The news coverage, by its nature, is a quick and superficial story, told by a 'fireman' reporter sent in from outside. In the words of an ABC producer, 'If it can't be done in three days, it hasn't happened.'[13] The overall result is a poor level of news about developing countries. And even though most people still receive most of their news via television, what they experience is 'random, fickle and incomplete ... news about the developing world is authorless, anchorless and impossible to understand or follow.'[14] This absence of sustained, informed coverage from the developing world has been particularly true of Africa. It has been badly reported since the post-colonial period and in many ways it still is today. Whilst there are experts and journalists with a detailed knowledge of the continent, they are the exception. The result is reporting that is without a real context and which therefore cannot give a properly nuanced view.

It is against this wider background of reporting Africa in the post-colonial period that the media coverage of Ethiopia, although so extensive, was so inadequate. A real political understanding and context were missing from the way in which the famine, and both its causes and effects, were characterized. In fact, the reporting about Ethiopia is part of a pattern where the media rarely cover African stories for their own sake and, on the rare occasions when they do so, they are liable to make mistakes. The Ethiopian famine is one example of several where there was a sudden focus of attention on an Africa story, but then, partly because there was so little context, the mainstream reporting got things wrong.

Within the BBC during this period there were particular reasons why the reporting of sub-Saharan Africa was so patchy and limited on the domestic services. Unlike other parts of the world, in particular the Indian sub-continent, there were no close links between the African Service and the domestic output. The African programming which came from Bush House and was destined for the wider world (including Africa itself) was certainly nuanced, well informed and comprehensive. Yet this did not filter through to the mainstream BBC output for domestic consumption. Another significant factor was that African governments in that period rarely showed any intense interest in the way they were portrayed to domestic UK audiences. Whereas in the case of the Indian sub-continent there was a stream of complaints about the way news from India was covered (especially on the BBC) and as a result the BBC devoted considerable care and attention to this output, which filtered through to other organizations, there were very few long-term correspondents who cared and lobbied within the BBC about how Africa was reported to domestic audiences and ensured that it was portrayed in a rounded and comprehensive way. Most crucially, there was simply not the same level of interest on the part of broadcasters (especially editorial figures setting the agenda in London) in reporting on Black Africa on a regular basis. Alasdair Milne recalls that as BBC director general (1982–87) he never issued a single invitation to an African High Commission, because in contrast to India 'it was simply not a priority'. He reflected later that black 'Africa was a distant land that never troubled us.'[15]

African governments or expatriates (with the exception of South Africa) never complained and the domestic BBC radio and television services, with rare exceptions in the wake of the various independence stories, rarely covered Black Africa. It was against this background that the news coverage and thereby the wider understanding of Africa were so much less informed. And it is because of this that it became possible for such misperceptions to occur in the reporting of Africa. In 1984 there was a rare explosion in the level of coverage about Africa, but then the media got things wrong. Had the same conditions prevailed for Africa as they did for India—for example, an alert audience awareness both among the diaspora in the UK and elsewhere, or a deep, ongoing editorial engagement up to the highest levels—it is certainly possible to argue that the same mistakes and misconceptions would not have taken place.[16]

Ten years after Ethiopia the crisis in Rwanda highlighted the continuing lacunae in media perceptions of Africa. When the killing began, it was difficult for editors to grasp what was happening and they initially did not give it enough attention. Organizations such as Oxfam[17] sent repeated warnings about imminent genocide, but there was little response. Crucially the timing coincided with the first democratic elections in South Africa and the feeling was that one African story at a time was enough; moreover all suitable expertise was busy in Johannesburg. The ignorance was compounded weeks later when the Hutu killers arrived in the camps in eastern Zaire. By then the elections were over in South Africa, and so there was an unseemly rush by both journalists and aid agencies to places like Goma to tell terrible tales about suffering refugees. For days there were misleading reports where many of the journalists, who knew little about the background, missed the point that the camps were not only ministering to fleeing victims of the slaughter but included also many of the recent killers and their relatives. George Alagiah covered this story for the BBC. He admitted later that for a whole week when he first reached Zaire he was in effect misleading the audience and he had 'lost the plot',[18] and was inadvertently telling the wrong story. Alagiah is no more to blame than the rest of the Western media in failing to understand what was going on. It took some time before the scale of the misrepresentation gradually emerged.[19]

According to some observers much media reporting of Africa has hardly moved on from the Victorian image of the dark continent.[20] This scandalous level of misinterpretation evident in the reporting of the post-genocide Rwanda refugee crisis would be unthinkable in most other parts of the world, but in Africa there is a sense that it is all too complicated and probably caused by some ancient tribal rivalries.[21] Others have drawn attention to this ongoing practice of 'double standards' when reporting on Africa.[22] There is evidence that practices taken for granted when reporting stories in the West are overridden when the subjects are Africans. Accuracy matters less and questions of taste and decency when dealing with subjects and victims are given a far looser interpretation. There is less inhibition about showing dead or mutilated bodies and less respect for individual privacy, demonstrating an ongoing sense of the 'other' in reporting on Africa.

Invisible wars

In the period following the end of the Cold War the problem of 'missing stories' has been compounded. Virgil Hawkins has written about the phenomenon of 'stealth conflicts'—and pointed out that the overwhelming proportion of these unreported wars have taken place in Africa.[23] The fighting in the Democratic Republic of the Congo (formerly Zaire), which was part of the fall-out from Rwanda, eventually claimed some estimated five million lives in a continuing war of attrition—yet for Western purposes it has been largely invisible. Indeed it is sometimes called 'Africa's hidden first world war', because as far as the rest of the world is concerned it is hardly ever reported, despite the enormous death toll.[24] 'The Congo war is so complex—involving the armies of six neighbouring states and an array of dubious mining interests that it never caught the public imagination ...'[25] Similarly the fighting in northern Uganda, where over a million people were displaced into camps—probably one of the biggest population displacements in the world at that time—rarely registered in international news coverage.[26] Bizarrely, some years later the controversial viral internet phenomenon known as *Kony 2012* (a Youtube video featuring the horror of the Lord's Resistance Army) received over 80 million hits in March 2012. Although by then Kony and his henchman had moved on from Uganda, it meant that finally (although far too late) the issue did get at least some kind of wider coverage.[27]

So the reporting of Ethiopia needs to be cast within a distinct pattern of the overall way Africa has been and in many ways continues to be covered. The famine was a dramatic episode in the reporting of Africa but it did not precipitate any shift in the way that we understand and relate to the continent. For much of the time stories about Africa, except those with a white or celebrity angle, are largely ignored—although it is interesting that 2005 saw an increase in developing country programming on mainstream channels on UK television, from an all time low in 2003. In the wake of the Commission for Africa report, the NGO Third World Eye (3WE) which monitors coverage of the developing world observed 'the unusual focus on Africa' which was responsible for some of this uplift.[28] Yet much of the output on Africa was still mediated through a white/celebrity angle, from Bob Geldof to Rolf Harris. And Jonathan Dimbleby noted in another report on TV coverage of developing countries that 'Despite the fact that 2005 saw more of the developing world on our TV screens than ever before, I doubt that we have a much deeper understanding of the people who live in Africa.'[29]

An ongoing lack of interest and engagement with Africa is not the only problem. It continues to be expensive and also complicated—both logistically and editorially—to operate from sub-Saharan Africa.[30] Satellite links alone cost far more than in other parts of the world.[31] News organizations do not invest much in covering Africa and tend to send in reporters when necessary. Occasionally a story in sub-Saharan Africa will attract major interest, but then the danger is that the news is covered by a specialist media 'flying squad'. In the absence of resident correspondents, a highly 'professional' reporter, well attuned to the needs and expectations of the various outlets, is flown in when disaster occurs and is expected to deliver something within days if not hours.[32] The 'emphasis is on expertise and house style above local knowledge … and values technical competence and speed over accuracy and content.'[33] There is little wider political understanding or adequate explanation of the background. The news appears as a random episode without any context and it is liable, like the reporting of the Ethiopian famine and other crises, to be subject to misinterpretation.

Africa, as in the case of the Ethiopian coverage, was covered in sudden bursts over a particular disaster. As far as the audience was concerned Black Africa was (and in many ways still is) a blank page of misery. Despite much handwringing and concern, surprisingly little has changed since the post-colonial period and in much of the reporting of Africa the same stereotypes still prevail.[34]

REPORTING DISASTERS

The Kenyan writer Binyavanga Wainaina wrote a brilliant and often quoted satire on 'How to Write about Africa' for *Granta* in 2005:

Never have a picture of a well-adjusted African on the cover … unless that African has won the Nobel Prize. An AK-47, prominent ribs, naked breasts—use these … Treat Africa as if it were one country. It is hot and dusty with rolling grasslands and huge herds of animals and tall, thin people who are starving … African characters should be colourful, exotic, larger than life—but empty inside with no dialogue …'[35]

In 2012 the Institute for Development Studies concluded two years of extensive research into the media portrayal of the Global South. It concluded that the Global South was still interpreted through a narrow prism of famine, war and corruption.[36] Despite periodic excitement about the number of mobile phones now used in Africa, the old tropes still prevail. There is still plenty of evidence of what Richard Dowden calls the 'New Orleans syndrome':[37] When Hurricane Katrina struck in 2005 there were plenty of other associations with New Orleans (picturesque historic city, jazz culture, etc.), and so the city was not branded with this one disaster story, because the media also offered other contexts; but when famine hit Ethiopia it was forever associated with this image and context and as a result, for much of the international audience, there are no other frames of reference for Ethiopia beyond that of the starving and the begging bowl. Even in an age of social media and other possibilities for telling and receiving stories, this syndrome endures.[38] Much of Africa is still reported as a land of war and poverty, rather than a complex system of societies like any other, full of normal people doing their best to make a life.

8

REAL MEDIA EFFECTS

'Foreign correspondents have a better chance of getting airtime or space in their papers if they play to stereotypical expectations at home. The focus in foreign reporting will be more than ever before on the negative, extraordinary and the sensational.'

Jurgen Kronig, *Die Zeit*[1]

The media reporting from Ethiopia in 1984 brought about immense change because it highlighted in the most dramatic way possible a tragic emergency. These broadcasts remain a part of collective and institutional memory because they were so compelling, had such an impact and have been so often revisited. In the short and medium-term, they mobilized opinion and generated a reaction. Since the Biafran famine in the 1960s, we have become accustomed to graphic disaster images in newspapers and on television screens. This coverage reached quite unprecedented levels with the Ethiopian famine in 1984/85; the response that it provoked put famine—especially in sub-Saharan Africa—on the global agenda and was responsible for huge aid campaigns. Arguably the long-term impact of the reports was even greater. When the *Guardian* organized a 2005 exhibition 'Imaging Famine' in London, an accompanying article concluded that 'The reverberations (of the Ethiopian coverage) are still being felt: Live 8, Make Poverty History and the global government campaigns for debt relief and increased aid are unthinkable without it.'[2] Yet despite this extraordinary media attention to the famine,

169

there are a number of paradoxes in the way that the media effects of the coverage played out in subsequent years.

The 1984 famine was—as we have seen—a 'celebrity' event in several ways.[3] It did produce real shifts and it has remained a vivid moment in contemporary history. It is often cited as an indisputable example of the impact of the media. The arresting media images produced a reaction that the events—on their own—would never have done. However, as it now appears, the overwhelming media coverage was also telling an inaccurate or at least a far from complete story. The account of the famine, as described by the media and in the fundraising, which has become part of the folk memory was a hugely simplified and depoliticized interpretation. One result of this—largely unconscious—manipulation was that the effect of the reporting and the corresponding response from public opinion was probably greater than if the media had given a more nuanced and complicated, although accurate, account. For the donor nations the coverage of the famine brought about a change in consciousness and awareness of the developing world, affecting and reaching out far wider than these issues had ever penetrated before. It changed the nature of charitable appeals and began a whole new genre of charity fundraising. More unexpectedly, the media coverage surrounding the famine also acted as a catalyst for the transforming growth of Northern aid agencies as institutions. Their size and overall significance within civil society completely changed during this period and this was to a considerable extent precipitated by the reaction to the media reporting of Ethiopia. The simplified, one dimensional story of a natural disaster with an obvious, straightforward solution was crucial in the public response to the media coverage.

A difficult story about famine as a social and political process with no easy answer—certainly not just soluble by sending large amounts of emergency relief aid to an authoritarian government—would perhaps have been unlikely to generate the same overwhelming reaction. It is self-evident that most of the popular media and in particular television prefer to deal with stories that have a clear solution rather than open-ended uncertainties. Yet there is an argument that points to the dramatic public response to the media coverage as a missed opportunity. The reporting and the aid agencies did not convey the complicated, long-term process of famine in Ethiopia. As a consequence the intervention that resulted was less effective than it might have appeared, because with a few exceptions, such as Médecins Sans Frontières (MSF), it never grappled with the complex and unpleasant political situation.[4] It addressed instead a media framed problem rather than the reality. Indeed the nature of the intervention which the media-prompted, especially by the UN, in some ways preserved the status quo by supporting the Ethiopian government in power. There was a great outpouring of effort and concern in response to the media, but there was no longer-term engagement with the process of development and the same problem of famine recurred soon afterwards. So a simple, but inaccurate story yielded an apparently extraordinary effect. The question is whether a more complicated story could have had a more sustained long-term effect on public education about faraway, poor countries and resulted in greater inclination and pressure to deal with the political realities?

Although the coverage of the famine had a dramatic effect upon public opinion and on NGOs, its demonstrable effect upon official policy in the UK was far less than might have appeared. As a result of the media furore there was pressure from public opinion upon government to 'do something' about the famine. Yet, despite appearances at the time, the result was really no change in official policy. This research shows the policy making process at the heart of government adapting to the public pressure, acting to assuage public sentiment, but ultimately resisting fundamental policy change. At every stage in the whole media-public opinion-policy process, it has revealed the intimate and previously private considerations of the BBC and of the government. Here the paradox is that the media coverage actually had a greater effect upon a later government than upon the Thatcher administration at the time.

When the Labour government under Tony Blair launched the Commission for Africa in February 2004, direct reference was made to the memory of Live Aid as a generational touchstone and an edifying occasion of altruistic outpouring and interest in Africa.[5] It was cited as an inspiration and the Commission was conceived in some ways as a means of capitalizing in retrospect upon the popular concern for Africa that had been expressed in 1984/85. Both Tony Blair and Gordon Brown, who proclaimed increased aid for Africa as central to their foreign policy, referred to Live Aid as a key historic development in that process, because of the awareness that it brought amongst domestic audiences. In contrast, the Thatcher government, whilst wanting to be seen as responsive, was not sympathetically inclined to the Live Aid movement.

It is a good example of how media effects may not necessarily be the short-term shifts which social scientists often look for but may in fact only really become evident in the much longer-term. Similarly, effects may also happen in rather more subtle, diverse and unexpected ways than the straightforward push and pull on immediate policy.

In 1984/85 the government faced a tidal wave of pressure to demonstrate its concern for the starving victims in Ethiopia, which despite appearances they largely resisted. The analysis of contemporary documents shows how civil servants and politicians grappled with the scale of the media coverage, but ultimately did as little as they could, whilst reaping the maximum political credit and, under the shadow of the Cold War, pursuing a clear ideological line. Foreign aid remained a low and diminishing priority for the Thatcher government and in the US for the Republicans. Again there is a paradox here in that the UK and US governments in 1984 may well have been doing the right thing, even if it was not necessarily for the right reason. Since much of the aid at that time was manipulated and in retrospect appears to have been used to prolong the civil wars or in forced resettlement, it is arguable that the Thatcher and Reagan governments were correct not to do more in contributing humanitarian relief at that point.

The Thatcher government's reservations about greater intervention in Ethiopia and the policy capacity to resist and manage public pressure both show the government's independence from the media. However hostile the Thatcher government was towards aid and development generally, like the US government it also, crucially, perceived this crisis through a Cold War perspective. This was a key reason why there was such resistance to helping a Marxist regime whose policies were part of the problem. This highlights in several ways how inadequate institutional history and media 'effects' research is without a proper historical context. The reason why the Ethiopia story became so significant in the first place depends upon understanding the interplay between theories about how the media work and real events. Media 'effects' cannot be studied meaningfully in an abstract and theoretical vacuum. Thus analyzing the way Western governments reacted, although it can be discussed within a theoretical framework of media effects also depends upon setting this within the historical developments of that time.

This research has revealed how an exemplary news event was produced and what its very long-term impact has been. In doing so it has argued that it can only be understood if it is situated properly in a precise historical framework. Both the news processes that made it possible and, perhaps more significantly, the politics of the moment determined and explain the making of the Ethiopian famine story, its reception and the sensation it caused. This historical sensitivity has been absent from many accounts in the media. Furthermore, examining this news reporting also reveals more general and enduring features of how many parts of Africa and other faraway places have continued to be reported and understood.

The period since 1984 has, to some extent, seen developments and some improvements in the way that crises in faraway places are reported and described. A considerable amount of the media rhetoric in 2005 surrounding the G8 events demonstrated at least some awareness about the far greater complexity of these problems. The narrative was no longer one of natural disasters solved by sending food aid. As a result the consciousness raising was focused at least partly upon political solutions and not just encouraging donations in fun ways and sending the money off to make things better. There is now, at least in some quarters, a more nuanced discussion of the boundaries of a natural disaster and a better understanding of the frequent interaction of social and political factors in complex emergencies. There is also greater awareness of how the victims are portrayed. Some, but not all, relief agencies, in reaction to the Ethiopian famine coverage, have reconsidered the way they use images, although 'media organisations have been slower to react'[6] and there was still criticism that Live 8 in 2005 recycled some of the 20-year-old stereotyped images. The media coverage of the Ethiopian famine was a key moment in the relationship between media and aid agencies. It precipitated some of this reflection and rethinking about images and about how disasters are understood and explained. There is also greater awareness in recent years of the need to let people affected speak for themselves, in their own voices, even if this does not always happen in practice.

Despite good intentions there are still many lapses in the way images are used and the portrayal of faraway victims. High pressure advertising uses convenient short cuts and stereotypes. Fundraising priorities, especially in times of economic uncertainty, still mean that agencies use inappropriate images, but there are attempts again to reinvigorate the messages of the original Red Cross code, and subsequently the Sphere

173

project has been an important development here. The same is true with the way in which news is reported and framed. More recent famine stories have sometimes been nuanced and tried to convey a more complicated picture. The East African famine in 2011 included some reporting of the Somali unrest and the behaviour of groups such as Al-Shabab as a cause of the suffering—rather than the usual 'lack of rains—please send money' narrative. But it is still patchy and there are many occasions where the simple account takes over.

The problem remains today that the consequences of the complicated relations between the media and the aid world, which were already apparent in the coverage of the Ethiopian famine, are rarely brought out into the open. Indeed the reporting of the Ethiopian famine and its successes and failures in itself made the media a more indispensable part of the aid industry. Yet the public is not necessarily aware of the extent to which the media are dependent upon aid agencies for access and stories. Equally important, the public needs to realize the way that aid agencies are reliant upon the media telling a dramatic story, as the key to their fundraising operation and the difficult compromises that this often entails. Better public understanding of this relationship is the only way to move away from what Tony Vaux calls the 'roulette wheel approach to disasters'. He argues that 'if we accept that the purpose of humanitarian agencies is to distribute aid according to where there is the greatest need then the current system is crazy … no way is it distributed according to need, but according to a knee jerk reaction by the western public which is galvanised by the media.'[7] Hilary Benn, as development secretary, argued strongly in support of the establishment of the UN Central Emergency Response Fund[8] to provide resources to alleviate crises that do not necessarily reap the benefit of the media bonanza. In the absence of this kind of regulating mechanism, it is invariably the disasters with a high media profile that are rewarded with funds, at the expense of those that are not reported. If the link between the scale of media coverage of crises in the developing world and the amount of aid is uncoupled, then this is one way of inserting some distance between NGOs and the media. An important effect of that would be a more balanced and sometimes sceptical reporting of agencies, as large and potentially powerful institutions, which warrant proper scrutiny.

It is not just agencies that could be better reported; foreign news altogether, especially about remote and difficult locations, in many instances does not serve audiences and readers well. In this way the continent of Africa is emblematic of those places we don't understand. Specialists can always find detailed information online, but general audiences do not seek this out. On several occasions Western reporting has got things badly wrong. The coverage of Ethiopia is just one example of an enduring problem in the reporting and unfolding of complex and difficult stories. In the years since 1984, the way in which the famine was reported is now seen as inadequate and misconceived, just as many other stories about disasters in faraway places have been similarly misreported or unreported. In many cases, including the Ethiopian famine, the media reports are all about a humanitarian crisis and focus on humanitarian solutions, whilst failing to engage with the underlying complex political issues. And the lessons have still not been learnt. Crises such as the post-election violence in Kenya in 2007/8 were reported, even in the most serious of publications, as 'atavistic' tribal violence, without proper attention to the (very significant) political background.[9]

Meanwhile other crises are so complicated, and unable to measure up to the accepted version of news values, that they are rarely covered at all. This need to grapple with complexity became even more apparent in the post-Cold War new world order. As part of their original analysis of foreign news in 1965 Galtung and Ruge gave a list of twelve policy implications which would improve the level of coverage and understanding. They suggest for example 'more emphasis on build up and background material', urging that 'journalists should be better trained to capture and report on long-term development' and concentrate less on 'events' and that 'a need to counterbalance the image of the world as composed of strings of dramatic events and more emphasis on complex and ambiguous events.'[10] These observations and prescriptions continue to be valid nearly fifty years later, as ways in which our comprehension of foreign news could be enhanced.

It is nevertheless easy to prescribe all the things that the media need to do if they are to give a more rounded and comprehensive account of faraway places, but slightly naive to simply assert what journalists should and ought to do better. Comprehensive and serious detailed coverage is obviously desirable in all kinds of fields, but the question is, how to achieve it? Galtung and Ruge (as many others have done since) exhort journalists to do better, but without a proper analysis of why journalism takes the form that it does, the remedies (if there are any) are likely to be inappropriate. It is more useful instead to examine the nature of the institutional pressures and look at the drivers which might enhance the quality of foreign coverage. One of the most obvious is the vital need for public service institutions as a necessary, if not sufficient, prerequisite for ensuring reliable foreign coverage. The resources and effort required for proper coverage of difficult foreign places have been gradually withdrawn from most non-public service media. The campaigning work of organizations that regularly draw attention to the need for serious foreign news and current affairs coverage has an important role to play in highlighting the ongoing need for allocating resources and commitment to well rounded and serious reporting.

The whole nature of foreign reporting has changed in the past decades. Technological advance and increased outlets have led to more emphasis on the fireman reporter and the 'dish monkey'—tethered to the satellite, providing hourly live updates from remote locations, but without much time or space to follow or even understand the story. Similarly a blizzard of social media and unverifiable citizen journalism may also not be a satisfactory alternative. It has a useful role to play but it cannot replace independent professionals who can interpret and explain.

Meanwhile serious analytical current affairs (as opposed to news) coverage of the developing world has become a disappearing genre, at least on mainstream channels. The paradox is that as communications and the ability to report have improved, our understanding of faraway places has in some ways diminished. There are all kinds of ways that stories can now be reported from faraway—incorporating social media, user generated content supplied by witnesses and crowd sourcing by sites such as Ushahidi which can incorporate a wide range of data. Yet as Nik Gowing observed already some years ago, 'Our capacity to broadcast real time pictures from places like the West Bank and the Middle East is now ahead of our ability to do journalism and to find the answers to the questions why, what, where, how and when?'[11] In some places rather less emphasis on fancy gadgetry and more on editorial understanding would be a good way to allocate resources.

The original Ethiopian famine reporting in October 1984 occurred in the same week as the coverage of the assassination of the Indian prime minister, Mrs Gandhi. The African story was a sudden burst of attention on a part of the world that rarely registered on mainstream domestic media outlets. It was presented as a simple and sudden story about drought, that failed to deal with the underlying causes and complexities. The Indian story, as it was told in the Western media, was part of an incremental and comprehensive pattern of coverage about a developing political crisis between the Congress government and the Sikhs. This contrast between the ways in which Africa and India were reported at that time offers some further suggestions for how foreign reporting might be enhanced. It is hardly possible to repeat the experience of the Raj, but the lesson of a large body of editorial staff who have a long-standing and well developed interest in a foreign place is certainly a good way to enhance foreign coverage. It is interesting that journalists like Mike Wooldridge or Richard Dowden, who have done sensitive and well nuanced reporting from developing countries, were influenced by doing volunteer work in Africa at the start of their careers. Multiple opportunities for journalists and those who normally reside behind their screens in editorial offices to experience and understand remote places would be another way of deepening understanding.

Perhaps the most compelling reason of all for good foreign reporting is that the demarcation between home and abroad is dissolving as never before. It is now a cliché that we live in an interconnected world. Audiences are more than ever international: diasporas live everywhere. In addition to the new problems and opportunities offered by multiethnic audiences, politically domestic and foreign matters intersect in an ever more complicated way. A London commuter worries about safety on the tube, or a Boston marathon-runner worries about safety on the streets, but this is linked to what is going on in Pakistan, Chechnya and elsewhere. There was a brief period after the end of the Cold War when foreign news did not seem to matter.[12] But now foreign news matters more than ever, which is why it should be able to give properly rounded explanations and not appear episodic and meaningless.

Understanding poor places is not a luxury. Not for them and not for us and not for the world. Good reporting, however it develops in a brilliant moment of technological innovation keeps local and international publics acute and holds local governments and business, international agencies and international governments to account.[13]

This research has explored the life history of an iconic news event. It has followed it through from the stories that prompted it, through the processes that created its importance to how the public mood received and responded to it, into its influence on government and NGOs and also into its long-term after-effects. The Ethiopian famine was an exceptional episode in foreign news reporting. It was a key moment in transformations such as that in the relationship between the media and aid agencies, and also in the process of understanding the way in which pure humanitarian action cannot operate in a vacuum. It highlighted the terrible paradox that the sight of faraway suffering might motivate thousands of individuals to offer their help, but that these good intentions are not enough and could even do more harm than good. Today it is not only the effects of the media coverage of the famine which continue to be felt; the (sometimes painful) lessons too are still being learned.

NOTES

INTRODUCTION: ARGUING ABOUT FAMINE

1. Norman Mailer interview with Robert McCrum, *Observer Magazine*, 4 February 2007.
2. BBC Written Archives Centre (WAC), R 9/1, 147/5 BBC Broadcaster's Audience Research Board (BARB) reports.
3. The combined audience for the three daily bulletins on 23 and 24 October 1984 was 17.4 million and 18.1 million respectively. BBC WAC, R 9/1, 147/5 BARB reports.
4. BBC *6 O'Clock News*, 23 October 1984.
5. John Simpson, *Strange Places, Questionable People* (London: Pan Macmillan, 1998), p. 368.
6. Jason Clay, 'Ethiopian Famine and the Relief Agencies' in Bruce Nichols and Gil Loescher (eds), *The Moral Nation: Humanitarianism and US Foreign Policy Today* (Notre Dame, IN: University of Notre Dame Press, 1989), p. 232.
7. Bernard Cohen, *The Press and Foreign Policy* (Princeton University Press, 1963), p. 13.
8. Glenda Cooper, *From their own Correspondent. New Media and the Changes in Disaster Coverage. Lessons to be Learnt* (Oxford: Reuters Institute, 2011).
9. David Rieff, *A Bed for the Night: Humanitarianism in Crisis* (London: Vintage, 2002), p. 38.
10. Frank Dikotter, *Mao's Great Famine* (London: Bloomsbury, 2010).
11. Jonathan Benthall, *Disasters, Relief and the Media*, 2nd edition (Wantage: Sean Kingston, 2010), p. 27.
12. Piers Robinson, *CNN Effect: The Myth of News, Foreign Policy and Intervention* (London: Routledge, 2002), p. 2.

13. Douglas Hurd speech to the Travellers Club, 9 September 1993, reported in *The Times*, 10 September 1993.
14. Report of speech, 'Hurd hits out again at media', *Daily Telegraph*, 10 September 1993.
15. George Kennan, 'Somalia through a glass darkly', *New York Times*, 30 September 1993.
16. Quoted in Ian Smillie and Larry Minear, *The Charity of Nations. Humanitarian Action in a Calculating World* (Bloomfield, CT: Kumarian Press, 2004), p. 177, and also in Danny Schechter, *The More You Watch the Less you Know* (New York: Seven Stories Press, 1997).
17. 'Doctrine of the International Community', speech by Tony Blair to Economic Club of Chicago delivered on 22 April 1999, www.globalpolicy.org/globaliz/politics/blair.htm (accessed 21 February 2007).
18. Philip Seib, *The Global Journalist* (Lanham, MD/Oxford: Rowman and Littlefield, 2002), p. 28.
19. Ibid., p. 27.
20. Amartya Sen, *Poverty and Famines: An Essay on Entitlement and Deprivation* (Oxford University Press, 1981).
21. Jean Drèze and Amartya Sen, *Hunger and Public Action* (Oxford University Press, 1989).
22. David Keen, *The Benefits of Famine* (Princeton University Press, 1994) gives a critique, and there are also criticisms in the Article 19 Report *Starving in Silence*.
23. Onora O'Neill, *Faces of Hunger: An Essay on Poverty, Justice and Development* (London: Allen and Unwin, 1986).
24. Linda Polman, *War Games: The Story of Aid and War in Modern Times* (London: Viking, 2011).
25. Craig Calhoun, 'The Imperative to Reduce Suffering: Charity, Progress and Emergencies in the Field of Humanitarian Action' in Thomas G. Weiss and Michael Barnett (eds), *Humanitarianism in Question: Power, Politics, Ethics* (Ithaca: Cornell University Press, 2008).
26. http://news.bbc.co.uk/1/hi/programmes/from_our_own_correspondent/8548412.stm
27. Rony Brauman "Refugee Camps, Population Transfers and NGOs" in Jonathan Moore (Ed) *Hard Choices: Moral Dilemmas in Humanitarian Intervention* (ICRC, Geneva, published Lanham, Maryland: Rowman and Littlefield, 1998), p. 188.
28. Ibid., p. 177.
29. Glasgow Media Group, *Viewing the World. A Study of British Television Coverage of Developing Countries News Content and Audience Studies* (London: Department for International Development [DFID], 2000). Third World

and Environment Broadcasting Trust (3WE), *Viewing the World: Production Study* (London: DFID, 2000). Caroline Dover and Steven Barnett, *The World on the Box: International Issues in News and Factual Programmes on UK Television 1975–2003*, University of Westminster, Communications and Media Research Institute/report for 3WE Broadcasting Project, 2004. Emily Seymour and Steven Barnett, *Bringing the World to the UK*, University of Westminster, Communications and Media Research Institute/report for 3WE Broadcasting Project, 2006. *Reflecting the Real World? How British TV Portrayed Developing Countries in 2005*, Voluntary Service Overseas (VSO) report, 2006.

30. Nikki van der Gaag and Cathy Nash, *Images of Africa* (Oxfam, 1987).
31. MacBride Report, *Many Voices One World* (UNESCO, 1980).
32. Oliver Boyd-Barrett and Daya Kishan Thussu, *Contra-Flow in Global News* (London: John Libbey, 1992), see for example pp. 19–22 for observations on the inadequate way that developing countries are reported.
33. Robin Palmer, 'Out of Africa, Out of focus', *Times Higher Education Supplement*, 12 December 1986; Mary Anne Fitzgerald, 'The News Hole: Reporting Africa', *Africa Report*, July-August 1989. More recent surveys include Suzanne Franks, 'The Neglect of Africa', *British Journalism Review* Vol. 16 No. 1, 2005 and Charlayne Hunter-Gault, *New News Out of Africa* (Oxford/New York: OUP, 2006).

1. HOW FAMINE CAPTURED THE HEADLINES

1. See for example Glasgow Media Group, *Viewing the World. A Study of British Television Coverage of Developing Countries*, London: DFID, 2000; VSO, *The Live Aid Legacy*, 2002; VSO, *Reflecting the Real World*, 2006. There is more discussion of this absence of foreign news and especially coverage from the developing world in chapter 7.
2. Peter Gill, *A Year in the Death of Africa* (London: Palladine, 1986).
3. Paul Harrison and Robin Palmer, *News out of Africa—Biafra to Band Aid* (London: Hilary Shipman, 1986), chapter 5, pp. 52–67.
4. Brian Phelan, 'Dying for News', *The Listener*, 28 February 1985.
5. BBC WAC, B 420–4–3 *Emergency Appeals Case file*. Script for Famine Appeal by Esther Rantzen 31 October 1983.
6. BBC WAC, B420–4–1 *Emergency Appeals Policy 1965–1985*. Summary of results from radio and television Disasters Emergency Committee (DEC) appeals (1966–83).
7. Interview, Mike Wooldridge, October 2004.
8. Interview, Mike Wooldridge.
9. Interview, Mike Wooldridge.

10. Bob Smith with Salim Amin, *The Man who Moved the World. The Life and Times of Mohamed Amin* (Nairobi: Camerapix Publishers International, 1998), pp. 212–13, quotes from Mo Amin's article for the *Daily Nation* which appeared under the banner headline 'Millions face death in Ethiopia', referring to the drought as 'one of Africa's greatest tragedies in the making'.

11. Interview, Libby Grimshaw, October 2004.

12. Interview, Libby Grimshaw. See also BBC WAC. File 405–3 *Current Affairs Programmes*, letter from Martin Bax, acting director of Christian Aid, to Alan Protheroe, assistant director general, 30 November 1984, reflecting on the way television news reported famine, and interview with Wendy Riches of Save the Children, quoted in Phelan, 'Dying for News'.

13. William Shawcross, *The Quality of Mercy* (London: Fontana paperback edition, 1985), p. 432.

14. Tony Vaux, 'The Ethiopia Famine 1984—Oxfam's Early Involvement', internal report, Oxfam, February 1985, and Robert Dodd, 'Oxfam's Response to Disasters in Ethiopia and the Sudan 1984–5', internal Oxfam report, Sept. 1986.

15. See for example Gill, *A Year in the Death of Africa*, or Graham Hancock, *Ethiopia: The Challenge of Hunger* (London: Gollancz, 1985) or Alexander Posten, 'The Gentle War: Famine Relief, politics and Privatization in Ethiopia, 1983–1986' in *Diplomatic History* Vol. 36 No. 2, 2012, pp. 399–425.

16. The National Archives (hereafter TNA; formerly the Public Record Office), Overseas Development Agency (ODA) 53/2, letter from Michael Smith, British Embassy, Addis Ababa, 8 December 1982.

17. TNA, ODA 53/3, telegram to FCO from Brian Barder, UK ambassador to Ethiopia, 25 March 1983.

18. TNA, ODA 53/6, report by Barder on the 'September Events' dated 5 October 1984.

19. FCO confidential paper 'The Ethiopian Famine: Policy Problems', 29 October 1984, obtained under the Freedom of Information Act (FOI).

20. TNA, ODA 53/5, memo from Malcolm Rifkind to Sir Geoffrey Howe, 8 October 1984.

21. See the following chapter for more detailed discussion of government response to the famine in the wake of extensive media coverage.

22. Interview, Mike Wooldridge.

23. Dawit Wolde Giorgis, *Red Tears: War, Famine and Revolution in Ethiopia* (Trenton, New Jersey: Red Sea Press, 1989).

24. Ibid., p. 141.

25. Mengistu fled to Zimbabwe in 1991, prior to the overthrow of his regime.

26. Giorgis, *Red Tears*, p. 136.

27. Shawcross, *The Quality of Mercy*, p. 432.
28. *Evil Days: Thirty Years of War and Famine in Ethiopia*, New York: Africa Watch Report, Human Rights Watch, 1991, p. i.
29. TNA, OD 53/4, telegram from Brian Barder to FCO, 30 November 1983. Reporting on a donors' meeting chaired by the United Nations Disaster Relief Organization (UNDRO), Barder (the UK ambassador to Ethiopia) reports on severe doubts cast on the logistical abilities of the Ethiopian Relief and Rehabilitation Commission to handle large quantities of aid, and in particular the capacity of the port at Assab.
30. Vaux, 'The Ethiopia Famine'.
31. Earthscan (environmental NGO), quoted in Gill, *A Year in the Death of Africa*, p. 94.
32. Christopher Bosso, 'Setting the Agenda: Mass Media and the Discovery of the Famine in Ethiopia' in Michael Margolis and Gary Mauser (eds), *Manipulating Public Opinion* (Belmont, California: Brooks/Cole Publishing Company, 1989), p. 162.
33. Peter Cutler, 'The Development of the 1983–85 Famine in Northern Ethiopia' (University of London, unpublished PhD thesis, 1988), p. 375.
34. Paul Harrison and Robin Palmer, *News out of Africa—Biafra to Band Aid* (London: Hilary Shipman, 1986), pp. 105–6.
35. See chapter 4 for a more detailed analysis of the Disasters Emergency Committee.
36. BBC WAC, B420–4–1 *Emergency Appeals—Policy 1965–85*, memo on 'Emergency Appeal for African Famine Relief' from Towyn Mason, assistant head of secretariat, to the secretary on 2 July 1984.
37. Interview, Michael Buerk, November 2004.
38. Interview, Michael Buerk.
39. Michael Buerk, *The Road Taken* (London: Hutchinson, 2004), p. 270.
40. Ibid., pp. 271–4.
41. BBC WAC, B 420–4–3 *Emergency Appeals Case file*. Script for DEC TV Famine Appeal broadcast on BBC 19 July 1984 by Frank Bough.
42. BBC WAC, B 420–4–1 *Emergency Appeals Policy 1965–85*, memo from Dennis Mann, appeals secretary to the BBC secretary, 1 August 1984.
43. Quoted in Mary Kay Magistad, 'The Ethiopian Bandwagon: The Relationship between News Media Coverage and British Foreign Policy towards the 1984–5 Ethiopian Famine' (unpublished Master's thesis, University of Sussex, 1985).
44. Giorgis, *Red Tears*, p. 158.
45. Vaux, 'The Ethiopia Famine'.
46. Interview with Jonathan Dimbleby in *Tourists of the Revolution*, BBC2, January 2000.

47. Harrison and Palmer, *News out of Africa*, p. 66.

48. In the *Daily Mail* report 'Economic facts which face the fund raisers' Andrew Alexander claimed it was $100 million (16 September 1985). However, UK government sources were quoting a figure of $250 million, which was used in the briefing for Timothy Raison's broadcast on 24 October 1984. Note from Denis Osborne, obtained under FOI.

49. Interview, Mike Wooldridge.

50. BBC WAC, B 420–4–3 *Emergency Appeals Case File*. Letter from Pam Pouncey, DEC secretary, to Dennis Mann, BBC appeals secretary, 4 September 1984.

51. Vaux, 'The Ethiopia Famine'.

52. BBC WAC, *Emergency Appeals case file* B 420–4–3, minutes of DEC meeting 25 March 1983.

53. Vaux, 'The Ethiopia Famine'.

54. Dodd, 'Oxfam's Response to Disasters'.

55. 'Ethiopia: The Green Famine in Wolayita and Kambat/Haydiya. The Report of a Visit by Marcus Thompson and Pat Diskett', internal Oxfam report, August 1984.

56. *TV Eye* film made by Peter Gill, *Bitter Harvest*, transmitted by Thames 25 October 1984.

57. Smith with Amin, *The Man Who Moved The World*, pp. 213–15.

58. Ibid., pp. 217–18.

59. Interview, Michael Buerk.

60. Buerk, *The Road Taken*, p. 293.

61. Interview, Chris Cramer, March 2006.

62. Interview, Michael Buerk.

63. BBC WAC, *Television Programme As Broadcast*, BBC1 *6 O'Clock News*, 23 October 1984.

64. BBC WAC, T67/370/1 *Six O'Clock News*, press Statement 8 August 1984.

65. Interview, Ron Neil, November 2005.

66. BBC WAC, T67/370/1, *Six O'Clock News*. Memo from Andrew Taussig, chief assistant, current affairs television to Chris Capron, head of current affairs, 17 May 1984.

67. There had been an ongoing debate in the BBC about the format of early evening scheduling on BBC1 since the late 1970s. See for example BBC WAC, T67/370/1, *Six O'Clock News*, or Anthony McNicholas, 'Wrenching the Machine around: EastEnders, the BBC and Institutional Change,' *Media Culture and Society* Vol. 26 (4), pp. 491–512.

68. Jackie Harrison, *Terrestrial TV News in Britain* (Manchester University Press, 2000), p. 169. (She is referring to John Birt who joined the BBC in 1987 as deputy director general and eventually director general. He imple-

mented changes throughout the news and current affairs departments with an emphasis on programmes which gave more in-depth explanation.)

69. Interview, Ron Neil.
70. BBC WAC. For BBC Audience figures see R 9/1, 147/5, *TV Audience Figures BARB*. Both *Six O'Clock News* and *Nine O'Clock News* audiences at this time were usually between 7.2 and 8.6 million.
71. Interviews with Ron Neil and Michael Buerk.
72. BBC WAC BBC Television *Programme as Broadcast*, BBC1, 24 October 1984.
73. Interview with Paddy Coulter 2004. See also article in *Morning Star*, 25 October 1984, 'Strike lifted for famine film to go ahead.'
74. Gill, *A Year in the Death of Africa*, p. 22.
75. Giorgis, *Red Tears*, p. 188.
76. See for example Johan Galtung and Mari Holmboe Ruge, 'The Structure of Foreign News', *Journal of International Peace Research*, 1965, pp. 64–90 for a classic summary of the drivers behind the values in foreign news coverage. The criteria were refined and updated by Tony Harcup and Deirdre O'Neill, 'What is News? Galtung and Ruge Revisited,' *Journalism Studies* Vol. 2 No. 2, 2001, pp. 261–80. Also Herbert Gans, *Deciding What's News* (Evanston, IL: Northwestern University Press, 2004); Michael Schudson, *The Sociology of News* (New York: Norton2003).
77. Gorm Rye Olsen, Nils Carstensen and Kristian Hoyen, 'Humanitarian Crises: Testing the CNN Effect', *Forced Migration Review* No. 16, January 2003.
78. Stijn Joye, 'The Hierarchy of Global Suffering: A Critical Discourse Analysis of Television News Reporting on Foreign Natural Disasters', *Journal of International Communication* Vol. 15, No. 2, 2009.
79. Harrison and Palmer, *News out of Africa*, pp. 112–14 discusses the content of *Bitter Harvest*, the *TV Eye* programme for Thames Television broadcast on 25 October 1984.
80. *Bitter Harvest*, ITV/Thames TV.
81. Interview, Ron Neil.
82. Buerk, *The Road Taken*, p. 304 describes the remarkable number of national and international awards which the famine item won.
83. Penny Kane, *Famine in China* (London: Macmillan, 1988) and Frank Dikotter, *Mao's Great Famine* (London: Bloomsbury, 2010).
84. Jonathan Benthall, *Disasters, Relief and the Media*, 2nd edition (Wantage: Sean Kingston, 2010). p. 12.
85. *International Herald Tribune*, 28 June 1996, 'Bringing humanitarian news into Prime Time.'
86. Interview, Ron Neil.

87. Interview, Brian Hanrahan, October 2004.
88. Interview, Nik Gowing, June 2006.
89. Michael Schudson, *The Sociology of News* (New York: Norton, 2003), pp. 48–9 discusses why the media were slow to cover the AIDS epidemic, concluding that 'aids is a slow moving disaster not a dramatic event of flood, fire or earthquake suddenness.'
90. Interview, Peter Gill, November 2004.
91. Interview, Ron Neil.
92. Interview, Chris Cramer, March 2006.
93. Harrison and Palmer, *News out of Africa*.
94. In 1973 Jonathan Dimbleby made his film for ITV, so that ITN had exclusive news access to the pictures.
95. Interview, Chris Cramer, March 2006.
96. Shudson, *The Sociology of News* (New York: Norton, 2003), p. 6.
97. For a more detailed analysis of the notion of sudden disasters see chapter 4.
98. Lloyd Timberlake, *Natural Disasters. Acts of God or Acts of Man?* Earthscan Press Briefing Document no. 39, London 1984, p. 95.
99. Harrison, *Terrestrial TV News in Britain* (Manchester University Press, 2000), p. 151.
100. Evan Davis (BBC Economics editor), 'Can the Media do Complexity?' Talk to Social Market Foundation, 13 July 2004.
101. According to BARB figures the 6 o'clock news figures averaged between 7 and 8 million in 1984 and the 9 o'clock news was between 7.5 and 9 million. This compares with 2007 figures for both bulletins of around 4 million. BBC WAC, R 9/1, 147/5 TV, audience reports. BBC Gateway http://acr/gateway/bbc/co.uk Audiences Online.
102. Interview, Michael Buerk.
103. Claire Phillips, 'Has there been a Discernible Change in the Way that Issues of Food Insecurity/Famine in Ethiopia have been Portrayed by CAFOD over the Last Twenty Years?' (unpublished Master's dissertation, University of London, 2003).
104. Interview with Ron Neil; Greg Philo, 'From Buerk to Band Aid' in John Eldridge (ed.), *Getting the Message: News, Truth and Power* (London: Routledge, 1993) gives a good account of the immediate impact of the news coverage on the aid agencies.
105. BBC WAC television programme as broadcast *Six O'Clock News*, 23 October 1984.
106. The PBS film *Faces in a Famine* by Robert Lieberman, shown on TV in the US in 1985, describes how the famine attracted assorted celebrities and voyeurs to Ethiopia over this period.
107. Schudson, *The Sociology of News* (New York: Norton, 2003), p. 180.

2. GLOBAL STORY: NATIONAL RESPONSE

1. TNA, OD 53/11, transcript of Giorgis's speech to donor conference, 12 December 1984.
2. Philip Seib, *The Global Journalist* (New York/Oxford: Rowman and Littlefield, 2002), p. 121.
3. Stephen Garrett, *Doing Good and Doing Well* (Westport, CT: Praeger, 1999), p. 85.
4. Michael Duffield, *Global Governance and the New Wars* (London: Zed Books, 2001), p. 76.
5. Mary Kay Magistad, 'The Ethiopian Bandwagon: The Relationship between News Media Coverage and British Foreign Policy towards the 1984–5 Ethiopian Famine' (Unpublished Master's thesis, University of Sussex, 1985).
6. Paul Harrison and Robin Palmer, *News out of Africa—Biafra to Band Aid* (London: Hilary Shipman, 1986), p. 101.
7. BBC WAC, B405–3 *Current Affairs Programmes*: letter from Fred O'Donovan to Stuart Young, 9 November 1984.
8. Interview, Mike Wooldridge.
9. BBC WAC, Radio 4 programme as broadcast, 22 October 1984.
10. BBC WAC, file B 405–3, *Current Affairs Programmes*, 'Action Ethiopia: The Television Pictures that Shocked the World', Visnews publication on coverage of Ethiopia, 3 December 1984.
11. Interview, Chris Cramer, March 2006.
12. Harrison and Palmer, *News out of Africa*, p. 123.
13. Interview, Chris Cramer, March 2006. He is referring to the scoop by Martin Bashir, interviewing Princess Diana on her marriage breakup in 1995.
14. BBC WAC, news and current affairs weekly meeting 20 November 1984, minute 454.
15. Harrison and Palmer, *News out of Africa*, p. 58.
16. Granada TV Programme *What the Papers Say*, 13 July 1968, quoted in Harrison and Palmer, *News out of Africa*, p. 32.
17. Harrison and Palmer, *News out of Africa*, p. 27.
18. Ondine Barrow and Michael Jenkins, 'Introduction: The Charitable Impulse' in Ondine Barrow and Michael Jenkins (eds), *The Charitable Impulse: NGOs and Development in East and North-East Africa* (Oxford: James Currey, 2001), p. 15.
19. See for example Barrow and Jenkins, *The Charitable Impulse*, or Jonathan Benthall, *Disasters, Relief and the Media* 2nd edition (Wantage: Sean Kingston, 2010), pp. 92–108, or Channel 4, 'The Hunger Business', 2000.
20. Harrison and Palmer, *News out of Africa*, p. 28.
21. Interview with John Wilkinson, formerly BBC director of public affairs, Witness Seminar 23 February 2004.

22. See chapter 5.
23. See Tim Allen and David Styan, 'A Right to Interfere? Bernard Kouchner and the New Humanitarianism', *Journal of International Development* Vol. 12, 2000, pp. 825–42 for an interesting background account to this.
24. Benthall, *Disasters, Relief and the Media*, p. 127.
25. As quoted in Fred Cate, 'The CNN Effect is far from Clear-cut', *Humanitarian Affairs Review*, Summer 2002, p. 5.
26. Colin Seymour-Ure, *The Political Impact of Mass Media* (London: Constable, 1974), p. 37.
27. Piers Robinson, *CNN Effect: The Myth of News, Foreign Policy and Intervention* (London: Routledge, 2002), p. 2.
28. Ibid., pp. 28–9. Also table on p. 122.
29. *Evil Days: Thirty Years of War and Famine in Ethiopia*, New York: Africa Watch Report, Human Rights Watch, 1991, p. 178.
30. Christopher Bosso, 'Setting the Agenda: Mass Media and the Discovery of Famine in Ethiopia' in Michael Margolis and Gary Mauser (eds), *Manipulating Public Opinion* (Belmont, California: Brooks/Cole Publishing Co., 1989), pp. 153–74.
31. This refers to papers released through Freedom of Information requests and also those available in The National Archives under OD 53.
32. Paper headed 'The Drought in Africa' prepared for Timothy Raison, minister for overseas development, 26 July 1984. Obtained under FOI.
33. Statement to House of Commons by Timothy Raison, ODA minister, 22 July 1985.
34. See also letters and memos from Malcolm Rifkind quoted in chapter 1.
35. Interview, Sir Malcolm Rifkind, June 2007.
36. There are many examples of briefings which report on the famine; for example, a telegram from the Addis Ababa embassy on 18 September 1984 refers to a briefing that 'Ethiopia is headed for disaster'. Obtained under FOI.
37. See reference to Cutler in previous chapter.
38. Peter Cutler, 'Famine Forecasting: Prices and Peasant Behaviour in Northern Ethiopia', *Disasters* Vol. 8 No. 1, 1984, pp. 48–56.
39. Memo from Tim Raison's private secretary to ODA officials, 28 December 1984. Obtained under FOI.
40. Memo from Malcolm Rifkind headed 'Famine in Africa', 17 October 1984. Obtained under FOI.
41. Feelings ran so high that MacKay even used a four letter obscenity in his oral evidence. He was asked about the government response to information about the famine and answered that 'They did f**k all.' Although the official record was changed to read 'Yes Sir.' MacKay was warned before doing a live BBC interview on the famine later that day that unless he gave an

undertaking not to use obscenities the interview would be cancelled. *Starving in Silence: a report on famine and censorship,* Article 19 Report, 1990.

42. *Famine in Africa, Foreign Affairs Select Committee Report with Proceedings, Evidence and Appendices.* 1984/5 HC 56, HMSO.
43. TNA, OD 53/5, minutes of meeting between Save the Children and ODA officials, 5 October 1984.
44. ODA Press Release 'British Government's Response to Famine in Ethiopia', 7 November 1984.
45. TNA, OD 53/6, memo from Barder entitled 'September Events' which included a report on the tenth anniversary celebrations of the Ethiopian regime, 5 October 1984.
46. Telegram from David Beaumont in Addis Ababa embassy to FCO, 10 October 1984. Obtained under FOI.
47. 'Ethiopia: Future Policy', 17 October 1984, memo from J. Buist. Obtained under FOI.
48. Telegram sent from British Embassy headed 'Official visits to view Ethiopian relief effort', 28 December 1984. Obtained under FOI.
49. Mary Kay Magistad, 'The Ethiopian Bandwagon: The Relationship between News Media Coverage and British Foreign Policy towards the 1984–5 Ethiopian Famine' (Unpublished Master's thesis, University of Sussex, 1985).
50. *Hansard* 22 November 1984, column 418.
51. TNA, OD 53/7, memo from Denis Osborne to Sir Crispin Tickell, 29 October 1984.
52. TNA, OD 53/8, memo from Denis Osborne to ODA department, 2 November 1984.
53. TNA, OD 53/8, minute to Ethiopian Drought Group by Denis Osborne, 3 November 1984.
54. TNA, OD 53/8, note from Osborne to Buist updating him after Buist's return from Ethiopia, 3 November 1984.
55. Ethiopian Drought: Situation report 6 November 1984. Obtained under FOI.
56. TNA, OD 53/8, note from Osborne to Buist updating him after Buist's return from Ethiopia, 3 November 1984.
57. Letter from Charles Powell to FCO headed 'Ethiopia: Famine Relief', 29 October 1984. Obtained under FOI.
58. Peter Gill, *A Year in the Death of Africa* (London: Palladine, 1986), p. 164.
59. BBC2 TV documentary *This World, Ethiopia—A Journey with Michael Buerk,* 11 January 2004.
60. Frederick Cuny, 'Politics and Famine Relief' in Bruce Nichols and Gil Loescher (eds), *The Moral Nation: Humanitarianism and US Foreign Policy Today* (Notre Dame, IN: University of Notre Dame Press, 1989), p. 281.

61. Interview, Timothy Raison, November 2004.
62. In her book *Statecraft* (London: HarperCollins, 2002) Mrs Thatcher made very clear her hostility to foreign aid as a means of assisting development in poor countries: pp. 442–4.
63. TNA, OD 53/3, transcript of news interview given by the prime minister to John Simpson.
64. Report on Anglo-German talks 14 November 1984 held in Bonn. Obtained under FOI.
65. Confidential briefing note for a House of Commons appearance by Tim Raison. Undated but appears to be late October 1984. Obtained under FOI.
66. TNA, OD 53/9, telegram from UK Moscow embassy, 16 November 1984.
67. Confidential telegram from UK embassy in Addis Ababa, 'Ethiopia Relief—Aid from Eastern Europe'. Sent from the ambassador, Brian Barder to Mr Wenban-Smith 29 October 1984. Obtained under FOI.
68. Robert Maxwell, owner of the *Daily Mirror*, had flown to Ethiopia on a '*Mirror* mercy mission' with aid donated by the paper's readers. His visit was very controversial and much criticized. See for example Buerk, *The Road Taken*, pp. 298–9.
69. TNA, OD 53/8, telegram from UK embassy in Ethiopia, 3 November 1984.
70. Telegram from UK embassy in Addis Ababa 7 November 1984. Obtained under FOI.
71. Telegram from UK embassy in Addis Ababa on 6 November 1984. Obtained under FOI.
72. Hugo Young, *One of Us* (London: Macmillan, 1989), p. 173.
73. John Campbell, *Margaret Thatcher, vol. 2: The Iron Lady* (London: Jonathan Cape, 2003), p. 339.
74. 'The Ethiopian Famine: Policy Problems' Confidential FCO paper prepared for ministerial meeting on 29 October 1984. Obtained under FOI from Cabinet Office.
75. Campbell, *Margaret Thatcher*, p. 340.
76. *Observer*, 18 November 1984.
77. Magistad, 'The Ethiopian Bandwagon', chapter 1, 'Relations between the News Media and the Government in the UK.'
78. Oxfam reports by Tony Vaux and Robert Dodds, cited in chapter 1.
79. Barrow and Jenkins, *The Charitable Impulse: NGOs and Development*, Introduction, p. 18.
80. Ibid. Quoting from M. Adams and M. Bradbury, 'Conflict and Development: organisations adaptations in conflict situations', Oxfam Discussion Paper 4 (Oxford: Oxfam, 1995), p. 18.

81. Ibid. Quoting from John Eriksson, *The International Response to Conflict and Genocide: Lessons from the Rwanda Experience* (Copenhagen: Steering Committee of the Joint Evaluation of Emergency Assistance to Rwanda), p. 18.

82. Kissinger quoted in Randolph C. Kent, *Anatomy of Disaster Relief* (London: Pinter, 1987) p. 81.

83. Alex de Waal, *Famine Crimes* (Oxford: James Currey, 1997), p. 123.

84. See *The Story of Band Aid*, Channel 4 December 2004, where the archive news footage is shown of Geldof confronting Mrs Thatcher and Geldof is then interviewed about the incident. See also Bob Geldof with Paul Vallely, *Is that It?* (London: Sidgwick and Jackson, 1986), pp. 314–15.

85. Peter Cutler, 'The Development of the 1983–85 Famine in Northern Ethiopia' (Unpublished PhD thesis, University of London, 1988), p. 400.

86. Letter from Charles Powell (foreign affairs adviser to PM) to C.R. Budd at Foreign Office, 29 October 1984. Obtained under FOI.

87. In fact, the Select Committee inquiry had been announced in July 1984 (when the first media coverage had taken place). However, the coverage in October gave it a new impetus and the hearings were held principally in November 1984.

88. *Famine in Africa, Foreign Affairs Select Committee Report*, HMSO.

89. *Famine in Africa. Government Observations on the Second Report from the Foreign Affairs Select Committee*, 1984/5 Cmnd. 9566, HMSO.

90. TNA, OD 53/7, letter, 2 November 1984.

91. TNA, OD 53/10, memo on 'Further Aid' from Mr Buist to minister, 27 November 1984.

92. Robert Kilroy-Silk and Nigel Spearing were amongst those MPs who pursued this point in Parliamentary Questions on 26 October 1984 and 23 November 1984.

93. TNA, OD 53/11, letter from Timothy Raison, ODA minister, to Sir Anthony Kershaw, chairman of the Foreign Affairs Select Committee 10 December 1984 (about an announcement made by Foreign Secretary Sir Geoffrey Howe on 23 November 1984).

94. *Observer*, 7 April 1985.

95. Parliamentary Question from Stuart Randall, MP, to Sir Geoffrey Howe, November 1984.

96. Confidential note to ministers from Mr Wenban-Smith, head of East Africa Department FCO, undated. Obtained under FOI.

97. TNA, OD 53/11, confidential memo from J. Buist to minister and permanent secretary, 5 December 1984.

98. TNA, OD 53/10, 'Ethiopia and Longer Term Aid', background briefing from J. Buist to minister, 21 November 1984.

99. Preston King, *An African Winter* (London: Penguin, 1986), p. 65.
100. Dawit Wolde Giorgis, *Red Tears: War Famine and Revolution in Ethiopia* (Trenton, New Jersey: Red Sea Press, 1989), p. 193.
101. TNA, OD 53/7, minute of meeting between Timothy Raison, Lord Trefgarne and Dawit Wolde Giorgis, 27 October 1984.
102. Giorgis, *Red Tears*, p. 192.
103. TNA, OD 53/11, briefing to minister for supplementary questions in debate on motion for the Christmas Adjournment, December 1984.
104. Giorgis, *Red Tears*, p. 195.
105. TNA, OD 53/8, note from Mr Budd, PS to foreign secretary, to Charles Powell, 2 November 1984.
106. See quote above from Tim Eggar; also interviews with Timothy Raison and Brian Barder. November 2004, made this point.
107. This is now quite a well recognized pattern and discussed in several places, for example Nicholas Wheeler, *Saving Strangers: Humanitarian Intervention in International Society* (Oxford University Press, 2000), p. 300.
108. Interview, Brian Barder, November 2004.
109. Telegram from Brian Barder, 13 December 1984. Obtained under FOI.
110. TNA, OD 53/11, telegram from Brian Barder, 14 December 1984.
111. 'Ethiopian Famine: Were early warnings Ignored?' Memo to Mr Wenban Smith, head of East Africa Department FCO from African Section of Research Department, 17 December 1984. Obtained under FOI.
112. Interview, Timothy Raison.
113. TNA, OD 53/11, briefing notes for Adjournment debate December 1984. Also undated briefing notes obtained under FOI for questioning in Parliament on Ethiopia.
114. Transcript of TVAM interview with Timothy Raison and Jonathan Dimbleby, 31 October 1984.
115. Interview, Timothy Raison.

3. A REVOLUTION IN GIVING

1. Interview in *Boston Globe*, 28 April 1985. Quoted in Christopher Bosso, 'Setting the Agenda: Mass Media and Discovery of Famine in Ethiopia' in Michael Margolis and Gary Mauser (eds), *Manipulating Public Opinion* (Belmont, California: Brooks/Cole Publishing Co., 1989), p. 168.
2. Interview, Michael Buerk.
3. Since then the Elton John song 'Candle in the Wind', written for the funeral of Princess Diana in 1997, has outsold Band Aid—but 'Do they Know it's Christmas?' continues to sell in various different versions. http://www.bobgeldof.info/Charity/bandaid.html (accessed 12/02/07).

4. Channel 4 documentary, *The Band Aid Story*, December 2004.
5. Michael Grade, *It Seemed Like a Good Idea at the Time* (London: Macmillan, 1999). pp. 196–7.
6. Mark Duffield, *War and Famine in Africa* (Oxfam Research Paper no. 5, 1991), p. 76.
7. Peter Burnell, *Charity, Politics and the Third World* (London: Harvester Wheatsheaf, 1991), p. 12.
8. Nikki van der Gaag and Cathy Nash, *Images of Africa*, Oxfam report, 1987.
9. Interview with Trevor Dann in 'The Inside Story of the Day Rock Changed,' *Word*, November 2004.
10. Interview, Mike Appleton, November 2004.
11. Grade, *It Seemed Like a Good Idea at the Time*, p. 197.
12. Burnell, *Charity, Politics and the Third World*, pp. 203–4. By the time Band Aid was wound up in 1987 it had raised a total of £174 million. Duffield, *War and Famine in Africa*, p. 76.
13. BBC WAC files. Minutes of TV Weekly Programme Review, 17 July 1985.
14. Daniel Dayan and Elihu Katz, *Media Events* (Cambridge, Mass. and London: Harvard University Press, 1992), p. 1.
15. Ibid., p. 21.
16. BBC WAC file on Outside Broadcasts B 220–002, 1973–89. The director of programmes (TV) reported to the board of management on 22 July 1985 that UK TV viewing figures for the Live Aid concert had been over 30 million. This is a reach measure throughout the day, not the number watching at a particular time. A BBC Press release claimed an estimated one and half billion viewers in over 100 countries and since then estimates have risen to two billion. See Joe Moran, *Armchair Nation* (London: Profile Books, 2013). But international TV viewing figures are notoriously unreliable. See Graham Mytton writing as head of International Broadcasting and Audience Research, BBC World Service, 'A Billion Viewers Can't be Right', *Intermedia*, Vol. 19 No. 3, May-June 1991.
17. *Sunday Times*, 14 June 1985.
18. Greg Philo, 'From Buerk to Band Aid' in John Eldridge (ed.), *Getting the Message: News, Truth and Power* (London: Routledge, 1993), p. 122.
19. BBC WAC B420–4–3 *Emergency Appeal Case File*. The appeal was officially closed in February 1985, having received £9.5 million. However, a further £5.2 million was donated through the DEC for Ethiopia over the next three months. Writing to the BBC appeals secretary, Denis Mann, the DEC secretary, Pam Pouncy, said that 'the public's response to our fundraising efforts has surpassed all expectations' (17 April 1985). (No previous DEC appeal had ever raised more than £6 million.)
20. Burnell, *Charity, Politics and the Third World*, p. 203.

21. Dayan and Katz, *Media Events*, p. 21.
22. Cathy Walker and Cathy Pharaoh, *A Lot of Give: Trends for Charitable Giving in the Twenty first Century* (West Malling: Charities Aid Foundation, 2002), p. 107.
23. Mark Ellen, 'The Longest Day', *Word*, November 2004. Ellen had been one of the presenters of Live Aid.
24. *From Seesaw to Wagon Wheel. Safeguarding Impartiality in the 21st Century*, BBC report published June 2007. Available on http://www.bbc.co.uk/bbctrust/research/impartiality.html (accessed 19 June 2007).
25. 'Not so much a programme more a green way of life', *Ariel*, 11 September 2007.
26. BBC WAC, Central Appeals Advisory Committee (CAAC) Agenda and Papers D34–4–6, paper on 'Broadcast Appeals: Policy and Research Issues' presented 25 September 1986.
27. For an explanation of the broadcasting of emergency appeals which operate under a different procedure see the following chapter.
28. BBC WAC, CAAC report.
29. Bob Geldof with Paul Vallely, *Is that It?* (London: Penguin, 1986), p. 392.
30. BBC *Annual Report and Handbook 1987*, p. 108.
31. BBC WAC, R2/83/18. Letter from Lady Marre to Joel Barnett, 6 October 1986.
32. BBC *Annual Report 1987*, p. 108.
33. BBC WAC, R78/2,633/1, 'Report on Children in Need Appeal' by Geoff Buck and John Wilkinson, G 180/86.
34. Martin Jacques and Stuart Hall, 'People Aid—A New Politics Sweeps the Land' in Stuart Hall, *The Hard Road to Renewal* (London: Verso, 1988), p. 253 (originally published in *Marxism Today*, July 1986).
35. Interview with Midge Ure, *Observer Music Monthly*, 'Rocking the World', October 2004.
36. Jonathan Benthall, *Disasters, Relief and the Media*, 2nd edition (Wantage: Sean Kingston, 2010), p. 86.
37. Paul Du Noyer, 'Deathknell for Rebellion', *Word*, November 2004.
38. Interview, Paddy Coulter, October 2004.
39. Tanja Müller, '"The Ethiopian Famine" Revisited: Band Aid and the Antipolitics of Celebrity Humanitarian Action,' *Disasters* Vol. 37 No. 1, 2013, pp. 61–79.
40. *Fran in Sudan* was made by Blakeway Productions and shown on ITV in 2005.
41. *Time* Magazine, 26 December 2005, 'The Year of Charitainment.'
42. After Live 8 in 2005 HMV produced a Live 8 Album Boost Chart: http://news.bbc.co.uk/1/hi/entertainment/4651309.stm (accessed 5 March 2007).

43. *Bob Geldof: Saint or Singer*, BBC1, 24 April 2004.
44. Jacques and Hall, 'People Aid—A New Politics Sweeps the Land', pp. 251–9.
45. Robert Allen, 'Bob's Not your Uncle', *Capital and Class* 1986: 30, pp. 31–7.
46. van de Gaag and Nash, *Images of Africa*.
47. Henrietta Lidichi, 'All in the Choosing Eye: Charity, Representation and the Developing World' (Unpublished PhD thesis, Open University, 1993), p. 114.
48. Robert Allen, 'Bob's Not your Uncle'.
49. Geldof quoted in *Guardian*, 24 May 1986.
50. Ian Smillie, *The Alms Bazaar*, (London: ITP, 1995), p. 144.
51. Geldof, for example, sat on the Commission for Africa in 2004/5 (becoming involved in discussions such as re-negotiating debt relief, improving governance within African states and changing the terms of trade with developing countries).
52. The charity One World Action specifically tried to engage with the political dimension of development, assisting projects that involved participation and widening democracy, usually by helping so-called Southern NGOs that promoted these values.
53. Glenys Kinnock speech as reported in *Guardian*, 9 May 1986.
54. Charles Elliott, *Comfortable Compassion? Poverty, Power and the Church* (London: Hodder and Stoughton, 1987), pp. 10–11.
55. Burnell, *Charity, Politics and the Third World*, p. 11.
56. For further discussion of changes within charities see chapter 6.

4. MISUNDERSTANDING THE FAMINE: TELLING THE STORY WRONG

1. Alex de Waal, *Famine Crimes*, (Oxford: James Currey, 1997), p. 132.
2. Irene Nemirovsky, *Suite Française* (London: Chatto and Windus, 2006), pp. 167–8.
3. Evan Davis (BBC Economics Editor), 'Can the Media do Complexity?' Talk to Social Market Foundation, 13 July 2004.
4. David Keen, *The Benefits of Famine* (Princeton University Press, 1994), p. 3.
5. Amartya Sen, *Poverty and Famines. An Essay on Entitlement and Deprivation* (Oxford University Press, 1981).
6. Tony Vaux, *The Ethiopian Famine 1984—Oxfam's Early Involvement*, report for Oxfam 1985.
7. See account of Dimbleby's film and its impact on Ethiopian politics in chapter 1.
8. Elizabeth Anderson, 'Sex, Ethics and Democracy' in Bina Agarwal (ed.),

Amartya Sen's Work and Ideas. A Gender Perspective (London: Routledge, 2005), p. 249.

9. BBC WAC, 10151372 India—BBC & media portrayal 30/04/73, memo from Noel Harvey, BBC Head of Liaison. BBC WAC, NCA 4/5/73 minute 302 and NCA 1/6/73 minute 372.

10. Frank Dikotter, *Mao's Great Famine* (London: Bloomsbury, 2010).

11. *Starving in Silence*, Article 19 Report, 1990.

12. 'History and the construction of national identity in China', Ben Pimlott memorial lecture given by Isabel Hilton at Institute for Historical Research, 21 May 2007.

13. Penny Kane, *Famine in China* (London: Macmillan, 1988).

14. *Starving in Silence*, 1990.

15. Stephan Haggard and Marcus Noland, *Famine in North Korea: Markets, Aid and Reform* (New York: Columbia University Press, 2007).

16. Mengistu and his family fled to Zimbabwe and he is even supposed to have had some influence on the policies of repression under Robert Mugabe. For an account of his life see www.bbc.co.uk/1/hi/world/africa/6171927.htm.

17. R.W. Johnson, 'In Time of Famine', *London Review of Books*, 22 February 2007; see also Winston Mano (ed.), 'The Media and Zimbabwe', Westminster Papers in Communication Special Issue November 2005, CAMRI, University of Westminster.

18. Jean Drèze and Amartya Sen, *Hunger and Public Action* (Oxford University Press, 1989).

19. Ibid., p. 264.

20. Ibid., p. 46.

21. *Famine: A Man Made Disaster?* Report for the Independent Commission on International Humanitarian Issues (London: Pan Books, 1985), p. 25.

22. Onora O'Neill, *Faces of Hunger: An Essay on Poverty, Justice and Development* (London: Allen and Unwin, 1986), p. 2.

23. Lloyd Timberlake, *Natural Disasters: Acts of God or Acts of Man?* Earthscan Briefing Document No. 39.

24. Interview with Mike Aaronson in 'Designing for Disasters', *Royal Society of Arts Journal*, April 2005.

25. BBC WAC, R108/79/1, *Political Balance*. Letter from Stuart Holland, MP to director general, 17 December 1984.

26. *Starving in Silence*, 1990.

27. *The Challenges of Drought: Ethiopia's Decade of Struggle in Relief and Rehabilitation*, (Addis Ababa: Relief and Rehabilitation Commission, 1986), as quoted in *Starving in Silence*.

28. Jason Clay and Bonnie Holcomb, *Politics and the Ethiopian Famine* (Cambridge, MA: Cultural Survival Inc., 1986), p. 4 and chapter 3.

29. Letters to the Editor, *The Times*, 7 November 1984.
30. Ondine Barrow, 'Charity Relief and Development: Christian Aid in Ethiopia 1960s-1990s' in Ondine Barrow and Michael Jenkins (eds), *The Charitable Impulse; NGOs and Development in East and North-East Africa* (Oxford: James Currey, 2001), p. 64.
31. Rony Brauman "Refugee Camps, Population Transfers and NGOs" in Jonathan Moore (Ed) *Hard Choices: Moral Dilemmas in Humanitarian Intervention* (ICRC, Geneva, published Lanham, Maryland: Rowman and Littlefield, 1998), p. 183.
32. TNA, OD 53/10, report to European Council by Jim O'Keefe, 27 November 1984.
33. Dawit Wolde Giorgis, *Red Tears: War Famine and Revolution in Ethiopia* (Trenton, New Jersey: Red Sea Press, 1989), p. 1.
34. Drèze and Sen, *Hunger and Public Action*.
35. *Our Common Interest: Report of the Commission for Africa* 2005. The very first point in the executive summary, p. 14, is headed 'Getting Systems Right: Governance and Capacity Building'; see also chapter 4, 'Getting Systems Right: Governance and Capacity Building', pp. 133-7.
36. Hilary Benn and William Easterly, 'Is Foreign Aid Working?' *Prospect*, November 2006.
37. *Eliminating World Poverty: Making Governance Work for the Poor*, DFID 2006 White Paper, http://www.dfid.gov.uk/wp2006 (accessed 14 March 2007).
38. Chidi Anselm Odinkalu, 'Human Rights in Africa', *African Topics*, October/November 1994, p. 7.
39. TNA OD 53/10, Barder report on Dawit Wolde Giorgis speech to an RRC donor conference on 12 December 1984.
40. BBC Summary of World Broadcasts ME 7788, 31 October 1984.
41. TNA, OD 53/11, telex from Barder Dec 84 telno 442 reports a protest by US Chargé to Ethiopian government after a report of an Ethiopian air force attack on Tigrayan refugees on or about 6 December.
42. TNA, OD 53/11, notes of meeting between War on Want and ODA minister Timothy Raison on 4 December 1984, including reports about bombing from Eritrea.
43. Interview with Jason Clay in *The Hunger Business*, Channel 4 documentary, November 2000.
44. Barrow and Jenkins, *The Charitable Impulse*, p. 65.
45. Drèze and Sen, *Hunger and Public Action*, pp. 274-5.
46. *Starving in Silence*, 1990 and Human Rights Watch/Africa Watch, *Evil Days: Thirty Years of War and Famine in Ethiopia* (New York, 1991).
47. Claire Bertschinger, *Moving Mountains* (London: Doubleday, 2005), p. 126.

48. *Starving in Silence*, 1990 and *Evil Days*, 1991; also Joanna Macrae and Anthony Zwi, 'Famine, Complex Emergencies and International Policy in Africa: An Overview' in Joanna Macrae and Anthony Zwi (eds), *War and Hunger: Rethinking International Responses to Complex Emergencies* (London: Zed Books, 1994), pp. 6–36.

49. Barbara Hendrie, 'Relief Aid behind the Lines: The Cross-Border Operation in Tigray' in Macrae and Zwi (eds), *War and Hunger*, p. 127.

50. Ibid., p. 126.

51. *Evil Days*, 1991, p. 177.

52. This argument was a common thread in the reporting and in *The Selfish Altruist* Tony Vaux discusses the unwillingness of journalists reporting on the famine to face up to the role of the fighting. See, for example, the *Economist* leader on 21 December 1984, 'Make Ethiopia stop shooting'.

53. Tony Vaux, *The Selfish Altruist*, (London: Earthscan Publications, 2001), p. 52.

54. Interview, Michael Buerk.

55. BBC WAC, Programme as Broadcast BBC News, 24 October 1984.

56. Interview for *Tourists of the Revolution*, BBC2, 2000.

57. Anna Jeffreys, 'Giving Voice to Silent Emergencies', *Humanitarian Exchange* No. 20, March 2002, ODI, London.

58. Allan Bell, *The Language of News Media* (Oxford: Blackwell, 1991); the classic definition of what makes foreign news is in the work of Johan Galtung and Mari Holmboe Ruge; see for example 'The Structure of Foreign News', *Journal of International Peace Research* Vol. 2 No. 1, March 1965, pp. 64–90. This was later refined by Tony Harcup and Deirdre O'Neill, 'What is News? Galtung and Ruge Revisited', *Journalism Studies* Vol. 2 No. 2, 2001, pp. 261–80.

59. *Our Common Interest: Report of the Commission for Africa*, 2005, p. 22.

60. Suzanne Franks, 'The CARMA Report. Western Media Coverage of Humanitarian Disasters', *Political Quarterly* Vol. 77 No. 2, April-June 2006.

61. Christopher Bosso, 'Setting the Agenda: Mass Media and Discovery of Famine in Ethiopia' in Michael Margolis and Gary Mauser (eds), *Manipulating Public Opinion* (Belmont, California: Brooks/Cole Publishing Co., 1989), p. 163.

62. BBC WAC, R 78/2, 578/1, *Emergency Appeals Policy*, introduction to DEC handbook August 1981.

63. Jonathan Benthall, *Disasters, Relief and the Media*, 2nd edition (Wantage: Sean Kingston, 2010), p. 42.

64. The five charities involved in the DEC from the start were Oxfam, Save the Children, War on Want, the British Red Cross and Christian Aid. War on Want resigned in 1979 and CAFOD (Catholic Agency for Overseas Devel-

opment) joined in 1973. During the 1980s several other charities applied to join and although this was resisted for some years (see, for example, note of meeting on 5 February 1985 between the chairman of the DEC and Lady Marre, chair of CAAC, in BBC WAC, R78/2, 578/1), eventually other aid agencies did gain membership. In 2013 there were 14 charities in the DEC.

65. Benthall, *Disasters, Relief and the Media*, p. 46.

66. For example, in the discussions between the DEC and BBC regarding an appeal for famine in the Horn of Africa in 1980 there was a tricky exchange of letters: 'we appreciate the service that the DEC gives … they do not have some right to television time on the two channels to make an appeal whenever they think some issue has arisen which justifies asking the public for support. I think once this principle is conceded we shall be in very great difficulty indeed.' Letter from Lewis Waddilove, chair of Central Appeals Advisory Committee, to BBC appeals secretary, 17 June 1980, BBC WAC, B 420–4–3 *Emergency Appeals Case File*. There was reluctance to agree to this appeal, and once it was eventually allowed the BOG minutes noted that 'The Board did not wish to receive many similar applications, given the terms of reference of the DEC': BOG 6 June 1980.

67. BBC WAC, R 78/2, 578/1, *Emergency Appeals Policy*, DEC handbook para 8.2.7.

68. BBC WAC, BOG minutes 25/2/82, minute 77.

69. BBC WAC, BOG paper 36/82.

70. BBC WAC, B420–4–3 *Emergency Appeals Case File*. See correspondence on El Salvador Appeal including, for example, letter from Lewis Waddilove, chair of CAAC, to Lord Hunt, chair of DEC: 'There may be a case for an emergency appeal for relief in Central America. In my view that case was not made', 29 March 1982.

71. Ian Black, 'Salvador gets TV plea from reluctant BBC', *Guardian*, 11 March 1982.

72. BBC WAC, board of management 22/2/82 minute 234.

73. DEC Indo-China emergency appeal 16 September 1979, BBC appeal made by Julian Pettifer.

74. BBC WAC, BOG 25/02/82, Minute 77.

75. BBC WAC, B420–4–3, *Emergency Appeals Case File*. Letter from BBC chairman George Howard to Lewis Waddilove, chair CAAC, 15 April 1982.

76. BBC WAC, BOG 29/04/82, minute 178.

77. BBC WAC, Radio Weekly Programme Review Board, 23 June 1982.

78. BBC WAC, B420–4–3, *Emergency Appeals Case File* memo from appeals secretary to director of public affairs, 17 June 1982.

79. *Guardian*, 19 June 1982, 'BBC 'blocking' Lebanon appeal.'

80. BBC WAC, BOG 8/07/82, minute 322.
81. BBC WAC, BOG 9/09/82, minute 364.
82. BBC WAC, DEC R 78/2, 578/1. *Emergency Appeals Policy 1965–85*, revised version of DEC handbook published September 1983. See also note 59 above.
83. BBC WAC, DEC R 78/2, 578/1, *Emergency Appeals Policy 1965–85*, DEC revised handbook: 10.1.5 'For man-made disasters, where political and other considerations may affect the likely response of the public and the means of providing and distributing aid, a request for an appeal may have to be deferred to scheduled meetings of the BBC's board of governors or of the ITC. For natural disasters, decisions may be taken by the respective chairs of the broadcasting authorities.'
84. Chris Tryhorn, 'Broadcasters veto Lebanon charity appeal', *Media Guardian*, 25 August 2006.
85. Suzanne Franks and Jean Seaton, 'Is Saving the World Journalism's Job?' *British Journalism Review* Vol. 20 No. 2, June 2009, pp. 13–21. Although the BBC and Sky News rejected the appeal, it was broadcast on other channels, ITV and Channel 4.
86. The DEC website in 2013 still referred to the 1984 Ethiopian appeal as follows: 'Lack of spring rains and disease which destroyed crops left … thousands dying of starvation.' www.dec.org.uk/appeals/appeals-archive
87. For a definition and discussion of the term complex emergencies see chapters in Robert Rotberg and Thomas Weiss (eds), *From Massacres to Genocide—The Media, Public Policy and Humanitarian Crises* (Washington: Brookings Institute, 1996), especially Peter Shiras, 'Big Problems Small Print. A Guide to the Complexity of Humanitarian Emergencies and the Media', pp. 93–114. The nature of complex emergencies is discussed at greater length in the following chapter.
88. BBC WAC, B 420–4–3, *Emergency Appeals Case File*, memo from appeals secretary Denis Mann to director of public affairs, 25 June 1982.
89. BBC WAC, RX27 B114–4–5 *Appeals Disasters Emergency Committee—India*. Memo from BBC appeals secretary to BBC chairman, 30 January 2001.
90. BBC WAC, B 420–4–3, *Emergency Appeals Case File*. For example, in a memo from the appeals secretary on 25 June 1982 he mentions a suspicion that the DEC was using 'the emergency arrangements as a means of achieving access to appeals broadcasting … we should therefore try to ensure that the distinction between regular and emergency appeals is properly defined …'
91. Ibid. Memo from Towyn Mason (assistant head of secretariat) to BBC secretary, 2 July 1984, and minutes of Disasters Emergency Committee meeting held at Red Cross HQ on 2 July 1984.

92. Ibid. Memo from Towyn Mason, 3 July 1984, 'Famine in Africa Emergency Appeal'. See also board of governors minute 220, 5 July 1984. Here the chairman Stuart Young made his reservations quite apparent: 'He believed the DEC in this instance had not consulted the broadcasters in a satisfactory fashion and were in breach of the spirit of the agreed rules for such appeal.'
93. BBC WAC, BOG 5 June 1980, minute 207.
94. Ian Smillie, *The Alms Bazaar*, (London: ITP, 1995), p. 101.
95. BBC WAC, B420–4–1, *Emergency Appeals Policy 1986–1992*. A review was made of the operation of the DEC over this period. Memorandum from DEC secretariat, 10 July 1992.
96. Giorgis, *Red Tears*, p. 363.

5. THE HUMANITARIAN DILEMMA

1. Frederick C. Cuny, 'Politics and Famine Relief' in Bruce Nichols and Gil Loescher (eds), *The Moral Nation: Humanitarianism and US Foreign Policy Today* (Notre Dame, IN: University of Notre Dame Press, 1989), p. 282.
2. 'Tourists of the Revolution', BBC2, 2000.
3. Jason Clay, 'Ethiopian Famine and the Relief Agencies' in Nichols and Loescher, *The Moral Nation*, p. 232.
4. Mark Duffield and John Prendergast, *Without Troops and Tanks—Humanitarian Intervention in Ethiopia and Eritrea* (Lawrenceville, NJ: Red Sea Press, 1994), p. 62.
5. Alex de Waal, *Famine Crimes*, (Oxford: James Currey, 1997), p. 124.
6. UN Emergency Office for Ethiopia (UNEOE) made this claim in a report released in August 1985 which reviewed the relief operations in Eritrea and Tigray. It was apparently written in four days and confined to a few garrisons in government held areas. No contact was made with the rebel relief organizations, the Eritrean Relief Association (ERA) and the Relief Society for Tigray (REST). The conclusions were later seen as 'manifestly untrue'. See *Evil Days: Thirty Years of War and Famine in Ethiopia*, Africa Watch Report, Human Rights Watch, New York, 1991, p. 368. See also Kurt Jansson, Michael Harris and Angela Penrose, *The Ethiopian Famine* (London: Zed Books, 1987) for a justification of how many famine victims the official operation reached in Tigray, p. 51.
7. David Korn, 'Ethiopia: The Dilemma for the West', *World Today*, January 1986, p. 5, quoted in Clay, 'Ethiopian Famine and the Relief Agencies', p. 235.
8. Alex de Waal, 'African Encounters', *Index on Censorship* Vol. 23, November/December 1994, p. 14. See also the polemic by Linda Polman, *War Games: The Story of Aid and War in Modern Times* (London: Viking, 2011).

9. There were exceptions to this, such as a film called *The Unofficial Famine*, broadcast by Yorkshire Television on 5 February 1985, which was about the situation in rebel-held Tigray.

10. Barbara Hendrie, 'Cross-Border Relief Operations in Eritrea and Tigray', *Disasters* Vol. 13 No. 4, 1989, pp. 351–60; Max Peberdy, *Ethiopia's Untold Story*, Relief Society of Tigray UK Support Committee 1985; and Duffield and Prendergast, *Without Troops and Tanks*, all give descriptions of the cross-border relief operation.

11. Jansson, Harris and Penrose, *The Ethiopian Famine*.

12. Tony Vaux, *The Selfish Altruist* (London: Earthscan Publications, 2001), p. 67.

13. See Jansson, Harris and Penrose, *The Ethiopian Famine*.

14. *Evil Days*, 1991, p. 367.

15. Peter Cutler, 'The Development of the 1983–85 Famine in Northern Ethiopia' (University of London: unpublished PhD thesis, 1988), p. 408.

16. Interview, Cathy Corcoran, November 2004.

17. Jonathan Dimbleby, 'A poor show', *Guardian*, 1 June 1998.

18. de Waal, 'African Encounters', p. 15.

19. A BBC World Service Assignment programme provoked a fierce debate on this in 2010. See http://www.bbc.co.uk/blogs/theeditors/2010/03/ethiopia.html and Suzanne Franks, 'Why Bob Geldof has got it wrong', *British Journalism Review* Vo. 21, No 2, 2010, pp. 51–6.

20. Interview with Dawit Wolde Giorgis on *The Hunger Business*, Channel 4 two-part series, November 2000, and BBC Monitoring, Summary of World Broadcasts ME 7788, reports on 'wheat aid' given to the troops.

21. *Evil Days*, p. 192.

22. de Waal, 'African Encounters', p. 15.

23. BBC WAC, T41/483/1, *Band Aid Trust File 2*, correspondence between Band Aid Trust and REST, January 1986.

24. Telegram sent to embassy in Addis Ababa, 5 December 1984. Obtained under FOI.

25. George Galloway, 'The Mengistu Famine', *Spectator*, 1 December 1984. Galloway was writing as director of war on want.

26. Memo from assistant private secretary Brian Donaldson to Malcolm Rifkind, 5 December 1984. Obtained under FOI.

27. Interview with Dawit Wolde Giorgis in Channel 4's *The Hunger Business*, 2000.

28. John Holmes, *The Politics of Humanity: The Reality of Relief Aid* (London: Head of Zeus, 2013), p. 319.

29. Jason Clay and Bonnie Holcomb, *Politics and the Ethiopian Famine* (Cambridge, MA: Cultural Survival Inc., 1986), p. 193. See also Donald Curtis,

Michael Hubbard and Andrew Shepherd, *Preventing Famine. Policies and Prospects for Africa* (London and New York: Routledge, 1988).

30. Fredrik Erikson was the opening speaker in the debate on 'Foreign aid to poor countries has done more harm than Good' Intelligence Squared Debate, Royal Geographical Society, London, 5 December 2006.
31. Jason Clay, 'Ethiopian Famine and the Relief Agencies' in Bruce Nichols and Gil Loescher (eds), *The Moral Nation: Humanitarianism and US Foreign Policy Today* (Notre Dame, IN: University of Notre Dame Press, 1989), p. 267.
32. William Shawcross, *The Quality of Mercy* (London: Fontana edition, 1985), pp. 431–51. This later edition of Shawcross's book on the Cambodian crisis included a final chapter on Ethiopia, examining the way the aid operation was manipulated by the government and drawing parallels with Cambodia.
33. Ibid., p. 451.
34. Dawit Wolde Giorgis, *Red Tears: War Famine and Revolution in Ethiopia* (Trenton, New Jersey: Red Sea Press, 1989), p. 289.
35. Clay and Holcomb, *Politics and the Ethiopian Famine*.
36. *The Hunger Business*, Channel 4, 2000.
37. Clay and Holcomb, *Politics and the Ethiopian Famine*, p. 5.
38. Graham Hancock, *Lords of Poverty* (London: Macmillan, 1989).
39. Germaine Greer, 'Resettlement, Ethiopia, 1985' in *The Madwoman's Underclothes, Essays and Occasional Writings* (London: Picador, 1986).
40. Alula Pankhurst, *Resettlement and Famine in Ethiopia. The Villagers' Experience* (Manchester University Press, 1992).
41. *New York Times*, 8 January 1985.
42. Giorgis, *Red Tears*, chapter 10, 'Resettlement and Villagization', pp. 281–308.
43. *Ethiopia: the Politics of Famine*, (New York, Freedom House, 1990).
44. Giorgis, *Red Tears*, p. 218.
45. TNA, OD 53/11, telexes from UK embassy in Addis in November/December 1984. These requests to use the aircraft for resettlement came up many times and were raised in particular on the various ministerial visits to Ethiopia.
46. BBC WAC, T41/483/1, *Band Aid Trust File 2*, minutes of Band Aid Trust Advisory Committee, 21 November 1985.
47. David Rieff, 'Dangerous Pity', *Prospect*, July 2005, pp. 34–9.
48. Vaux, *The Selfish Altruist*, pp. 60–61.
49. Clay, 'Ethiopian Famine and the Relief Agencies' in Nichols and Loescher, *The Moral Nation*, p. 272.
50. Laurence Binet 'Famine and forced Relocations in Ethiopia (1984–86)' in Case Studies: Médecins Sans Frontières Speaks Out, 2009.

51. Rony Brauman "Refugee Camps, Population Transfers and NGOs" in Jonathan Moore (Ed) *Hard Choices: Moral Dilemmas in Humanitarian Intervention* (ICRC, Geneva, published Lanham, Maryland: Rowman and Littlefield, 1998), pp. 188–9.

52. Interview with Michael Priestly in *The Hunger Business*, Channel 4, 2000.

53. Eyal Weizman, *The Least of all Possible Evils. Humanitarian Violence from Arendt to Gaza* (London: Verso, 2012).

54. BBC WAC, B420–4–1, *Emergency Appeals Policy, part 2 (1986–1992)*, 'DEC Appeals Since 1980'.

55. Vaux, *The Selfish Altruist*, p. 56.

56. Daniel Wolf, 'What happened to the f***ing money?' *Spectator*, 23 October 2004.

57. For a further discussion of the coverage of Biafra see chapter 2 and also Ian Smillie, *The Alms Bazaar*, (London: ITP, 1995), pp. 101–6.

58. Michael Maren, *The Road to Hell: The Ravaging Effects of Foreign Aid and International Charity* (New York: Free Press, 1997), pp. 205–6.

59. Urs Boegli, 'Thoughts on the Relationship between Humanitarian Agencies and the Media', based on talk at 'Dispatches from Disaster Zones' symposium 1998. Published in *International Review of the Red Cross* No. 325, pp. 627–31.

60. Rony Brauman 'Refugee Camps, Population Transfers and NGOs', p. 183.

61. David Rieff, *A Bed for the Night: Humanitarianism in Crisis* (London: Vintage, 2002), p. 39.

62. See Fiona Terry, *Condemned to Repeat: The Paradox of Humanitarian Action* (Ithaca: Cornell University Press, 2002) for a comprehensive account of this, based upon her experience in Médecins Sans Frontières (MSF).

63. Mark Duffield, *Global Governance and the New Wars* (London: Zed Books, 2001), p. 82.

64. Quote attributed to the United States Agency for International Development director Peter McPherson as quoted in Cuny, 'Politics and Famine Relief', p. 282. Also echoed by Michael Priestly (former head of UN Special Office in Ethiopia) in interview for *Tourists of the Revolution*, BBC2, 2000.

65. *The Legacy of Live Aid*, BBC World Service, BBC World Report 6 July 1995.

66. Ibid.

67. *The Hunger Business*, Channel 4, 2000; interview with Save the Children Fund (SCF) representative.

68. Ondine Barrow and Michael Jenkins (eds), *The Charitable Impulse; NGOs and Development in East and North-East Africa* (Oxford: James Currey, 2001), p. 14.

69. Rony Brauman "Refugee Camps, Population Transfers and NGOs" in Jonathan Moore (Ed) *Hard Choices: Moral Dilemmas in Humanitarian Inter-*

vention (ICRC, Geneva, published Lanham, Maryland: Rowman and Littlefield, 1998), p. 181.

70. Interview with Rony Brauman in *The Hunger Business*, Channel 4, 2000.
71. Barrow and Jenkins, *The Charitable Impulse*, p. 67.
72. Polman, *War Games*, has further examples.
73. Rieff, *A Bed for the Night*, chapter 5, pp. 155–93, 'Rwanda', gives an uncompromising account of humanitarianism which causes harm.
74. Barrow and Jenkins, *The Charitable Impulse*, p. 24.
75. Interview, Paddy Coulter, October 2004.
76. Rieff, *A Bed for the Night*, p. 53.
77. Duffield, *Global Governance*, p. 81.
78. David Rieff, 'Dangerous Pity', *Prospect*, July 2005.
79. Barrow and Jenkins, *The Charitable Impulse*, p. 29.
80. Ed Miliband, MP, speech to Charity Commission/BBC conference 'Building Participation through Innovation', City University, 19 March 2007.

6. TOO TIGHT AN EMBRACE? THE AGENCIES AND THE MEDIA

1. Timothy Weaver, 'Prostituting the Facts in Time of War and Humanitarian Crisis' in Edward Girardet (ed.), *Somalia, Rwanda and Beyond: The Role of the International Media in Wars and Humanitarian Crises* (Dublin: Crosslines Communications, 1995), p. 203.
2. See chapter 3.
3. Maggie Black, *Oxfam—The First Fifty Years* (Oxford University Press, 1992), p. 300.
4. Interview with Hilary Blume in 'Designing for Disasters' views of 6 experts in *Royal Society of Arts Journal*, April 2005.
5. Michael Maren, *The Road to Hell: The Ravaging Effects of Foreign Aid and International Charity* (New York: Free Press, 1997), p. 263.
6. Interview with Tony Vaux, 8 June 2005. Vaux has also written several of the independent evaluation reports on DEC appeals which raise some of these issues. See below.
7. Ross Clark, 'Tsunami of Cash', *Spectator*, 19 November 2005.
8. *Humanitarian Exchange*, the Magazine of the Humanitarian Practice Network (March 2002) focused on 'Silent Crises' and the following (July 2002) issue was on 'Noisy Emergencies'. Many organizations publish lists of 'Forgotten Crises' to try and rectify this problem of attention.
9. Ian Smillie, *The Alms Bazaar* (London: ITP, 1995), p. 101.
10. Interview quoted in Henrietta Lidichi, 'All in the Choosing Eye: Charity, Representation and the Developing World' (Open University: Unpublished PhD thesis, 1993), p. 128.

11. Ondine Barrow and Michael Jenkins (eds), *The Charitable Impulse; NGOs and Development in East and North East-Africa* (Oxford: James Currey, 2001), p. 9.

12. Nicholas Deakin, *In Search of Civil Society* (London: Palgrave, 2001), pp. 167–71.

13. Barrow and Jenkins, *The Charitable Impulse*, p. 64.

14. Ibid., p. 15.

15. Peter Gill, *A Year in the Death of Africa* (London: Palladine, 1986), p. 87.

16. See, for example, the biography of James Wolfensohn (for ten years the World Bank president) by Sebastian Mallaby, *The World's Banker* (London: Yale University Press, 2005), which shows that he devoted considerable energy to this question.

17. See for example Katharine Quarmby, 'Why Oxfam is failing Africa', *New Statesman*, 30 May 2005, or Barrow and Jenkins, *The Charitable Impulse*, p. 6 or Lidichi, 'All in the Choosing Eye', p. 107.

18. Gill, *A Year in the Death of Africa*, p. 87.

19. Ibid.

20. Nicholas Deakin, 'Civil Society' in Paul Addison and Harriet Jones (eds), *A Companion to Contemporary Britain 1939–2000* (Oxford: Blackwell, 2005), pp. 407–26.

21. Interview with Nicholas Deakin, June 2006.

22. There was an ongoing debate between Short and the aid agencies. See for example 'Well Said, Clare Short', *Independent on Sunday*, 7 June 1998 or Semin Abdulla, 'Aiding a Difference?' on www.open2.net/society/international_development/aid_projects_difference_p.html.

23. Deakin, *In Search of Civil Society*, p. 169.

24. David Rieff, *A Bed for the Night: Humanitarianism in Crisis* (London: Vintage, 2002), p. 104.

25. Peter Burnell, *Charity, Politics and Third World* (London: Harvester Wheatsheaf, 1991), p. 198.

26. Barrow and Jenkins, *The Charitable Impulse*, p. 24.

27. 'Haiti and the Truth about NGOs', BBC Radio 4 documentary 11 January 2011.

28. Alex de Waal, *Famine Crimes*, (Oxford: James Currey, 1997), p. 122.

29. Nikki van der Gaag and Cathy Nash, *Images of Africa: The UK Report*, Oxfam, 1987.

30. Anne Mackintosh, 'International Aid and the Media', *Contemporary Politics* Vol. 2 No. 1, Spring 1996.

31. Maggie Black, *Oxfam—The First Fifty Years* (Oxford University Press, 1992), p. 110.

32. Bob Geldof with Paul Vallely, *Is That It?*, (London: Penguin, 1986), p. 309.

33. Memo headed 'Ethiopian Drought Problem' sent from Mr Wenban-Smith (East Africa Department, Foreign Office) to Malcolm Rifkind and Timothy Raison, 19 October 1984. Obtained under FOI.

34. Fred Cate, 'The CNN Effect is far from Clear-cut', *Humanitarian Affairs Review*, Summer 2002, p. 5.

35. Randolph C. Kent, *Anatomy of Disaster Relief* (London: Pinter, 1987), p. 105.

36. Peter Gill, *A Year in the Death of Africa* (London: Palladine, 1986), p. 94.

37. Fred Cate, 'Communications, Policy-making and Humanitarian Crises' in Robert Rotberg and Thomas Weiss (eds), *From Massacres to Genocide—The Media, Public Policy and Humanitarian Crises* (Washington: Brookings Institute, 1996), p. 18.

38. Humanitarian Logistics 'Die First Aid Later' http://www.hu-online.org/index.php/j-stuff/category-blog/351-die-first-aid-later

39. Philip Seib, *The Global Journalist* (New York/Oxford: Rowman and Littlefield, 2002), p. 12.

40. Ibid., quotes from article by Rick Grant, 'Manufacturing Content', *Ottawa Citizen*, 20 April 2000, p. 12.

41. Clare Phillips, 'Has there Been a Discernible Change in the Way that Issues of Food Insecurity/Famine in Ethiopia have been Portrayed by CAFOD over the Last Twenty Years?' (Unpublished MSc dissertation, London University, 2003)

42. See chapter 1.

43. Claire Bertschinger, *Moving Mountains* (London: Doubleday, 2005).

44. David Styan, 'Misrepresenting Ethiopia and the Horn of Africa? Constraints and Dilemmas of Current Reporting' in Tim Allen and Jean Seaton (eds), *The Media of Conflict* (London: Zed Books, 1999), p. 292.

45. BBC WAC, news and current affairs weekly meeting 6 November 1984, minute 427.

46. Interview, Chris Cramer, March 2006.

47. Press release headed 'A Television Documentary on a Dying Continent' issued by Mo Productions c/o Camerapix and Visnews March 1985.

48. BBC WAC, news and current affairs coverage—B405/B510–22, *African Famine. Nov 84–Jan 86*. This file contains material relating to the row over the *African Calvary* programme transmitted on 2 April 1985 on BBC2.

49. BBC management registry N2674 'Christian Aid', undated memo from the programme's producer, Christopher Olgiati, to *Panorama* editor Peter Ibbotson.

50. Germaine Greer, *The Madwoman's Underclothes* (London: Picador, 1986), p. 302.

51. BBC WAC, BOG 18 April 1985.
52. BBC WAC, minutes of Television Weekly Programme Review, 3 April 1985 discussing the programme *African Calvary*.
53. BBC WAC, BOM 1/4/85, minute 179.
54. BBC WAC, R78/2, 578/1, *Emergency Appeals Policy 1965–85*. In 1985 a group of agencies—Action Aid, Help the Aged, The Salvation Army, War on Want and UNICEF—made representations to join the DEC which they criticized as an unfair 'monopoly'. World Vision also protested at being excluded from the Emergency Appeal system. They were all turned down but in later years the membership of the DEC was expanded. See also chapter 4.
55. BBC WAC, management registry N2674 'Christian Aid', letter from Martin Bax, acting director, Christian Aid to John Wilkinson, BBC director of public affairs, 26 February 1985.
56. BBC WAC, Management Registry N2674, Christian Aid, letter from John Wilkinson, director of public affairs to Christian Aid, 21 March 1985.
57. BBC WAC, minutes of TV Programme Review, 3 April 1985.
58. Witness Seminar on BBC Enterprises with Michael Checkland *et al.*, 1 July 2004.
59. Interview, Derek Warren, DFID, November 2004.
60. 'Reporting War in Africa', seminar at St Antony's College, Oxford, 4 November 2004.
61. Interview, David Loyn, March 2007.
62. Maren, *The Road to Hell*, p. 269.
63. Urs Boegli, 'Thoughts on the Relationship between Humanitarian Agencies and the Media', *International Review of the Red Cross* No. 325, 1998, pp. 627–31.
64. Seib, *The Global Journalist*, p. 12.
65. Glenda Cooper, *From their own Correspondent. New Media and the Changes in Disaster Coverage. Lessons to be Learnt* (Oxford: Reuters Institute, 2011).
66. Wolf also produced the *Hunger Business* programme about the famine for Channel 4.
67. Daniel Wolf, 'What happened to the f***ing money?' *Spectator*, 23 October 2004.
68. Interview with Dimbleby on *Tourists of the Revolution*, BBC2.
69. Mark Duffield, *War and Famine in Africa* (Oxfam Research Paper No. 5, 1991).
70. Bertschinger, *Moving Mountains*, p. 129.
71. Alex de Waal, 'African Encounters', *Index on Censorship* 6, 1994, p. 16.
72. Cate, 'CNN Effect', p. 6.
73. Jean Drèze and Amartya Sen, *Hunger and Public Action* (Oxford University Press, 1989), p. 69.

74. Laura Seay, 'How not to write about Africa', *Foreign Policy*, 25 April 2012.

75. Jonathan Benthall, *Disasters, Relief and the Media*, 2nd edition (Wantage: Sean Kingston, 2010), p. 220.

76. Jason Clay, 'Ethiopian Famine and the Relief Agencies' in Bruce Nichols and Gil Loescher (eds), *The Moral Nation: Humanitarianism and US Foreign Policy Today* (Notre Dame, IN: University of Notre Dame Press, 1989), p. 240.

77. Tony Vaux, *The Selfish Altruist* (London: Earthscan Publications, 2001), p. 61.

78. de Waal, 'African Encounters', pp. 14–15.

79. As well as some of those sources cited above, for example de Waal, Clay, Vaux, Smillie, see Graham Hancock, *Lords of Poverty* (London: Macmillan, 1989). The UK based journalist Ian Birrell has also focused on this in recent years. See www.ianbirrell.com

80. For further discussion of this see Suzanne Franks, 'The Neglect of Africa and the Power of Aid' in *International Communication Gazette* Vol. 72 No. 1, 2010, pp. 71–84 and 'Aid Agencies: are we Trusting too Much?' *Political Quarterly* Vol. 79 No. 3, July 2008.

81. For example www.ngoperformance.org or www.alnap.org

82. Karen Rothmyer, 'Hiding the Real Africa. Why NGOs Prefer Bad News', *Columbia Journalism Review*, March/April 2011.

83. Lidichi, 'All in the Choosing Eye', p. 107.

84. Ibid., p. 133.

85. Interview, David Loyn.

86. Thomas Keneally, *Three Famines: Starvation and Politics* (New York: Public Affairs, 2011), p. 276.

87. van de Gaag and Nash, *Images of Africa*.

88. Red Cross Code of Conduct, Clause 10.

89. VSO, *The Live Aid Legacy* (VSO, 2002).

90. Paddy Coulter, 'Pretty as a Picture', *New Internationalist* 194, April 1989.

91. *Independent Evaluation: The DEC Response to the Earthquake in Gujarat*, December 2001 at www.dec.org.uk/uploads/documents/india_earthquake2002_report_summary.pdf—(accessed 22 May 2007).

92. *Independent Evaluation of the DEC Tsunami Crisis Response*, December 2005, was available at www.dec.org.uk (accessed 22 May 2007). This evaluation has since been removed from the DEC website but it is still available on the BBC link below.

93. *Tsunami Report: Before and After*, transmitted 12 January 2006.

94. de Waal, *Famine Crimes*, p. 139.

95. Cate, 'CNN Effect', p. 5.

96. Timothy Weaver 'Prostituting the Facts', p. 205.

97. Richard Dowden, Interview, 2006.
98. See Jean Seaton, 'The Numbers Game: Death, Media and the Public', 6 October 2005 http://www.opendemocracy.net/media-journalismwar/numbers_2902.jsp for an examination of the way that numbers of deaths are so significant in the reporting of crises. (accessed 15 June 2007.)
99. Johan Galtung and Mari Holmboe Ruge, 'The Structure of Foreign News', *Journal of International Peace Research* Vol. 2 No. 1, 1965.
100. Michael Holman, 'Media and Development', Presentation given at Case-study symposium on African Development held at City University, London, 31 October 2006.
101. Boegli, 'Thoughts on the Relationship between Humanitarian Agencies and the Media'.
102. Charles Elliot, *Comfortable Compassion? Poverty and Power and the Church* (London: Hodder and Stoughton, 1987). p. 11.
103. Press reports of speech by Clare Short, MP, to One World '98 conference, June 1998, for example, Fran Abrams, 'Short attacks aid agencies and press,' *Independent*, 4 June 1998.
104. Robin Poulton and Michael Harris, *Putting People First* (London: London,1988), p. 7.
105. BBC WAC files B405–3, *Current Affairs Programmes*, letter from Martin Bax, acting director, Christian Aid to Alasdair Milne, 12 November 1984.
106. Humanitarian Logistics 'Die First, Aid Later' http://hu-online.org/index.php/j-stuff/category-blog/351-die-first-aid-later
107. Cate in Rotberg and Weiss, *From Massacres to Genocide*, p. 21.
108. Interview with Dereje Wordofa, Head of Regional Policy, Oxfam, *Famine, Aid and Media* Seminar, Frontline Club, November 2004.
109. Interview with John Seaman, *Famine, Aid and Media* Seminar, November 2004.
110. Stephen Rattien, 'The Role of the Media in Hazard Mitigation and Disaster Management', *Disasters* Vol. 14, 1990, p. 36.
111. Interview with Sarah La Trobe, policy officer for climate change and disasters, Tearfund, in 'Designing for Disasters'.
112. Clare Short speech to One World '98 conference, June 1998, as quoted in Suzanne Moore 'Clare Short is right—there is more to the Third World than famine', *The Independent*, 5 June 1998.
113. Christopher Bosso, 'Setting the Agenda: Mass Media and Discovery of Famine in Ethiopia' in Michael Margolis and Gary Mauser (eds), *Manipulating Public Opinion* (Belmont, California: Brooks/Cole Publishing Co., 1989), p. 171.
114. Ibid., p. 154. This refers to a Reuters news item on page 10 of the Boston *Globe* of 23 October 1984.

115. Smillie, *The Alms Bazaar*, p. 144.
116. Oxfam Briefing Paper (2009), *Band Aid and Beyond. Tackling disasters in Ethiopia 25 years after the famine.*
117. Bob Geldof keynote speech to *Africa 2015*: Conference organized by the BBC and Corporation of London to coincide with launch of the Commission on Africa Report, 18 March 2005.
118. *Bob Geldof: Saint or Singer?* BBC1, 2004.
119. Bob Smith with Salim Amin, *The Man who Moved the World. The Life and Times of Mohamed Amin* (Nairobi: Camerapix Publishers International, 1998).
120. Karen Rothmyer, *They Wanted Journalists to say 'Wow'. How NGOs affect Media Coverage of Africa*, Joan Shorenstein Center Discussion Paper 61, January 2011.
121. David Rieff, 'Dangerous Pity', *Prospect*, July 2005, p. 35.

7. INTERPRETING AFRICA

1. Alan Philps, 'Motorcycle Diaries', *Prospect*, August 2007.
2. Suzanne Franks, 'Global Media and the War on Terror. Why Some Wars Matter', *Journal of African Media Studies* Vo. 4, No. 1, 2012.
3. Interview, Graham Mytton, BBC Africa Service, August 2005.
4. Oliver Boyd-Barrett and Daya Kishan Thussu, *Contra-Flow in Global News* (London: John Libbey, 1992), p. 143.
5. Tim Allen and Jean Seaton (eds), *The Media of Conflict* (London: Zed Books, 1999), or see 'If it's Africa, it must be a tribe', Africa News Service editorial 1 December 1990, posted on http://allafrica.com/stories/200101080391. html (accessed 12 May 2007).
6. Alex de Waal, 'Counter-Insurgency on the Cheap', *London Review of Books*, 5 August 2004 and Julie Flint and Alex de Waal, *Darfur: A Short History of a Long War* (London: Zed Books, 2005). Mahmood Mamdani, *Saviors and Survivors: Darfur, Politics and the War on Terror* (London: Verso, 2009).
7. Suzanne Franks, 'Lacking a Clear Narrative. Foreign Reporting after the Cold War' in John Lloyd and Jean Seaton (eds), *What Can Be Done Making the Media and Politics Better* (Oxford: Blackwell, 2006).
8. Ethiopia is, interestingly, the only country in Africa that was never colonized.
9. Laura Seay, 'How not to Write about Africa', *Foreign Policy*, April 2012.
10. Interview, John Seaman, November 2004.
11. Bosah Ebo, 'American Media and African Culture' in Beverly G. Hawk (ed.), *Africa's Media Image* (New York: Prager, 1992), p. 20, quoting Mary Ann Fitzgerald, 'In Defence of the Fourth Estate', *Africa Report* (March-April 1987).

12. According to the 3WE reports which monitor television coverage of developing countries, in 2003 the total number of programmes of this type on terrestrial TV reached an all time low. It had dropped by 49 per cent since 1989. See Steven Barnett and Caroline Dover, *The World on the Box: International Issues in News and Factual Programmes on UK Television 1975–2003*, University of Westminster, Report for the Third World and Environment Broadcasting Project, 2004 and successive reports on www.ibt.org.

13. Stephen Garrett, *Doing Good and Doing Well* (Westport, Connecticut: Praeger, 1999), p. 82, quoting Edward Girardet, 'Public Opinion, The Media and Humanitarianism' in *Humanitarianism Across Borders*, p. 51.

14. Ian Smillie, *The Alms Bazaar* (London: ITP, 1995), p. 133.

15. Interview, Alasdair Milne, 2007.

16. Suzanne Franks, 'BBC Reporting in India in the 1970s and 1980s. Globally Connected Media ahead of its Time', *Historical Journal of Film, Radio and Television* Vol. 32 No. 3, 2012.

17. Anne Mackintosh, 'International Aid and the Media', *Contemporary Politics* Vol. 2 (Spring 1996).

18. George Alagiah, *A Passage to Africa* (London: Little Brown, 2001), p. 120.

19. There are many accounts of how in retrospect the reporting of the refugee camps in Goma in 1994 was completely misinformed. See references to this in previous chapters, especially David Rieff. *A Bed for the Night: Humanitarianism in Crisis* (London: Vintage, 2002), and Fiona Terry, *Condemned to Repeat: The Paradox of Humanitarian Action* (Ithaca: Cornell University Press, 2002).

20. Tami Hultman in Beverly G. Hawk (ed.), *Africa's Media Image* (New York: Prager, 1992)

21. Allen and Seaton, *The Media of Conflict.*

22. Seay, 'How not to Write about Africa'.

23. Virgil Hawkins, *Stealth Conflicts: How the World's Worst Violence is Ignored* (Aldershot: Ashgate, 2008).

24. Speech by Hilary Benn, MP, as secretary of state for international development, 'Awareness, Understanding and Response', given at BBC-World Service Trust/DFID conference 'The Media and Development; Communication and the Millennium Development Goals', 24 November 2004, http://www.dfid.gov.uk/news/files/speeches/bennmedia24nov04.asp (accessed 24 June 2007).

25. Philps, 'Motorcycle Diaries'. Even in 2007, five years after there was a supposed peace agreement in the Congo, thousands were still dying in the fighting—more than in the Darfur crisis.

26. Tim Allen, *Trial Justice. The International Criminal Court and the Lord's Resistance Army* (London: Zed Books, 2006).

27. http://www.guardian.co.uk/politics/reality-check-with-polly-curtis/2012/mar/08/kony-2012-what-s-the-story

28. See *Bringing the World to the UK*, 3WE Emily Seymour and Steven Barnett, University of Westminster, *Bringing the World to the UK: Factual International Programming on UK Public Service TV 2005*. Third World and Environment Broadcasting Project, 2006. Also available on www.ibt.org.uk, which demonstrates how developing coverage in 2005 increased in the period since the previous report, especially on the BBC and on terrestrial channels, in part because of the Africa coverage. Nevertheless, factual developing country coverage on ITV in 2005 was principally 'Celebrity Love Island'!

29. Foreword to *Reflecting the Real World*, Joe Smith, Lucy Edge and Vanessa Morris, VSO and others, 2006. Available on www.ibt.org.uk.

30. Winship and Hemp in Hawk (ed.), *Africa's Media Image*, p. 238.

31. Jon Snow presentation to 'Development, Government and the Media: The role of the media in building African society.' POLIS/LSE/DFID Conference 22 March 2007, report available http://www.lse.ac.uk/collections/polis/publications.htm (accessed 12 August 2007).

32. Lara Pawson, 'Reporting Africa's Unknown Wars' in Sarah Maltby and Richard Keeble (eds), *Communicating War: Memory, Media and Military* (Bury St Edmunds: Arima, 2007).

33. David Styan, 'Misrepresenting Ethiopia and the Horn of Africa? Constraints and Dilemmas of Current Reporting' in Allen and Seaton, *The Media of Conflict*, p. 290.

34. Afua Hirsch, 'The West's lazy reporting of Africa', *Guardian*, 15 April 2012.

35. Binyavanga Wainaina, 'How to Write about Africa', *Granta 92, The View from Africa*, 2005.

36. http://www.ids.ac.uk/news/ids-film-examines-how-british-media-portray-global-south, 11 January 2012.

37. Richard Dowden, *Africa. Altered States, Ordinary Miracles* (London: Portobello Books, 2008).

38. Seay, 'How not to Write about Africa'.

8. REAL MEDIA EFFECTS

1. Jurgen Kronig, 'Elite versus Mass: the Impact of TV in an Age of Globalisation', *Historical Journal of Film, Radio Television* Vol. 20 No. 1, *News Into the Next Century*, March 2000.

2. Luke Dodd, 'Whose Hunger?' article accompanying *Guardian* exhibition 'Imaging Famine', 6 August 2005.

3. Tanja Müller, '"The Ethiopian Famine" Revisited: Band Aid and the Anti-

politics of Celebrity Humanitarian Action,' *Disasters* Vol. 37 No. 1, 2013, pp. 61–79.

4. Laurence Binet 'Famine and forced Relocations in Ethiopia (1984–86)' in *Case Studies: Médecins Sans Frontières Speaks Out*, 2009.

5. Launch of Commission for Africa, February 2004. Reference was made to the Live Aid anniversary at the press launch. See also www.commissionforafrica.info.

6. Ibid.

7. Interview, Tony Vaux.

8. Hilary Benn, discussion at 'Media and Politics' seminar, Nuffield College, Oxford University, 13 October 2006. See http://ochaonline.un.org/cerf

9. Rothmyer, *They Wanted Journalists to say 'Wow'. How NGOs affect Media Coverage of Africa*. Joan Shorenstein Center Discussion Paper 61, January 2011, quoting the *New York Times*.

10. Galtung and Ruge, 'The Structure of Foreign News', *Journal of International Peace Research* 1, 1965, pp. 64–90.

11. Nik Gowing, 'Journalists and War: the Troubling New Tensions post 9/11' in Daya Thussu and Des Freedman (eds), *War and the Media* (London: Sage, 2003), p. 235.

12. Geoffrey Hodgson, 'The End of the Grand Narrative and the Death of News', *Historical Journal of Film, Radio and Television* Vol. 20 No. 1, March 2000.

13. Jean Seaton, 'Being Objective: Changing the World' in *Global Voices: Britain's Future in International Broadcasting* (London: Premium Publishing, 2007), p. 54.

BIBLIOGRAPHY

Primary Sources

BBC Written Archive Centre, Caversham

Individual files and reference numbers are all listed in the footnotes. The following is a list of the principal file series which I consulted.

Board of management minutes and papers (BOM).
Board of governors minutes and papers (BOG).
Television programme review minutes.
Radio programme review minutes.
News and current affairs minutes.
Programme as broadcast summaries.
Central Advisory Appeals Committee meetings and papers.
TV and radio audience research files.
BBC summaries of World Broadcasts.
Files relating to Disasters Emergency Committee and to Emergency Appeals Broadcasts.
Files relating to Band Aid Trust.
News and current affairs coverage, radio and television.
Management registry and World Service registry files relating to India.

The National Archives

Overseas Development Administration file series OD 53: *Humanitarian aid including food aid and disaster relief in Ethiopia 1982, 1983, 1984*

OD 53/2 to OD 53/11.

Papers obtained under Freedom of Information

Requests to Cabinet Office and DFID (formerly ODA) in 2006.

BIBLIOGRAPHY

Oxfam Archive:

Oxfam Briefing Paper (2009) *Band Aid and Beyond: Tackling disasters in Ethiopia 25 years after the famine.*

'Ethiopia: The Green Famine in Wolayita and Kambat/Haydiya The report of a visit by Marcus Thompson and Pat Diskett', Oxfam internal report, August 1984.

Hugh Goyder, field director report on visit to Korem, Wollo, 8–10 October 1984.

Robert Dodd, *Oxfam's Response to Disasters in Ethiopia and the Sudan 1984–5*, Oxfam internal report, September 1986.

Tony Vaux, *The Ethiopia Famine 1984—Oxfam's Early Involvement*, Oxfam internal report, February 1985.

Nikki van der Gaag and Cathy Nash, *Images of Africa: The UK Report*, Oxfam, 1987.

Books and articles

Abdulla, Semin, 'Aiding a Difference', Open2.net/society/international_development/aid_projects_difference_p.html (accessed on 8 May 2007).

Adichie, Chimamanda Ngozi, *Half of a Yellow Sun* (London: Harper, 2007).

Agarwal, Bina, Jane Humphries and Ingrid Robeyns (eds), *Amartya Sen's Work and Ideas. A Gender Perspective* (London: Routledge, 2005).

Alagiah, George, *A Passage to Africa* (London: Little Brown, 2001).

Allen, Robert, 'Bob's Not Your Uncle', *Capital and Class* Vol. 30, 1986.

Allen, Tim, 'International Interventions in War Zones', *Contemporary Politics* Vol. 2 No. 1 (Spring 1996).

———— *Trial Justice. The International Criminal Court and the Lord's Resistance Army* (London: Zed Books, 2006).

———— and Jean Seaton (eds), *The Media of Conflict* (London: Zed Books, 1999).

———— and David Styan, 'A Right to Interfere, Bernard Kouchner and the New Humanitarianism', *Journal of International Development* Vo. 12 No. 6 (August 2000).

Barrow, Ondine and Michael Jenkins (eds), *The Charitable Impulse; NGOs and Development in East and North-East Africa* (Oxford: James Currey, 2001).

Bell, Allan, *The Language of News Media* (Oxford: Blackwell,1991).

Bell, Martin, *In Harm's Way* (London: Penguin, 1996).

Benthall, Jonathan, *Disasters, Relief and the Media*, 2nd edition (Wantage: Sean Kingston, 2010).

Bertschinger, Claire with Fanny Blake, *Moving Mountains* (London: Doubleday, 2005).

Binet, Laurence "Famine and Forced Relocation in Ethiopia 1984–6", Case

BIBLIOGRAPHY

Studies: Médecins Sans Frontières Speaks Out, Paris 2009. http://www.msf-crash.org/en/publications2009/06/08/288/famine-andforced-relocation-in-ethiopia-(1984–1986).

Black, Maggie, *Oxfam—The First Fifty Years* (Oxford University Press, 1992).

Boegli, Urs, 'Thoughts on the Relationship between Humanitarian Agencies and the Media', *International Review of the Red Cross* No. 325, 1998, pp. 627–31.

Boltanski, Luc, *Distant Suffering* (Cambridge University Press, 1999).

Bosso, Christopher, 'Setting the Agenda: Mass Media and Discovery of Famine in Ethiopia' in Michael Margolis and Gary Mauser (eds), *Manipulating Public Opinion* (Belmont, California: Brooks/Cole Publishing Co., 1989), pp. 153–174.

Bowen, Jeremy, *War Stories* (London: Pocket Books, 2007).

Boyd-Barrett, Oliver and Daya Kishan Thussu, *Contra-Flow in Global News* (London: John Libbey, 1992).

Briggs, Asa, *The History of Broadcasting in the United Kingdom, Volume V, Competition* (Oxford University Press, 1995).

Buerk, Michael, *The Road Taken* (London: Hutchinson, 2004).

———— 'Going back', *Sunday Times*, 4 January 2004.

Burnell, Peter, *Charity, Politics and Third World* (London: Harvester Wheatsheaf, 1991).

Butcher, Tim, *Blood River: A Journey to Africa's Broken Heart* (London: Chatto and Windus, 2007).

Calhoun, Craig, 'The Imperative to Reduce Suffering: Charity, Progress and Emergencies in the Field of Humanitarian Action' in Thomas G. Weiss and Michael Barnett (eds), *Humanitarianism in Question: Power, Politics, Ethics*, (Ithaca: Cornell University Press, 2008).

Campbell, John, *Margaret Thatcher, vol. 2: The Iron Lady* (London: Jonathan Cape, 2003).

Carruthers, Susan, *The Media at War* (London: Macmillan, 2000).

Cate, Fred, 'The CNN Effect is far from Clear-cut', *Humanitarian Affairs Review*, Summer 2002.

Chouliaraki, Lilie The Spectatorship of Suffering (London: Sage, 2006).

Clark, Ross, 'Tsunami of Cash', *Spectator*, 19 November 2005.

Clay, Jason and Bonnie Holcomb, *Politics and the Ethiopian Famine* (Cambridge, MA: Cultural Survival Inc., 1986).

Cohen, Bernard, *The Press and Foreign Policy* (Princeton University Press, 1963).

Cooper, Glenda, *From their own Correspondent. New Media and the Changes in Disaster Coverage. Lessons to be Learnt* (Oxford: Reuters Institute, 2011).

Coulter, Paddy, 'Pretty as a Picture', *New Internationalist* 194, April 1989.

Curtis, Donald, Michael Hubbard and Andrew Shepherd, *Preventing Famine: Policies and Prospects for Africa* (London and New York: Routledge 1988).

BIBLIOGRAPHY

Cutler, Peter, 'The Development of the 1983–85 Famine in Northern Ethiopia' (University of London: unpublished PhD thesis, 1988).

————— 'Famine Forecasting: Prices and Peasant Behaviour in Northern Ethiopia', *Disasters* Vol. 8 No. 1, 1984, pp. 48–56.

Dayan, Daniel and Elihu Katz, *Media Events* (Cambridge, MA and London: Harvard University Press, 1992).

Deakin, Nicholas, *In Search of Civil Society* (London: Palgrave, 2001).

————— 'Civil Society' in Paul Addison and Harriet Jones (eds), *A Companion to Contemporary Britain 1939–2000* (Oxford: Blackwell, 2005).

Dikotter, Frank, *Mao's Great Famine* (London: Bloomsbury, 2010).

Dimbleby, Jonathan, 'A poor show', *Guardian*, 1 June 1998.

Dodd, Luke, 'Whose Hunger?' *Guardian*, 6 August 2005.

Dover, Caroline and Steven Barnett, *The World on the Box: International Issues in News and Factual Programmes on UK Television 1975–2003*, University of Westminster, Report for the Third World and Environment Broadcasting Project, 2004.

Dowden, Richard, *Africa. Altered States, Ordinary Miracles* (London: Portobello Books, 2008).

Drèze, Jean and Amartya Sen, *Hunger and Public Action* (Oxford University Press, 1989).

Duffield, Mark, *War and Famine in Africa* (Oxfam Research Paper no. 5, 1991).

————— *Global Governance and the New Wars* (London: Zed Books, 2001).

————— and John Prendergast, *Without Troops and Tanks: Humanitarian Intervention in Ethiopia and Eritrea* (Trenton, New Jersey: Red Sea Press, 1994).

Easterly, William and Hilary Benn, MP, 'Is Foreign Aid Working?' *Prospect*, November 2006.

Economist, 'Here is the News', 4 July 1998, pp. 13–14 and 'The New Business', pp. 19–23.

Elliott, Charles, *Comfortable Compassion? Poverty and Power and the Church* (London: Hodder and Stoughton, 1987).

Fenton, Tom, *Bad News: The Decline of Reporting the Business of News and the Danger to us All* (New York: HarperCollins, 2005).

Firebrace, James (ed.), *The Future of Television's Coverage of Global Issues* (Third World and Environment Broadcasting Project/International Broadcasting Trust, 1990).

Fitzgerald, Mary Anne, 'The News Hole: Reporting Africa', *Africa Report* Vol. 34 No. 4, July-August 1989.

Franks, Suzanne, 'The Neglect of Africa', *British Journalism Review* Vol. 16 No. 1, 2005, pp. 59–65.

————— 'The CARMA Report. Western Media Coverage of Humanitarian Disasters', *Political Quarterly* Vol. 77 No. 2, April-June 2006.

BIBLIOGRAPHY

———— 'How Famine Captured the Headlines', *Media History* Vol. 12 No. 3, December 2006, pp. 291–313.

———— 'Lacking a Clear Narrative. Foreign Reporting after the Cold War' in John Lloyd and Jean Seaton (eds), *What Can Be Done? Making the Media and Politics Better* (Oxford: Blackwell, 2006), pp. 91–102.

———— 'Aid Agencies: are We Trusting too much?' *Political Quarterly* Vol. 79 No. 3, July-2008.

———— 'Is Saving the World Journalism's Job?' (with Jean Seaton), *British Journalism Review* Vol. 20 No. 2, June 2009, pp. 13–21.

———— 'The Neglect of Africa and the Power of Aid', *International Communication Gazette* Vol. 72 No. 1, 2010, pp. 71–84.

———— 'Why Bob Geldof has Got it Wrong', *British Journalism Review* Vol. 21 No. 2, 2010, pp. 51–6.

———— 'BBC Reporting in India in the 1970s and 1980s. Globally Connected Media Ahead of its Time', *Historical Journal of Film, Radio and Television* Vol. 32 No. 2, 2012, pp. 207–224.

———— 'Global Media and the War on Terror. Why Some Wars Matter', *Journal of African Media Studies* Vol. 4 No. 1, 2012.

Galloway, George, 'The Mengistu Famine', *Spectator*, 1 December 1984.

Galtung, Johan and Mari Holmboe Ruge, 'The Structure of Foreign News', *Journal of International Peace Research* Vol. 2 No. 1, 1965.

Gans, Herbert, *Deciding What's News* (Evanston, Ill: Northwestern University Press, 2004).

Garrett, Stephen, *Doing Good and Doing Well* (Westport, Connecticut: Praeger, 1999).

Geldof, Bob with Paul Vallely, *Is That It?* (London: Penguin, 1986).

Gill, Peter, *A Year in the Death of Africa* (London: Palladine, 1986).

———— *Famine and Foreigners* (Oxford University Press, 2010).

Giorgis, Dawit Wolde, *Red Tears: War Famine and Revolution in Ethiopia* (Trenton, New Jersey: Red Sea Press, 1989).

Girardet, Edward (ed.), *Somalia, Rwanda and Beyond: The Role of the International Media in Wars and Humanitarian Crises* (Dublin: Crosslines Communications, 1995).

Golding, Peter and Philip Elliot, *Making the News* (London: Longman, 1979).

Gowing, Nik, 'Real-time Television Coverage of Armed conflicts and Diplomatic Crises: Does it Pressure or Distort Foreign Policy Decisions?' 1994, http://www.ksg.harvard.edu/presspol/publications/papers.htm.

———— *Media Coverage: Help or Hindrance in Conflict Prevention* (New York: Carnegie Corporation, 1997).

———— '"Noisy" Emergencies and the Media', *Humanitarian Exchange* No. 21 (London: ODI, July 2002).

BIBLIOGRAPHY

Grade, Michael, *It Seemed Like a Good Idea at the Time* (London: Macmillan, 1999).

Greer, Germaine, *The Madwoman's Underclothes: Essays and Occasional Writings 1968–85* (London: Picador, 1986).

Hachten, William A. and James F. Scotton, *The World News Prism* (Ames, Iowa: Iowa State Press, 2002).

Haggard, Stephan and Marcus Noland, *Famine in North Korea: Markets, Aid and Reform* (New York: Columbia University Press, 2007).

Hallin, Daniel, *The Uncensored War: The Media and Vietnam* (Berkeley: University of California Press, 1986).

Hancock, Graham, *Ethiopia: the Challenge of Hunger* (London: Gollancz, 1985).

———— *Lords of Poverty* (London: Macmillan, 1989).

Harcup, Tony and Deirdre O'Neill, 'What is News? Galtung and Ruge Revisited', *Journalism Studies*, Vol. 2 No. 2, 2001, pp. 261–80.

Harrell-Bond, Barbara, *Imposing Aid* (Oxford University Press, 1986).

Harrison, Jackie, *Terrestrial TV News in Britain* (Manchester University Press, 2000).

Harrison, Paul and Robin Palmer, *News out of Africa—Biafra to Band Aid* (London: Hilary Shipman, 1986).

Hawk, Beverly G. (ed.), *Africa's Media Image* (New York: Prager, 1992).

Hawkins, Virgil, *Stealth Conflicts: How the World's Worst Violence is Ignored* (Aldershot: Ashgate 2008).

Hellinger, Doug, 'NGOs and the Large Aid Donors: Changing the Terms of Engagement', *World Development* Vol. 15, October 1987, pp. 135–43.

Hendrie, Barbara, 'Cross-Border Relief Operations in Eritrea and Tigray', *Disasters* Vol. 13, 1989, pp. 351–60.

Hesmondhalgh, David, 'Media Coverage of Humanitarian Emergencies: A Literature Survey' (London: Goldsmiths College Dept of Media and Communications, 1993, unpublished).

Hirsch, Afua, 'The West's lazy reporting of Africa', *Guardian*, 15 April 2012.

Hodgson, Geoffrey, 'The End of the Grand Narrative and the Death of News', *Historical Journal of Film, Radio & Television* Vol. 20 No. 1, March 2000.

Holmes, John, *The Politics of Humanity: The Reality of Relief Aid* (London: Head of Zeus, 2013).

Humanitarian Practice Network, *Humanitarian Exchange*, 'Silent Crises', March 2002.

———— 'Noisy Emergencies', July 2002.

Hunter-Gault, Charlayne, *New News out of Africa* (Oxford/New York: OUP, 2006).

Ignatieff, Michael, *The Warrior's Honor* (London: Chatto and Windus, 1998).

BIBLIOGRAPHY

Jacques, Martin and Stuart Hall, 'People Aid—A New Politics Sweeps the Land' in Stuart Hall, *The Hard Road to Renewal* (London: Verso, 1988).

Jakobsen, P.V., 'Focus on the CNN Effect Misses the Point. The Real Media Impact on Conflict Management is Invisible and Indirect', *Journal of Peace Research* Vol. 37 No. 2, 2000.

Jansson, Kurt, Michael Harris and Angela Penrose, *The Ethiopian Famine* (London: Zed Books, 1987).

Jeffreys, Anna, 'Giving Voice to Silent Emergencies', *Humanitarian Exchange* (London: ODI, March 2002).

Joye, Stijn, 'The Hierarchy of Global Suffering: A Critical Discourse Analysis of Television News Reporting on Foreign Natural Disasters', *Journal of International Communication* Vol. 15 No. 2, 2009.

Kane, Penny, *Famine in China* (London: Macmillan, 1988).

Keen, David, *The Benefits of Famine* (Princeton University Press, 1994).

Keneally, Thomas, *Three Famines: Starvation and Politics* (New York: Public Affairs, 2011).

Kent, Randolph, *Anatomy of Disaster Relief* (London: Pinter, 1987).

King, Preston, *An African Winter* (London: Penguin, 1986).

Kronig, Jurgen, 'Elite versus Mass: the Impact of TV in an Age of Globalisation', *Historical Journal of Film, Radio Television* Vol. 20 No. 1, March 2000.

Lean, Geoffrey, 'The Meanest Giver', *Observer*, 7 April 1985.

Lidichi, Henrietta, 'All in the Choosing Eye: Charity, Representation and the Developing World' (Open University: Unpublished PhD thesis, 1993).

Livingstone, Steven, 'Clarifying the CNN Effect: An Examination of the Media Effects According to Type of Military Intervention', 1997. http://www.ksg.harvard.edu/presspol/publications/papers.htm.

Mackintosh, Anne, 'International Aid and the Media', *Contemporary Politics* Vol. 2 (Spring 1996).

Macrae, Joanna and Anthony Zwi (eds), *War and Hunger: Rethinking International Responses to Complex Emergencies* (London: Zed Books, 1994).

Magistad, Mary Kay, 'The Ethiopian Bandwagon: The Relationship between News Media Coverage and British Foreign Policy towards the 1984–5 Ethiopian Famine' (Unpublished Master's thesis, University of Sussex, 1985).

Mallaby, Sebastian, *The World's Banker* (London: Yale University Press, 2005).

Mamdani, Mahmood, *Saviors and Survivors: Darfur, Politics and the War on Terror* (London: Verso, 2009).

Mano, Winston (ed.), 'The Media and Zimbabwe', Westminster Papers in Communication Special Issue, CAMRI, University of Westminster, November 2005.

Maren, Michael, *The Road to Hell: The Ravaging Effects of Foreign Aid and International Charity* (New York: Free Press, 1997).

BIBLIOGRAPHY

McNicholas, Anthony, 'Wrenching the Machine Around: EastEnders, the BBC and Institutional Change', *Media Culture and Society* Vol. 26 No., pp. 491–512.

Milne, Alasdair, *Memoirs of a British Broadcaster* (London: Hodder and Stoughton, 1988).

Moeller, Susan D., *Compassion Fatigue* (New York and London: Routledge, 1999).

Moore, Jonathan (ed.), *Hard Choices: Moral Dilemmas in Humanitarian Intervention* (ICRC, Geneva, published Lanham, Maryland: Rowman and Littlefield, 1998).

Müller, Tanja, '"The Ethiopian Famine" Revisited: Band Aid and the Antipolitics of Celebrity Humanitarian Action,' *Disasters* Vol. 37 No. 1, 2013, pp. 61–79.

Mytton, Graham, 'A Billion Viewers Can't be Right', *Intermedia* Vol. 19 No. 3, May-June 1991.

Nichols, Bruce and Gil Loescher (eds), *The Moral Nation: Humanitarianism and US Foreign Policy Today* (Notre Dame, IN: University of Notre Dame Press, 1989).

Du Noyer, Paul, 'Deathknell for Rebellion', *Word*, November 2004.

Observer Music Monthly, 'Rocking the World', October 2004.

Odinkalu, Chidi Anselm, 'Human Rights in Africa', *African Topics*, October/November 1994.

Olsen, Gorm Rye, Nils Carstensen and Kristian Høyen, 'Humanitarian Crises: Testing the CNN Effect', *Forced Migration Review* No. 16, January 2003.

O'Neill, Onora, *Faces of Hunger: An Essay on Poverty, Justice and Development* (London: Allen and Unwin, 1986).

Pankhurst, Alula, *Resettlement and Famine in Ethiopia. The Villagers' Experience* (Manchester University Press, 1992).

Palmer, Robin, 'Out of Africa. Out of Focus', *Times Higher Education Supplement*, 12 December 1986.

Park, Robert, 'The Natural History of the Newspaper', pp. 80–99 in Robert E. Park, Ernest W. Burgess and Roderick D. McKenzie, *The City* (University of Chicago Press 1925).

Pawson, Lara, 'Reporting Africa's Unknown Wars' in Sarah Maltby and Richard Keeble (eds), *Communicating War: Memory, Media and Military* (Bury St Edmund's: Arima, 2007).

Peberdy, Max, *Ethiopia's Untold Story*, Relief Society of Tigray UK Support Committee, 1985.

Phelan, Brian, 'Dying for News', *The Listener*, 28 February 1985.

Phillips, Clare, 'Has there Been a Discernible Change in the Way that Issues of Food Insecurity/Famine in Ethiopia have been Portrayed by CAFOD over

BIBLIOGRAPHY

the Last Twenty Years?' (Unpublished MSc dissertation, London University, 2003).

Philo, Greg (ed.), Glasgow Media Group, *Message Received* (London: Longman, 1999).

———— 'From Buerk to Band Aid', chapter 5 in John Eldridge (ed.), *Getting the Message: News, Truth and Power* (London: Routledge 1993).

Polman, Linda, *War Games: The Story of Aid and War in Modern Times* (London: Viking, 2011).

Poster, Alexander, 'The Gentle War: Famine Relief, Politics and Privatization in Ethiopia, 1983–1986,' *Diplomatic History* Vol. 36 No. 2, 2012, pp. 399–425.

Poulton, Robin and Michael Harris, *Putting People First* (London: Macmillan, 1988).

Rieff, David, *A Bed for the Night: Humanitarianism in Crisis* (London: Vintage, 2002).

———— 'Dangerous Pity', *Prospect*, July 2005.

Robinson, Jenny, *Development and Displacement* (Oxford University Press, 2002).

Robinson, Piers, 'World Politics and Media Power: Problems of Research Design', *Media Culture and Society* Vol. 22, 2000, pp. 227–32.

———— *The CNN Effect: The Myth of News, Foreign Policy and Intervention* (London: Routledge, 2002).

Rotberg, Robert and Thomas Weiss (eds), *From Massacres to Genocide—The Media, Public Policy and Humanitarian Crises* (Washington: Brookings Institute, 1996).

Rothmyer, Karen, *They Wanted Journalists to say 'Wow'. How NGOs affect Media Coverage of Africa*, Joan Shorenstein Center Discussion Paper 61, January 2011.

———— 'Hiding the Real Africa. Why NGOs Prefer Bad News', *Columbia Journalism Review* March/April 2011.

Schechter, Danny, *The More You Watch the Less You Know* (New York: Seven Stories Press, 1997).

Schlesinger, Philip, *Putting 'Reality' Together* (London: Methuen, 1987).

Schudson, Michael, *The Sociology of News* (New York: Norton, 2003).

Seaton, Jean, 'Media and Misery', *Contemporary Politics* Vol. 2 No. 2 (Summer 1996).

———— *Carnage and the Media* (London: Penguin Books, 2005).

———— 'The Numbers Game: Death, Media and the Public' (6 October 2005), http://www.opendemocracy.net/media-journalismwar/numbers_2902.jsp.

Seay, Laura, 'How not to Write about Africa', *Foreign Policy*, April 2012.

BIBLIOGRAPHY

Seib, Philip, *The Global Journalist* (New York/Oxford: Rowman and Littlefield, 2002).

Sen, Amartya, *Poverty and Famines: An Essay on Entitlement and Deprivation* (Oxford University Press, 1981).

Seymour, Emily and Steven Barnett, University of Westminster, *Bringing the World to the UK: Factual International Programming on UK Public Service TV 2005*. Third World and Environment Broadcasting Project, 2006. Also available on www.ibt.org.uk.

Seymour-Ure, Colin, *The Political Impact of Mass Media* (London: Constable, 1974).

Shaw, Martin, *Civil Society and Media in Global Crises* (New York: Pinter, 1996).

Shawcross, William, *The Quality of Mercy* (London: Fontana edition, 1985).

Simpson, John, *Strange Places, Questionable People* (London: Macmillan, 1998).

Smillie, Ian, *The Alms Bazaar* (London: ITP, 1995).

Smillie, Ian, and Larry Minear, *The Charity of Nations: Humanitarian Action in a Calculating World* (Bloomfield, Connecticut: Kumarian Press, 2004).

Smith, Bob with Salim Amin, *The Man who Moved the World. The Life and Times of Mohamed Amin* (Nairobi: Camerapix Publishers International, 1998).

Taylor, Philip M., 'Television: Force Multiplier or Town Crier in the Global Village?' *Corporate Communications*, Bradford, 1999, Vol. 4 No. 2, http://ics.leeds.ac.uk/papers.

Terry, Fiona, *Condemned to Repeat: The Paradox of Humanitarian Action* (Ithaca: Cornell University Press, 2002).

Thatcher, Margaret, *Statecraft* (London: HarperCollins, 2002).

Thussu, Daya Kishan and Des Freedman (eds), *War and the Media* (London: Sage Publications, 2003).

Timberlake, Lloyd, *Natural Disasters—Acts of God or Acts of Man?* (London: Earthscan Briefing Document no. 39, 1984).

——— *Africa in Crisis* (London: Earthscan Publications, 1985).

Turner, Steve, 'Pictures that Rocked the World', *Radio Times*, 11 July 1985.

Twose, Nigel, *Fighting the Famine* (London: Pluto Press, 1985).

Vaux, Tony, *The Selfish Altruist* (London: Earthscan Publications, 2001).

de Waal, Alex, 'African Encounters', *Index on Censorship* 6, 1994, pp. 14–31.

——— *Famine Crimes* (Oxford: James Currey, 1997).

——— 'Counter-Insurgency on the Cheap', *London Review of Books*, 5 August 2004.

——— and Julie Flint, *Darfur: A Short History of a Long War* (London: Zed Books, 2005).

BIBLIOGRAPHY

Wainaina, Binyavanga, 'How to Write about Africa', *Granta 92 The View from Africa*, Winter 2005.

Walker, Catherine and Cathy Pharaoh, *A Lot of Give: Trends for Charitable Giving in the Twenty first Century* (West Malling: Charities Aid Foundation, 2002).

Wallis, Roger and Stanley Baran, *The Known World of Broadcast News: International News and Electronic Media* (London: Routledge, 1990).

Weizman, Eyal, *The Least of all Possible Evils: Humanitarian Violence from Arendt to Gaza* (London: Verso, 2012).

Wheeler, Nicholas, *Saving Strangers: Humanitarian Intervention in International Society* (Oxford University Press, 2000).

Wolf, Daniel, 'What happened to the f***ing money?' *The Spectator*, 23 October 2004.

Young, Hugo, *One of Us* (London: Macmillan, 1989).

Other reports and online resources

Alertnet (Reuters website) 'Alerting Humanitarians to Emergencies' http://www.alertnet.org.

Band Aid details http://www.bobgeldof.info/Charity/bandaid.html.

BBC *Annual Report and Handbook 1987*

'Bob, Band Aid and How the Rebels bought their arms.' Blog about the World Service Assignment programme March 2010, www.bbc.co.uk/blogs/theeditors/2010/03/ethiopia.html.

'Development, Government and the Media: The role of the media in building African society.' POLIS/LSE/DFID Conference 22/03/07. Report available on http://www.lse.ac.uk/collections/polis/publications.htm (accessed 12/08/07).

'Designing for Disasters', *Royal Society of Arts Journal*, April 2005.

Disasters and the Mass Media: Proceedings of the Committee on Disasters and the Mass Media Workshop, National Academy of Sciences, February 1979, Washington. (Simpson).

Economist Development Report (ed. Mark Malloch-Brown for the *Economist*), London 1984

Eliminating World Poverty: Making Governance Work for the Poor, DFID 2006 White Paper http://www.dfid.gov.uk/wp2006 (accessed 14 March 2007).

Ethiopia. The Politics of Famine (New York, Freedom House,1990).

Evil Days: Thirty Years of War and Famine in Ethiopia, Africa Watch Report, Human Rights Watch, New York, 1991.

Famine in Africa 1984–5, House of Commons Foreign Affairs Select Committee, HMSO, Session 1984/5.

BIBLIOGRAPHY

Famine: A Man Made Disaster? Report for the Independent Commission on International Humanitarian Issues (London: Pan Books, 1985).

Famine, War and Corruption. How British Media Portray the Global South, Institute of Development Studies, University of Sussex. http://www.ids.ac.uk/news/ids-film-examines-how-british-media-portray-global-south 2012.

Global Voice. Britain's Future in International Broadcasting, BBC Global News, Premium Publishing, 2007, 'If it's Africa, it must be a tribe', Africa News Service editorial 1 December 1990 posted on http://allafrica.com/stories/200101080391.html (accessed 12 May 2007).

Imaging Famine, Guardian, 2005. Report issued in conjunction with exhibition at the Newsroom, Guardian visitor centre. http://www.imaging-famine.org/blog/.

Independent Evaluation: The DEC Response to the Earthquake in Gujarat, December 2001 at www.dec.org.uk/uploads/documents/india_earthquake 2002_report_summary.pdf—(accessed 22 May 2007).

Independent Evaluation of the DEC Tsunami Crisis Response, Disasters Emergency Committee, December 2005.

The Live Aid Legacy, Voluntary Service Overseas (VSO), 2002.

Many Voices One World, MacBride Report, UNESCO, 1980.

The Media and Africa since Independence: Past Trends and Future Prospects, Symposium, African Studies Association of the UK, London, 6 December 1986 (transcript).

Our Common Interest: Report of the Commission for Africa, 2005. Subsequently published in the UK as *Our Common Interest: An Argument* (London: Penguin, 2005). Report and other background information available on www.commissionforafrica.org.

Reflecting the Real World, Joe Smith, Lucy Edge and Vanessa Morris, VSO and others, 2006. Available on www.ibt.org.uk.

From Seesaw to Wagon Wheel. Safeguarding Impartiality in the 21st Century, BBC report, published June 2007. Available on http://www.bbc.co.uk/bbctrust/research/impartiality.html (accessed 19 June 2007).

Starving in Silence: A Report on Famine and Censorship, Article 19, April 1990.

UN Central Emergency Response Fund. http://ochaonline.un.org/cerf/.

Viewing the World. A Study of British Television Coverage of Developing Countries, News Content and Audience Studies, Glasgow Media Group, DFID, London, 2000.

Viewing the World: Production Study, Third World and Environment Broadcasting Trust (3WE) (London: DFID, 2000).

Video/Audio Material

BBC TV

Heart of the Matter, BBC2, 20 September 1984.

BIBLIOGRAPHY

BBC News programmes 23 and 24 October 1984.

BBC Live Aid Coverage, 13 July 1985.

Open Space: Framing the Famine by Oxfam, 3 June 1991.

Tourists of the Revolution, part: 3 The Waking Giant, BBC2, 1 April 2000.

This World: Ethiopia, A Journey with Michael Buerk, BBC2, 11 January 2004.

Bob Geldof: Saint or Singer, BBC1, 24 April 2004.

Band Aid: The Song that Rocked the World, BBC3, 21 October2004.

BBC Radio

Aid for Arms in Ethiopia, BBC World Service Assignment programme which led to complaints from Band Aid and Bob Geldof 11 March 2010 (was subsequently removed from BBC Website).

Haiti and the Truth about NGOs, Radio 4 documentary 11 January 2011, presented by Edward Stourton.

Never Again, Archive Hour, presented by Mike Wooldridge on the Ethiopian famine, Radio 4, 2 October 2004.

World Report: Aid, the Legacy of Live Aid, BBC World Service, 6 July 1995.

Non-BBC material

The Unknown Famine, ITV/Thames TV, October 1973.

Seeds of Despair, ITV/Central TV, July 1984.

Bitter Harvest, ITV/Thames TV, October 1984.

The Unofficial Famine, ITV/Yorkshire TV, February 1985.

The Hunger Business, Channel 4, 2 part series, November 2000.

The Story of Band Aid, Channel 4, December 2004.

Faces in a Famine, film made by Robert Lieberman for Ithaca Movies Inc in 1984/85 and shown on PBS channels in the United States.

Mo and Me, film about the life of Mohamed Amin presented by his son Salim, Camerapix/Al Jazeera International, 2006.

INDEX

INDEX

INDEX

INDEX

INDEX